YEOVIL COLLEGE
LIBRARY

WITHDRAWN
FROM LIBRARY

D0550840

PaintShop Pro X6 for Photographers

Yeovil College

Y0074427

PaintShop Pro X6
for Photographers

YEOVIL COLLEGE
LIBRARY

Ken McMahon

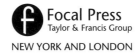

Focal Press
Taylor & Francis Group

NEW YORK AND LONDON

First published 2014 by Focal Press
70 Blanchard Road, Suite 402, Burlington, MA 01803

and by Focal Press, 2 Park Square, Milton Park, Abingdon, Oxon OX14 4RN

Focal Press is an imprint of the Taylor & Francis Group, an informa business

© 2014 Taylor & Francis

The right of Ken McMahon to be identified as author of this work has been asserted by him in accordance with sections 77 and 78 of the Copyright, Designs and Patents Act 1988.

All rights reserved. No part of this book may be reprinted or reproduced or utilised in any form or by any electronic, mechanical, or other means, now known or hereafter invented, including photocopying and recording, or in any information storage or retrieval system, without permission in writing from the publishers.

Notices
Knowledge and best practice in this field are constantly changing. As new research and experience broaden our understanding, changes in research methods, professional practices, or medical treatment may become necessary.

Practitioners and researchers must always rely on their own experience and knowledge in evaluating and using any information, methods, compounds, or experiments described herein. In using such information or methods they should be mindful of their own safety and the safety of others, including parties for whom they have a professional responsibility.

Product or corporate names may be trademarks or registered trademarks, and are used only for identification and explanation without intent to infringe.

Foreword and screen shots copyright © 2014 Corel Corporation. All Rights Reserved.

Corel, the Corel logo, PaintShop, CorelDRAW, Painter, VideoStudio, and WordPerfect are trademarks or registered trademarks of Corel Corporation and/or its subsidiaries. Patent: www.corel.com/patent.

The statements and opinions in this publication are solely those of the individual Author and Publisher and do not necessarily reflect those of Corel Corporation. The appearance of screen shots, images and other material related to PaintShop Pro in this publication is not a warranty, endorsement or approval of this publication by Corel Corporation and are used with permission.

Library of Congress Cataloging in Publication Data
McMahon, Ken, author.
    PaintShop Pro X6 for photographers / Ken McMahon.
        pages cm
    Summary: "Written for photographers of all levels, PaintShop Pro X6 for Photographers is packed with inspirational, full-color images and easy-to-follow step-by-step projects that will have you producing great images in PaintShop Pro in no time! Everything you need to enhance and improve your digital photography is right here in this Corel
    ISBN: 978-0-415-74525-3 (pbk.)
        1. PaintShop Pro. 2. Photography—Digital techniques. 3. Image processing—Digital techniques. I. Title. II. Title: PaintShop Pro X6 for photographers.
    TR267.5.P35M36 2014
    006.6'96—dc23
                                        2013045204
ISBN: 978-0-415-74525-3 (pbk)
ISBN: 978-1-315-79802-8 (ebk)

Typeset in Myriad Pro
Project Managed and Typeset by: diacriTech

Printed in Canada

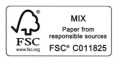

Bound to Create

You are a creator.

Whatever your form of expression — photography, filmmaking, animation, games, audio, media communication, web design, or theatre — you simply want to create without limitation. Bound by nothing except your own creativity and determination.

Focal Press can help.

For over 75 years Focal has published books that support your creative goals. Our founder, Andor Kraszna-Krausz, established Focal in 1938 so you could have access to leading-edge expert knowledge, techniques, and tools that allow you to create without constraint. We strive to create exceptional, engaging, and practical content that helps you master your passion.

Focal Press and you.

Bound to create.

> We'd love to hear how we've helped
> you create. Share your experience:
> **www.focalpress.com/boundtocreate**

Focal Press
Taylor & Francis Group

Contents

YEOVIL COLLEGE LIBRARY

Contents

Contents

Foreword

A Note from Corel

In every photographer's heart rests a desire to produce an amazing photograph. That's why we at Corel make PaintShop Pro – to help photographers get to their best ever photo. Corel® PaintShop® Pro X6 delivers the complete set of editing tools needed to create professional-looking photos. And now thanks to the addition of 64-bit support and new quick selection tools, creating stunning images is faster than ever! By combining Ken McMahon's photographic expertise and insight from his years of experience with the powerful yet easy-to-use features of Corel PaintShop Pro X6, you will be able to fix all kinds of photo problems from quick and easy color corrections to full-blown restoration projects, enhance photos by replacing unwanted elements, experiment with exciting new developments in digital photography like HDR and learn how to keep all of your photos organized so that they're easy to find.

Corel PaintShop Pro X6 was designed with the needs of photographers in mind. Whether you are new, or a seasoned veteran, PaintShop Pro X6 provides the image-perfecting tools needed to take your photos to the next level, and Ken McMahon teaches you how. Corel, Ken and Focal Press have worked closely together in order to create a book that helps anyone who desires to create, not just a great photo, but their best photo ever.

Sara Chesiuk
Public Relations Manager, Corel Photo & Video
Ottawa, Ontario
December 2013

About Corel

Corel is one of the world's top software companies providing some of the industry's best-known graphics, productivity and digital media products. Boasting the most comprehensive portfolio of innovative software, we've built a reputation for delivering solutions that are easy to learn and use, helping people achieve new levels of creativity and productivity. The industry has responded with hundreds of awards for innovation, design and value.

Used by millions of people around the world, our product lines include CorelDRAW® Graphics Suite, Corel® Painter®, Corel® PaintShop® Pro, Corel® VideoStudio® and Corel® WordPerfect® Office. For more information on Corel, please visit www.corel.com.

Introduction

As photographers, we're all interested in the same thing, how to take and make better pictures. Pressing the shutter release is just the start, though, and these days what happens after the 'decisive moment' very often has just as much impact on the making of great photos.

If you're reading this, you may already be using Corel PaintShop Pro X6 or one of the earlier versions of the application. And you've probably discovered that, while it makes some things very simple and straightforward, there are depths to it that you've yet to explore and understand. I've written *PaintShop Pro X6 for Photographers* to help you do just that, develop a comprehensive knowledge of PaintShop Pro X6 and build the skills you'll need to use its tools more effectively to produce great looking photos.

PaintShop Pro's great strength is that it's really easy to use for most every-day editing jobs, but it also provides some very powerful and sophisticated features that you can use, not just to rescue your mistakes, but to transform good images into great ones. In *PaintShop Pro X6 for Photographers*, I've taken a similar approach, starting off with the simple stuff and graduating to more advanced topics only once you've got the skills and experience to tackle them with confidence.

The book begins with an overview of PaintShop Pro X6 and introduces the three workspaces – Manage, Adjust, and Edit – that you'll use to organize and work on your photos, along with the most important tools and features that you'll be using. Managing a growing library of many thousands of photos can be a daunting task and so I've given over a whole chapter to it. If you've got a sprawling collection of photos spread over hard disks, DVDs and memory sticks head straight to Chapter 2, The Manage Workspace, where you'll find out how to manage, tag and easily find any of your photos from among many thousands.

Subsequent chapters cover everything you're likely to need or want to know about using PaintShop Pro X6 including improving your photos with basic editing techniques. Chapter 4, subtitled *Beyond the Basics*, takes your editing and image manipulation skills to the next level. The following chapters cover, among other things, working with selections and text, combining images with layers and how to use masks, special effects and advanced editing techniques, and Printing. Finally I show you how to use PaintShop Pro X6's sharing features to upload photos to Flickr, Facebook and Google+ as well as the best way to prepare images for upload to your own websites.

Each chapter concludes with step-by-step projects where you can learn not just by reading about, but by actually completing real-life photo editing projects. You can download the images used in the projects from gopaintshoppro.co.uk, before moving on to use the techniques demonstrated on your own work. The step-by-step projects, like much of the material in the rest of the book, is applicable to earlier versions of PaintShop Pro, so if you're still using PaintShop Pro X1 to X5, there's plenty you'll find useful (but you really should upgrade to X6!)

If you want to take your skills further still, you'll find more information and tutorial projects on the companion website gopaintshoppro.co.uk. You can also keep up with me on social media; on Flickr I'm @photosensitive, feel free to circle me on Google+ where I'm +KenMcMahon, on Instagram I'm kenmcmahon, or follow me on Twitter @kenmcmah0n (that's a zero instead of an 'o'.)

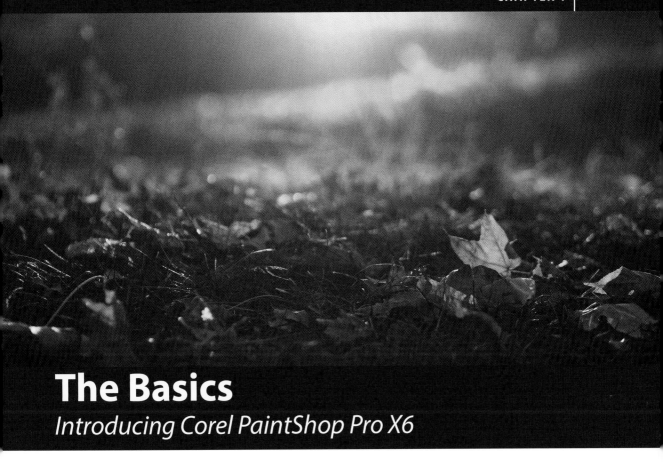

CHAPTER 1

The Basics
Introducing Corel PaintShop Pro X6

What's Covered in this Chapter

- This chapter explains what PaintShop Pro X6 can do and how it works. If you're new to the program I'd strongly recommend you start at the beginning and read this chapter right through, it'll put you in a much better position when it comes to some of the basic photo editing in Chapter 2. In fact, for beginners, taking things in a linear fashion chapter by chapter is the best way to use the book as the simple stuff is dealt with early on and it gets gradually more advanced as you go.
- Unlike the other chapters, there isn't a lot of hands-on stuff here, it's mostly an explanation of how PaintShop Pro X6 works. All the same, I'd recommend you prop the book open in front of you while you're at your computer so you can play with the menus, tools and features while you're reading about them.
- First off, the chapter covers PaintShop Pro X6's basic tools including the Learning Center which is by far the best place to start if you're new to the application. If you're in a big hurry to get started on your own stuff, by the time you reach page 6 you'll know enough to download your photos from your camera and carry out basic guided tasks using the Learning Center.

- Next, I provide an overview of PaintShop Pro's three workspaces – Manage, Adjust and Edit.
- The Manage workspace is where you organize your photos into collections, assign star ratings, caption them and add keyword tags. There are lots of other things you can do in the Manage workspace, I'll describe them in a little more detail later in this chapter and Chapter 2 is devoted entirely to organizing your Photos using the Manage workspace.
- The Adjust workspace is where you go to make quick, everyday edits like rotating and cropping photos. It also has some clever one-step filters designed to improve image quality and other easy-to-use tools for making tonal adjustments. I look at the Adjustment workspace in more detail in Chapter 3 – Improving your Photos: Basic editing.
- Finally, the Edit workspace is for full-on image editing; the only limits to which are your skill and imagination. The Edit workspace offers a huge array of tools that provide massive scope for control over image adjustment and editing. I'll look at some of them later in this chapter and from Chapter 4 onwards; most of what we'll be doing involves working in the Edit workspace.
- Following on are brief descriptions of some of PaintShop Pro X6's editing tools, then I take a look at the features in this latest version. In addition to the brand new stuff, I also take a look at features that were introduced in earlier versions.
- The four step-by-step projects – Exploring the Learning Center, Straightening an image, Perspective correction and Cropping pictures can each be completed in just a few minutes with little or no previous knowledge of the program – are a nice easy start!

Installation: 32 or 64 bit?

Before we get onto working with PaintShop Pro X6, if you've yet to install the program there are one or two things that you should be aware of. One of the biggest features of this new version of PaintShop Pro is 64-bit compatibility. The 64-bit version of PaintShop Pro X6 is the fastest yet and, on the right hardware, runs much more quickly than earlier 32-bit versions. You'll notice the speed increase mostly when performing processor-intensive tasks like applying transformations and filters to images, or cataloguing batches of photos, but it also makes a difference for everyday operations like cropping, retouching and making tone and color adjustments.

To run the 64-bit version of PaintShop Pro X6 you'll need to be running a 64-bit version of Windows on your PC. If you're not sure if your version of Windows is 32- or 64-bit you can easily find out by clicking the Start button, clicking Control Panel, clicking System and Maintenance and then clicking System. This will display a panel which tells you the system type i.e. 32- or 64-bit.

If you're not running a 64-bit version of Windows don't worry, you can still install and use PaintShop Pro X6. The installer gives you the option of installing the either 32- or 64-bit versions of the program, or both. Why would you want to install both 32- and 64-bit versions? Well, the 64-bit version of PaintShop Pro X6 is compatible with many 64-bit Photoshop plug-ins, see the section on using plug-ins in Chapter 8 for more details. The problem is, it can't run older 32-bit plug-ins, so if you have a favorite plug-in that you've used with an earlier version of PaintShop Pro, you'll need to run the 32-bit version of PaintShop Pro X6 to use it. If you choose to install both 32- and 64-bit versions of PaintShop Pro X6, each is installed as a separate application with its own shortcut on the Windows desktop.

Introduction: Basic Tools and Functions

Over the next few pages, I'll explain the various features of the PaintShop Pro X6 workspace and how to use them to carry out basic photo editing tasks. I'd recommend you read through the following section while in front of your PC, so that you can try things out and familiarize yourself with the basics of uploading, organizing and editing your photos.

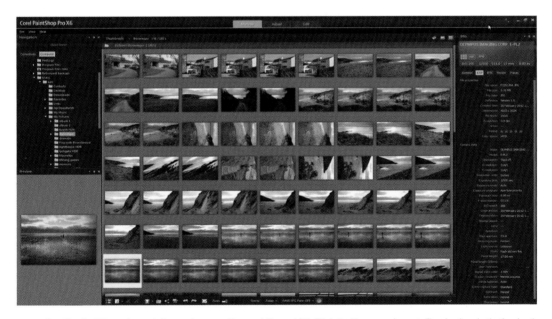

FIG 1.1 PaintShop Pro X6's interface with three workspaces — Manage, Adjust and Edit. This is the Manage workspace in Thumbnail mode, the thumbnails shown are of photos in a folder called Maurellas which is in the My Pictures folder and is highlighted in the Navigation palette on the left. On the right information about the currently selected thumbnail is displayed.

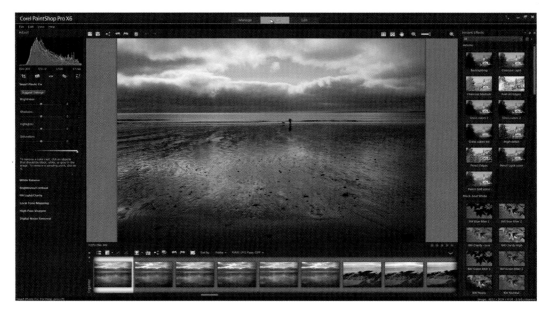

FIG 1.2 This is the Adjust workspace which is used to make quick adjustments using Smart Photo Fix (shown in the Adjust palette on the left and other quick fix tools). Notice the Organizer palette containing thumbnails is now displayed at the bottom of the screen.

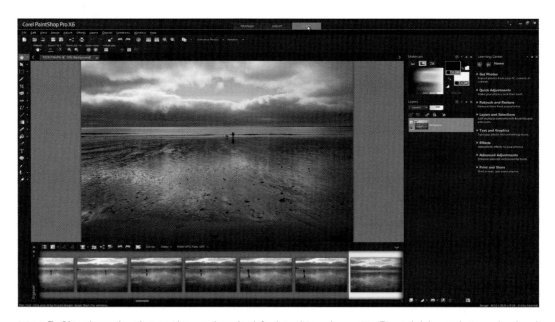

FIG 1.3 The Edit workspace, shown here, provides more advanced tools for photo editing and composition. These include layers, selections and masks and an extensive range of retouching tools. The Learning Center, shown on the right, can help you find your way around and walk you through editing tasks.

The Manage Workspace

More likely than not, you already have some photos stored on your hard disk and you'll want to open these in PaintShop Pro X6. There are a number of ways you can do this, but try to get into the habit of using the Manage workspace from the start. Figure 1.1 shows what the Manage workspace looks like, if yours doesn't look like this you need to click the Manage tab in the middle of the top edge of the screen.

Chapter 2 explains in more detail how the Manage workspace works, for now it will help you to know that it makes finding and opening photos much easier than selecting File > Open, though you're welcome to do it that way if you prefer.

The Manage workspace has four elements, the Navigation palette on the left which shows files and folders on your hard drive, a large thumbnail area in the middle of the screen, called the Organizer palette, which shows thumbnails of all the photos in the currently selected folder in the Navigation palette, and a preview of the selected thumbnail in the bottom left corner. Finally, the Info palette on the right displays metadata for the selected image including the exposure details, time and date and IPTC metadata such as captions, keyword tags and ratings.

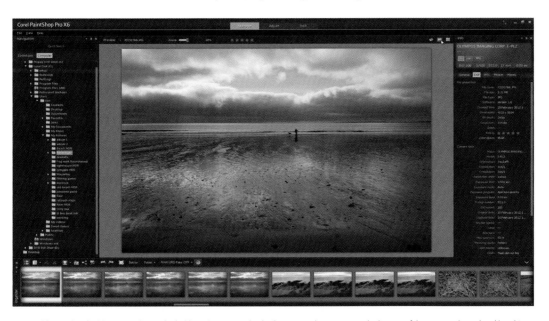

FIG 1.4 This is what the Manage workspace looks like in Preview mode, the Organizer palette moves to the bottom of the screen to be replaced by a big preview. This is useful if you want a good look at your photos, but for organizing them thumbnail mode (shown in Figure 2.1) is best.

There are a few important things about the way the Manage workspace functions that you might find helpful to know at this stage. The first is that there are three viewing modes: the one we've been looking at is called Thumbnail mode, and the others are called Preview mode and Map Mode. To change between them click one of the three mode buttons at the top right of the Manage workspace. When you enter Preview mode the preview image in the bottom left expands to fill the area in the center of the screen replacing the thumbnail view and the Organizer palette is displayed as a strip at the bottom of the screen.

Map mode displays the location of all the photos in the currently selected folder on a Map of the World and is great for viewing the location of photos you've shot while travelling. In order for Map mode to work, though, your photos will need to have the location information present in their metadata. Some cameras have a built in GPS that does this automatically; others allow you to tag your photos with location data using the GPS in your smartphone. If you have neither a GPS-equipped camera nor one that can connect with your smartphone via Wi-Fi you can use the Map view to manually add location information to your photos.

The Navigation palette has two tabs labelled Collections and Computer. The Computer tab shows the files and folders on your hard drive. This is quite useful to begin with as you can locate a folder of images anywhere on your PC, but there's a lot of clutter – folders that have nothing to do with your photos – getting in the way. Click the Collections tab at the top of the Navigation palette and you'll see a list that includes your Pictures folder, some Smart Collections, which are collections of photos selected using saved search criteria, and the option to display thumbnails based on their star rating. The Collections tab provides a far more useful way to organize and find your photos because you can decide exactly what appears on it and which images are displayed in the Organizer palette. More about that in the next chapter.

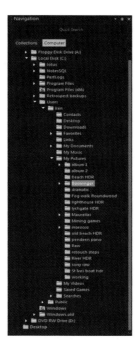
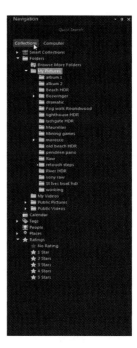

FIG 1.5 The Navigation palette tabs. The Computer tab (left) displays the files and folders on your PC, useful for finding photos if you know where you put them, but there's a lot of clutter. The Collections tab (right) shows only those folders you choose.

For now, let's take a quick look at some of the functions of the Navigator palette and how you can use it to browse for photos on your PC. Start by clicking the Computer tab at the top of the Navigator palette, then click the triangle icon next to the hard drive on which Windows is installed, it's probably called Local Disk (C:). Click the triangle next to the Users folder, followed by the + sign next to your username (in my case, ken). You should now be able to see the My Pictures folder. Mine has sub-folders in it so I need to select one of these to display the thumbnails of the photos it contains in the Organizer palette. When I do that the first image is automatically selected and its information is displayed in the Info palette on the right below the preview.

Now click the Collections tab, click the triangle next to Folders and you'll see your My Pictures folder right there. It's automatically added to the Folders collection and it's much easier to get to without all that other stuff in the way. You can easily add other folders by clicking Browse more folders at the top of the folders list.

Notice there are five tabs on the Info palette labelled General, EXIF, IPTC, People and Places. The first of these tells you the file name, the date the photo was taken, the rating, which you can change by clicking on the stars, what keyword tags have been applied and, if you scroll down, the caption and some other information. EXIF stands for Exchangeable Image File format and it contains non-editable information recorded by the camera at the time of exposure. Click the EXIF tab and you'll see the exposure details, date and time, camera make and model, resolution and a lot of other stuff. EXIF information can include all kinds of things down to the kind of metering mode you used, whether the flash was fired and the focal length of the lens.

IPTC stands for International Press Telecommunications Council (these acronyms, usually named from the organizations and committees that define these standards, aren't particularly useful to know, but there you are) and is a standard for adding metadata to digital photos after they've been taken. IPTC metadata can include things like your name and address, a copyright statement and caption. The distinction between EXIF and IPTC metadata is that the former is recorded by the camera at the time of exposure and is usually non-editable and the latter is subsequently added by people and can be edited. The Info palette and the information it displays are described in more detail in Chapter 2. The People tab displays the name tags you've added to photos of people you know. You can use PaintShop Pro's face recognition feature to automatically find and identify people or you can tag images manually. I'll explain more about people tagging in Chapter 2. Finally, the Places tab shows the location of images that contain geopositional metadata. It's essentially a mini version of the Map View and I'll explain more about using geopositional data in your photos in Chapter 2.

The Organizer palette can be displayed in all three workspaces which makes it easy to select any photo from the currently selected folder or from a tray to adjust or edit. The Navigator palette only appears in the Manage workspace. To display it in the Adjust and Edit workspaces click the Show/Hide Navigation

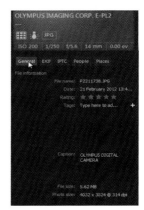

FIG 1.6 The General tab of the Info palette tells you the file name, date taken, rating, tags and caption as well as file size and pixel dimensions. More information is available on the EXIF and IPTC tabs.

7

button on the Organizer palette. If you select an image in the Organizer palette in the Manage workspace, when you switch to the Adjust or Edit workspaces that image is open and ready to work on. Alternatively you can right-click the thumbnail and select Adjust Photo or Edit Photo from the menu.

The Adjust Workspace

The Adjust workspace was introduced in PaintShop Pro X4. If you're working with PaintShop Photo Pro X3 or Paintshop Pro Photo X2 you'll have something called Express Lab which is similar, though less well integrated. As I've said, the Adjust workspace is where you carry out routine adjustments like cropping and straightening, correcting color and exposure problems, fixing red-eye caused by on-camera flash and touching up spots and blemishes. I'm going to go into more detail here than I did for the Manage workspace because if you only read this chapter and the next you'll be well equipped to carry out the most important tasks – organizing and basic photo editing.

The Adjust workspace is shown in Figure 1.2. As you can see, it's divided into four areas; there's the Organizer palette, familiar from the Manage workspace, at the bottom of the screen, the Adjust palette on the left, a large preview area occupying most of the screen on the top right and the Instant Effects palette on the right.

Most of what goes on in the Adjust workspace happens, appropriately enough, in the Adjust palette, but before we look in detail at that I'll explain what some of the other controls are for. Above the Preview area there's a toolbar with a row of buttons top left and top right. The buttons on the left are for saving your work, sharing it, rotating photos left and right, deleting and undo and redo. On the right are view buttons for zooming to 100% view, fit in window, a Pan tool for grabbing the image and moving it around in the preview window when you're zoomed in and, on the extreme right, a zoom slider with + and – magnifiers. Incidentally, if you get to the Adjust workspace and find the image you want to adjust is located in a different folder you can display the Navigation palette by clicking the Show/Hide Navigation button on the top left corner of the Organizer palette.

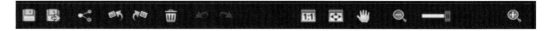

FIG 1.7 The Adjust workspace toolbar buttons are divided into two groups. On the left – save, save as, share, rotate left, rotate right, delete, undo and redo. On the right – zoom to 100%, fit image to window, pan tool and zoom tool.

At the top of the Adjust palette there's a histogram display. I look at histograms and how to interpret and work with them in Chapter 3. Below the histogram the (EXIF) exposure information is displayed and below that is a toolbar containing four tools – Crop, Straighten, Red-eye, Makeover and a Clone brush. If you want to know how to use some of these tools take a look at the step-by-step projects at the end of this chapter.

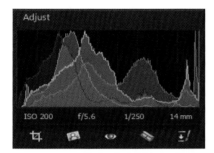

FIG 1.8   The Adjust palette toolbar (l–r) Crop tool, Straighten tool, Red-eye tool, Makeover tool and Clone Brush.

Below the Adjust palette toolbar is the Smart Photo Fix panel. Unless you've clicked on one of the tools above the Smart Photo Fix panel (in which case just click the Smart Photo Fix header to expand the panel) the control sliders will be displayed. You can experiment with these to try and improve image quality but it's called 'Smart' photo fix for a reason; click the 'Suggest Settings' button and it will do the hard work for you, analyzing the image and deciding what settings to apply to get the best results.

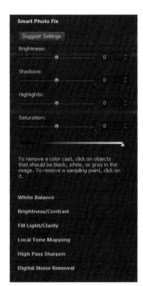

Below the Smart Photo Fix panel you'll find a range of other tools designed to produce improvements to your photos quickly and easily. These include Color Balance, Fill Light/Clarity, High Pass Sharpen and Digital Noise removal. These are 'simplified' versions of tools which are available in the Edit workspace and described briefly later in this chapter and demonstrated throughout the book. They're included in the Adjust workspace so that you can quickly access and apply them without having to think too much about the process. The point of the Adjust workspace is to provide a place where you can scan through all of your images from an event and apply adjustments to those that need it.

FIG 1.9   The Smart Photo Fix panel has sliders for Brightness, Shadows, Highlights and Saturation, but a click on the Suggest settings button is often all that's required.

Of course, no matter how quick and simple the adjustment you make, if you have to apply them individually to hundreds of photos, its going to add up. Thankfully PaintShop Pro X6 allows you to 'capture' the changes you make to a photo in the Adjust or Edit workspaces and apply them to others.

The Edit Workspace

The Edit workspace is where you go for serious photo editing work. The Adjust workspace is fine for quick edits, the Edit workspace has the tools you'll need to carry out more substantial work. In the Edit workspace you can create

9

layers, superimposing photos on top of each other and you can add masks to layers that work like stencils, hiding some areas of the layers below and revealing others. Sophisticated selection tools allow you restrict edits and adjustments to parts of an image and these selections can form the basis for masks, which do the same thing only more flexibly.

As well as a wide range of editing tools, the Edit workspace has a raft of special effects filters as well as controls for adjusting tone, color and just about every other factor that affects how a digital photo appears. Using these tools you can fix exposure problems, remove color casts, change the color of individual objects in photos, sharpen or blur them, remove scratches and digital noise, remove people, cats, lamp posts or anything else, make old photos look like new and new ones look old, produce one good photo from several not so good ones and a lot more besides.

Figure 1.3 shows the Edit workspace. The main components of this workspace are the Menu bar and Standard toolbar at the top of the screen, below that the Tool Options palette, then the image window and at the bottom of the screen the by now familiar Organizer palette. The Tools toolbar is the long narrow strip on the left which contain all of the Edit workspace tools. When you hover over a tool its name is displayed in a tool tip and its function is explained in the status bar at the very bottom of the screen. Finally on the right of the screen is the Learning Center palette.

The Learning Center

The Learning Center appears on the right of the screen in the Edit workspace and shows you how to get things done. If you can't see the Learning Center select View > Palettes > Learning Center, or press the F10 key on your keyboard.

For simple tasks, like rotating photos, the Learning Center just does it for you. For more complex tasks involving several steps, the Learning Center walks you through, step-by-step, selecting the tools for the job at the appropriate moment.

Because the Learning Center selects the tools for you and tells you how to use them, after a while, you'll find you no longer need it for common tasks like cropping, straightening and rotating photos – when you know how, it's quicker and easier to do it yourself. When the time comes you can close the Learning Center palette (press F10 again) to make more room for your photos and other palettes.

The Learning Center works like a website. The home page contains seven topics – Get Photos, Adjust, Retouch and Restore, Collage, Text and Graphics, Effects and Print and Share. You can return to this page at any time by clicking the Home button at the top of the palette.

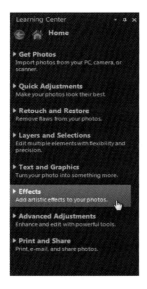

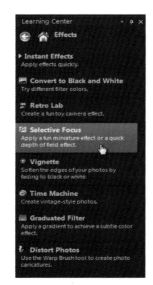

FIG 1.10 The Learning Center home.   **FIG 1.11** The Effects tab.

Each topic has a number of projects, click Effects and you'll find eight projects that demonstrate, among other things how to use the Time Machine to create vintage-style photos, converting photos to black and white and distorting photos. Click either the Home or Back buttons at the top of the palette to return to the home page. I'm not going to go through each of the projects in the Learning Center because they don't need any explanation. Why not try them out for yourself.

The Menu Bar

PaintShop Pro X6's menu system gives you access to most of the program's tools, commands and features. There are other ways to access them, but the Menu bar lays them all out for you in a logical organized fashion. If you're not sure where something is, a quick skim through the menus will usually reveal it. For example, if you want to apply a special effects filter there's a good chance you'll find what you're looking for somewhere in the Effects menu. Anything to do with making tonal and color adjustments is on the Adjust menu and stuff to do with displaying tool bars, palettes, grids, guides and organizing the workspace is on the View menu (except workspace presets which, for some reason, are on the File menu).

Some menu items are nested in sub-menus. When I refer to these in the book, they are denoted using the > character. For example, the Levels command on the Brightness and Contrast sub-menu of the Adjust menu is shown as Adjust > Brightness and Contrast > Levels.

Another useful piece of information you'll find on menus is keyboard shortcuts. You'll probably be familiar with Ctrl-c and Ctrl-v to copy and paste, after a while it will become second nature to you to press Shift-H to adjust Hue/Saturation/Lightness rather than selecting Adjust > Hue and Saturation > Hue/Saturation/Lightness.

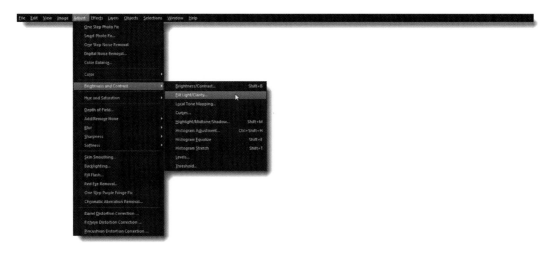

FIG 1.12   The menu bar with Adjust and Brightness and Contrast sub-menus selected.

Toolbars

Now that you know how to use the Organizer to find and open photos into PaintShop Pro X6 and you can carry out simple guided projects using the Learning Center, it's time to take a look at some of the other parts of the PaintShop Pro X6 Edit workspace.

The narrow strip of buttons running down the left side of the screen is the Tools toolbar. If you need to select part of a photo, crop it, straighten it, retouch it, add text or fix problems like red eye, this is where you'll find the tools for the job.

PaintShop Pro X6 displays tool tips when you hover with your mouse pointer over each of the tools and this is a good way to familiarize yourself with each tool's function. As well as the tool tips, the Status bar at the very bottom of the screen provides some guidance on how to use each tool.

There are several other toolbars, some of them, like the Standard toolbar, are visible in the default workspace and some need to be activated by selecting them from the Toolbars sub-menu of the View menu.

The different toolbars group together similar tools and functions which you're likely to need for a specific photo editing task or which it seems logical to keep in the same place. On the Standard toolbar at the top of the screen you'll find tools for creating, opening and saving photos, scanning and printing, resizing, rotating and displaying photo information.

Other toolbars include the Effects, Photo, Script and Web toolbars. Some of these you'll use rarely, or possibly not at all, which is one of the reasons they're tucked away, so as not to clutter up the workspace. I've already mentioned that you can toggle the toolbars on and off by selecting them from the View > Toolbars menu, (you can also hide toolbars and palettes by clicking their close box) and you can float or dock any of the toolbars by dragging the title bar. To dock a toolbar, drag it to one of the top, bottom or side edges of the main picture window where it will snap into place. To float a toolbar, drop it anywhere away from one of the docking edges.

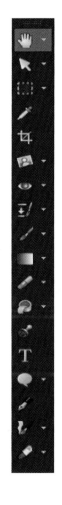

FIG 1.13 The Tools toolbar sits on the left of the main picture window. Hover over the tools to display a tooltip naming the tool and a brief explanation of its function in the Status bar at the bottom of the screen. From the top: Pan + Zoom tool, Pick + Move, Selection + Freehand Selection + Magic Wand, Dropper, Crop, Straighten + Perspective Correction, Red-Eye +Makeover, Clone Brush + Scratch Remover + Object Remover, Paint Brush + Airbrush, Lighten/Darken + Dodge + Burn + Smudge + Push + Soften + Sharpen + Emboss + Saturation Up/Down + Hue Up/Down + Change to target + Color Replacer, Eraser + Background Eraser, Flood Fill + Color Changer, Picture Tube, Text tool, Preset Shape tool + Rectangle + Ellipse + Symmetric Shape, Pen tool, Warp Brush + Mesh Warp, Oil Brush + Chalk + Pastel + Crayon + Colored Pencil + Marker + Palette Knife + Smear + Art Eraser.

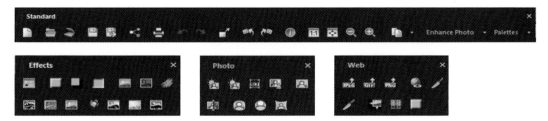

FIG 1.14 To activate toolbars select them from the View>Toolbars menu. The Standard Toolbar appears in the default workspace and contains among other things filing commands, rotate buttons, undo and redo commands, zoom buttons and the palettes menu.

Tip

To reset Preferences, including the default workspace layouts, hold down the shift key when you launch PaintShop Pro Photo X4.

Have a play around with showing, hiding and re-arranging the PaintShop Pro X6 workspace elements. Before you do though, first select File > Workspace > Save and save your existing setup as 'default_workspace' or something similar. When you've everything setup the way you want, save this new arrangement as 'favorite_workspace'. Now, to return the workspace to either of these arrangements you just need to select Workspace > load and choose the one you want.

Photo Toolbar

If you deal with scanned or digital photos, this is the toolbar to get friendly with. The Backlighting and Fill Flash tools help to correct exposure problems caused by problematic lighting conditions, and the Chromatic Aberration and Digital Camera Noise Removal filters help reduce colored fringing and noise problems that can occur in digital photos. You can add tools for common photo enhance operations like Levels, for example, by right-clicking any of the toolbar buttons and selecting Customize from the contextual menu.

Effects Toolbar

If you have had no experience using PaintShop Photo Pro but are curious how its effects might look when applied to a picture, click the first button on the Effects toolbar – the Browse Presets button. This loads and displays the Effects Browser, displaying all of the available adjustment and effect filter presets. Click on a folder to see the entire contents, all of the artistic effects for example, or choose an individual preset from within one of the folders. Double-click the effect you like the look of in the Browser, and PaintShop Photo Pro transfers it to the photo in the work area. In this way you can preview the filter effect and save time by only trying effects that you like the look of.

What else is there on the Effects toolbar? Buttonize, Drop Shadow, Inner Bevel, Gaussian Blur, Hot Wax, Brush Strokes, Colored Foil, Emboss, Fur, Lights, Polished Stone, Sunburst and Topography. All are preset filter effects that can be applied to a selection, or globally, depending on application. All can be customized through the displayed options window. Customized filter sets can also be saved in the same way as customized tools.

Script Toolbar

While strictly not a tool as such, scripting offers incredible power to anyone with a bit more than the most basic of photo-editing requirements. What's scripting all about? As the name might suggest, a script is a file of instructions that produce a series of actions or effects – much in the same way that a play's script, when followed by a group of actors, produces actions that result in a play.

PaintShop Pro ships with a wide range of pre-recorded scripts but the fun really begins when you start to record your own. The Script toolbar is set up just like a video recorder. Press 'Record'; perform the actions you want on the selected picture (i.e. rotate + change contrast + save). It's that easy. Once saved, the script can be run on other pictures in the work area. It's a great way to automate jobs that require repetitive actions applied to multiple pictures (e.g., in website design).

Web Toolbar

Put together specifically for web designers, this small toolbar contains an 'Image Slicer' tool, an 'Image Mapper' tool, 'JPEG', 'GIF' and 'PNG' image optimizers plus a 'Web Browser Preview' feature, 'Seamless Tiling' and a 'Buttonize' feature – most of the tools, in fact, needed to prepare images for your own website.

Tool Options and Other Palettes

A tool wouldn't be very useful if it did only one thing, and PaintShop Pro X6's tools are nothing if not versatile. The Tool Options palette is what gives tools their versatility, allowing you to change settings that modify the selected tool's behavior.

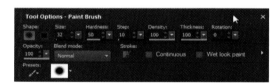

FIG 1.15 Tool options for the Paint Brush.

Tip

For lacklustre digital photos, start with the One Step Photo Fix. This versatile command applies six different processes to the image: Automatic Color Balance, Automatic Contrast Enhancement, Clarify, Automatic Saturation Enhancement, Edge Preserving Smooth and Sharpen.

The Tool Options palette automatically displays the available settings for the selected tool. So, when you select the Paint Brush Tool, the Tool Options palette displays size, shape, density opacity and other options. Switch to the Selection tool and the Tool Options palette displays selection type, mode, feathered edge and other selection options.

Try selecting a few different tools and looking at what aspects of their behavior can be modified using the Tool Options palette. Don't worry if it's not clear at this stage what they do or how they work. As you progress through the book, you'll discover how to use them in practice. Right now it's enough to know that, along with the Tools toolbar, the Tool Options palette is one of PaintShop Pro X6's most useful assets.

We've already talked about two other palettes – the Learning Center and Organizer. PaintShop Pro X6's other palettes include the Layers, Materials, Histogram and History palettes. The Materials palette is used to select colors, gradients and patterns for all of the painting a drawing tools.

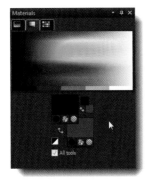

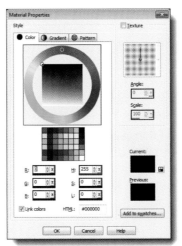

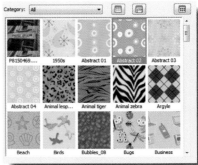

FIG 1.16 The Materials palette (1) is used for selecting foreground and background colors, gradients and patterns for all the painting and drawing tools. The Material Properties dialog (2) (click the foreground or background swatch) is used to fine-tune color selection, create gradients and choose pattern and texture swatches (3).

Other Features

The final part of this first chapter is a brief introduction to some of the other useful tools and features that PaintShop Pro X6 has to offer. Some of these features, for example Skin smoothing and One Step Purple Fringe Fix, are mentioned here because, although they can be very useful, there isn't space to include a more detailed explanation of how they work or examples of them in use. Others, like HDR, Camera RAW Lab, Instant Effects and the Smart Carver, you'll be finding out more about in the upcoming chapters and projects.

Smart Selection Brush

The Smart selection brush is new to PaintShop Pro X6 and provides a very quick and simple way to make accurate selections of elements that previously would have been a challenge even for experienced photo editors. It's a brush tool, so you just paint over the area you want to select and the Smart selection brush does the rest, automatically detecting edges and snapping your selection to them. You can find out more about the Smart selection brush and how to use it in Chapter 5.

Auto Selection Tool

Like the Smart selection brush the Auto selection tool is a new introduction to PaintShop Pro X6 that simplifies the job of making complex selections. Imagine a rectangular selection tool that shrinks to fit elements within its boundary – draw a box around something, a dog, a tree, a cloud, whatever – and the Auto selection tool automatically works out where it begins and ends and draws a tight-fitting selection boundary around it. Simple.

Instant Effects Palette

The Instant effects palette was introduced in PaintShop Pro X5; it shows all of PaintShop Pro's effects filters organized by category and allows you to browse and apply them more easily than using the Effects browser. The Instant effects palette is displayed by default in the Adjust workspace, but you can use it in either of the other workspaces, just select View > Palettes > Instant Effects or press Shift-F2. Double-click a thumbnail to apply it to the current image.

Retro Lab

The Retro Lab is designed to produce a variety of effects ranging from a Lomo style toy camera effect to vintage film stock, but it's actually quite versatile and you can use it to create a wide variety of grungy effects which, as with most other PaintShop Pro effects, you can then save as a preset. It has several presets of its own, but there's a lot more to be gained if you experiment with the numerous controls it provides.

Find People

If you never take photos of people you know, this one won't be of any interest. But if like most of us you've got lots of photos of friends and family, Find people will be enormously useful. It allows you to attach name tags to photos of people you know, either manually or by using PaintShop Pro's face recognition software. Once they're tagged it's easy to find pictures of people. You'll find more on how to do that in Chapter 2.

Photo Mapping

I introduced Photo mapping a little earlier in this chapter and I'll explain how it works in more detail in the step-by-step project at the end of chapter 2. Like Find people, it relies on metadata in your photos – in this case geoposition co-ordinates identifying the geographic location where the picture was taken. This can be added automatically in a GPS-equipped camera, or you can do it manually later. Using the data in the images PaintShop Pro can show you the location of your photos on a map.

Share My Trip

Share my trip allows you to include up to 200 photos in a map-based interactive slideshow that you can post to your blog or to Dropbox.

HDR

HDR stands for High Dynamic Range. The dynamic range in a photo is the range of tones that are represented, from pure white to solid black. PaintShop Pro X6's HDR tools combine several bracketed exposures to better represent the wide tonal range in some subjects and avoid blown-out highlights and filled-in shadows. Earlier versions of PaintShop Pro had HDR Photo Merge, but PaintShop Pro X6 improves the merge algorithm and introduces a new batch merge feature.

Photo Blend

Photo Blend lets you combine two or more photos of the same scene so that you can swap or remove unwanted details. This is perfect for group shots where, for example, one person has their eyes closed. You can combine the best bits from several photos to make one really good one.

Selective Focus

Selective Focus simulates the shallow depth of field that's typical of a specialist tilt-shift lens and often makes real-life subjects look like miniaturized models. It's an effect that has become very popular – if you haven't seen it before (where have you been?) got to flickr.com and search tilt-shift.

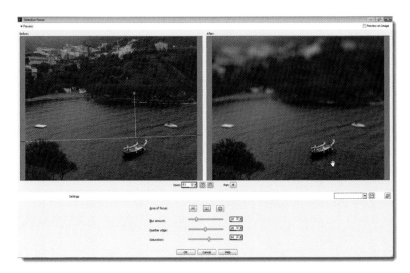

FIG 1.17 PaintShop Pro X6's selective focus feature simulates the shallow depth of field produced by specialist tilt-shift lenses.

Fill Light/Clarity

Fill light/Clarity is a new adjustment that comes in two parts. Fill light works a bit like the existing Fill Flash, which is more effective at brightening shadows without affecting other areas. According to Corel Clarity 'enhances subtle yet important details', the overall effect is to make lifeless detail 'pop'.

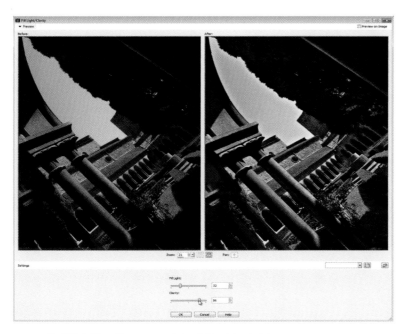

FIG 1.18 The Fill light/Clarity filter in action – before (left) and after (right).

Social Media Integration

You can share your photos on Flickr, Facebook and Google+ directly from PaintShop Pro X6. In Chapter 10, I explain how it works as well as looking at other ways of using photos on the Web.

Camera RAW Lab

Camera RAW Lab is PaintShop Pro X6's module for processing camera RAW files. It's recently been enhanced with an improved histogram and new highlight recovery options.

Quick Review

Quick review isn't new, but it's been recently updated and is now much more useful than its slideshow-based predecessor. It's an Organizer feature that displays a full-screen preview of the Organizer palette. Quick Review can be used to scan through a folder of images, delete the ones you don't want and rate and rotate the rest. It's full-screen, so you get a good look at the images and you can use the keyboard to navigate. To launch it double-click any thumbnail in the Manage workspace.

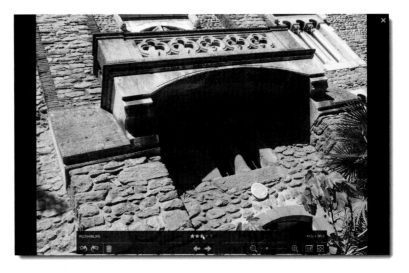

FIG 1.19 The Quick Review space is great for quickly rating your photos.

Multi-photo Editing

PaintShop Pro provides an easy way to apply all of the edits you make to a photo to other photos in the Organizer. This is an extremely useful thing to be able to do and has the potential to drastically reduce the amount of time you spend for editing. Let's say you've downloaded a card full of images from your camera and want to prepare them for a slideshow presentation. You select the first image, open it in the Adjust workspace, apply the Smart Photo Fix, adjust the color using Color Balance, then sharpen it before saving the image.

These are general edits that you'd like to apply to every image, so back in the Organizer you select the image and click the Capture Editing button on the toolbar. Now you just need to select the photos you want to apply the same editing process to and click the Apply Editing button and you're done. There are other ways to apply a sequence of editing steps to multiple photos, but none are as quick and easy as this.

Smart Carver

The Smart Carver is like an intelligent crop tool. It changes the dimensions of a photo without distorting the content by removing parts of the image that have little structural detail. You can also use the Smart Carver to target specific parts of the image that you want to remove. Used in this way, it's great for removing unwanted and distracting bits of photos like lamp posts, cars, trees or even people.

Object Extractor

The Object extractor makes it easy to isolate and cutout part of an image from its background. While the conventional selection tools require some skill and patience to get a good result, using the Object extractor is a much simpler process. You just paint an outline around the thing you want to extract, fill the area inside then click process to preview the result. You can then refine the result using Edit Mask.

Vibrancy

To adjust the saturation of colors in a photo you can use the Hue/Saturation/Lightness controls. The problem with increasing saturation, though, is that some colors can become over-saturated and unnatural-looking. Vibrancy is a more subtle saturation controller – it increases saturation, but rather than a blanket increase only those colors that lack saturation are boosted. This makes it ideal for giving a boost to skin tones in portraits and in other images which have a mix of strongly saturated and more muted hues.

Raw Format Support

PaintShop Pro X6 can open and edit images shot in your camera's – proprietary camera RAW format. For advanced photographers, there are many advantages to doing this not the least of which is the potential to produce better quality images than if you shoot using the jpg file format to capture images. The Organizer can display thumbnails for RAW images and when you open them they are initially processed using Camera Raw Lab. PaintShop Pro X6 extends the range of camera RAW formats supported; you can find a list of supported camera RAW formats on the Corel website at www.corel.com. You can find out more about processing RAW files in Chapter 2 and in the Step-by-step project at the end of Chapter 3.

Auto-Preserve Originals

It's always a good idea to back up your photos onto a CD or DVD so that, should the worst happen, you've always got the originals somewhere safe. Likewise, before you begin work on a photo in PaintShop Pro X6 it's always a good idea to leave the original untouched and work on a copy. One way of doing this is to select 'Save As' from the File menu and save the photo with a different name and/or in a different location (I sometimes create a folder inside the folder containing the downloaded photos and call it 'edited').

PaintShop Pro X6's Auto-Preserve Originals feature takes care of this for you by saving the original in a sub-folder of the current folder. You can either use this in addition to the backup steps I've already suggested or instead of using 'Save As' to create a copy. Auto-Preserve Originals is on by default, to turn it off select File > Preferences > General Program Preferences, select Auto-Preserve from the list on the left then uncheck the box and click OK.

Layer Styles

Layer Styles are live editable effects that can be applied to raster and vector layers. There are six Layer styles – Reflection, Outer Glow, Bevel, Emboss, Inner Glow and Drop Shadow. To apply Layer styles, double-click a layer in the Layers palette and select the Layer styles tab in the Layer Properties dialog box. Most of the Layer styles have basic controls – to adjust the size, position and opacity of a drop shadow, for example. You can edit Layer styles at any time by reopening the Layer Properties Dialog box and adjusting the settings. And when you edit a layer which has a Layer style applied, the style automatically updates.

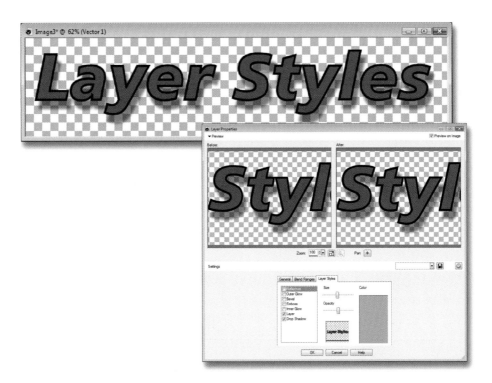

FIG 1.20 PaintShop Pro X6 Layer Styles include Reflection, Outer Glow, Bevel, Emboss, Inner Glow and Drop Shadow.

Visible Watermarks

Watermarking your images is one way of preventing copyright theft. PaintShop Pro X6's visible watermarks make it easy for you to add a logo, or other text or graphic to your photos. You'll find a step-by-step project that shows you how to add a visible watermark and copyright message to your photos at the end of Chapter 10.

Color Changer Tool

The Color Changer tool lets you change pixel colors at a stroke and provides sophisticated, but easy-to-use, selection methods so that only those pixels you want to recolor are affected. You can use the Color Changer tool to change the color of clothing, paintwork or pretty much anything at a stroke. There's a step-by-step project using the Color Changer tool at the end of Chapter 8.

Skin Smoothing

Removing wrinkles and blemishes is one of the most difficult retouching tasks; even professional retouchers find it a challenge. PaintShop Photo Pro's Skin Smoothing feature makes it easy to remove wrinkles and skin blemishes, taking years off your portrait subjects.

Riff File Format Support

You can save PaintShop Photo Pro files in the Riff file format used by Corel Painter and Corel Painter Essentials. These programs provide natural media painting effects and tools, which can be used to simulate traditional media.

Time Machine

Some photo applications have an 'antique' effect; PaintShop's Time Machine filter goes much further, providing a range of effects that simulate historical photographic processes such as the Daguerreotype and Platinotype.

Film and Filters

Film and Filters does two things. First it allows you to simulate the particular look of some color film stock. In the days of film, photographers would choose a particular emulsion for the look. Portrait photographers would choose a film for the way it rendered skin tones; for landscapes an emulsion that rendered rich earth tones and natural looking blue skies would be appropriate. Film and Filters has seven film looks to choose from including Muted Reds, Vibrant foliage and Glamour. Additionally you can apply creative filters from a range of six including Night Effect, Warming, Orange, Champagne and Sunset. You can also create your own custom filters.

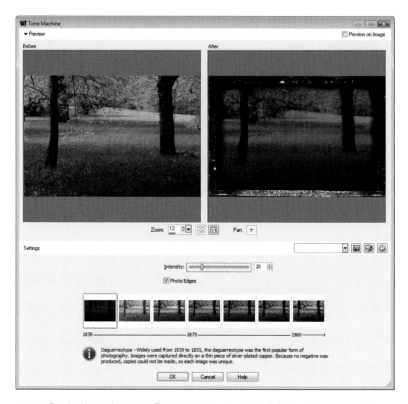

FIG 1.21 Time Machine applies ageing effects to photos based on historical photographic processes – this one simulates the Daguerreotype; also available, in chronological order, are Albumen, Cyanotype, Platinum, Autochrome, Box camera and Cross process – a more recent photo lab technique.

Depth of Field

Creating artificial depth of field effects to simulate using a wide aperture and throwing the background out of focus isn't difficult, but it takes time and a little skill. Corel PaintShop Pro's Depth of Field effect makes it a lot simpler.

Makeover Tools

The Blemish Fixer, Toothbrush and Suntan Brush can give your portraits an instant lift with very little effort. The Blemish Fixer can also be used for where a more subtle effect than the Clone Brush is needed.

Red-Eye Tool

A much more straightforward tool than PaintShop Pro's earlier red-eye removal tool; just set the tool size and click on the eyes.

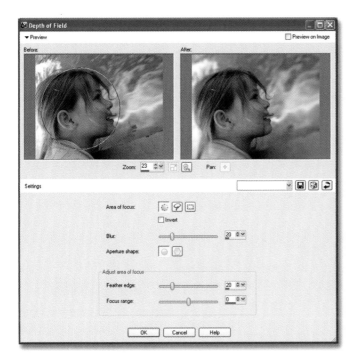

FIG 1.22 The Depth of Field effect simulates narrow depth of field achieved in camera by shooting with a wide open lens aperture.

Object Remover

Like the Clone Brush, but easier to use, the Object Remover seamlessly replaces unwanted detail in a photo, such as a lamp post, tree or other distracting background detail, with another part of the image.

One Step Purple Fringe Fix

A common problem with digital cameras, purple fringing is caused by lens aberrations. Purple fringing usually shows up as a purple fringe around high-contrast edges like tree branches against a bright sky. The One Step Purple Fringe Fix does exactly what it says.

High-Pass Sharpen

High-pass sharpening is a professional sharpening technique that has some advantages over conventional unsharp masking, mainly it's less likely to exaggerate noise and produce haloing.

Color Balance

If you don't know your additive from your subtractive primaries, then PaintShop Pro's new Color Balance tool is the one for you. It automatically adjusts the white balance to remove color casts, then all you need to decide is whether you want to warm the colors up, or cool them down. There's also an advanced mode.

Black and White and Infra-Red Conversion Filters

These effects allow you to easily convert your images to black and white and to simulate shooting with infra-red and black and white film with colored filters for enhanced tonal reproduction.

One Step Noise Removal

PaintShop Pro's Digital Noise Removal provides powerful tools for cleaning up noisy images providing you have the time and know-how to use it effectively. For everyone else, there's One Step Noise Removal.

Color Management

PaintShop Pro's color management engine lets you work with embedded image color profiles to improve screen-to-print color matching.

IPTC Metadata Support

Most metadata that's saved with images when you shoot them – the camera model and exposure settings, for example – isn't editable. But IPTC fields are designed to allow you to record information about the photographer, the location of the scene and searchable keywords. You can add and edit IPTC metadata in PaintShop Pro.

File Open Pre-Processing

This feature allows you to run a script on files as they are opened. It's a time-saver if you want to automatically apply the same process to all images you open, such as the One Step Photo Fix. Or you might use it to automatically downsample 16-bit images to 8-bit, or anything else you have, or can write a script for.

Step-by-Step Projects

Exploring the Learning Center

Whether you're new to PaintShop Pro, or an old hand, it's worth taking a little time to explore the Learning Center and see what it has to offer. As well as taking you step-by-step through basic editing techniques, like cropping and rotating images, the Learning Center can help you with more ambitious projects like producing a photomontage and advanced editing techniques like digital camera noise removal.

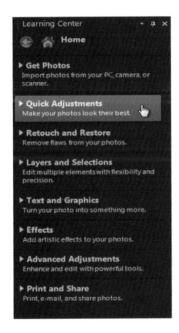

STEP 1 First make sure you're in the Edit workspace and if not click its tab. If the Learning Center isn't on the home page, click the Home button. Topics are divided into eight categories: Get Photos, Quick Adjustments, Retouch and Restore, Layers and Selections, Text and Graphics, Effects, Advanced Adjustments and Print and Share. Click on any of these to view the list of available projects. You can get back to the home page either by clicking the Home button, or the Back button at the top of the Learning Center palette, just like in a web browser.

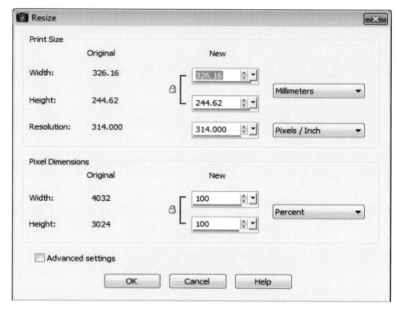

STEP 2 Click the second option on the Learning Centre Home page, Quick Adjustments, and on the next page click the last option on the list – Resize. The resize dialog box is automatically opened for you and the Learning Center explains what the various fields are for and how to use them. We don't want to resize this image just now so click the close box to get of the Resize dialog and click the Home button at the top of the Learning Center palette.

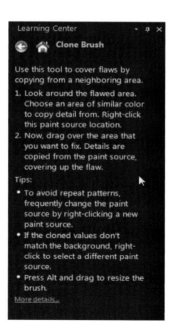

STEP 3 Now select retouch and restore from the Learning Center Home page and choose Clone brush from the Retouch and Restore menu. This time the Learning Center selects the Clone brush from the Tools toolbar and tells you what do with it. The Learning Center provides step-by-step instructions for a wide variety of tasks and selects the tools you need or opens the appropriate dialogs to help get you going. In the next two Step-by-step projects we'll look at how to straighten a photo and how to correct perspective with the help of the Learning Center.

Straightening an Image

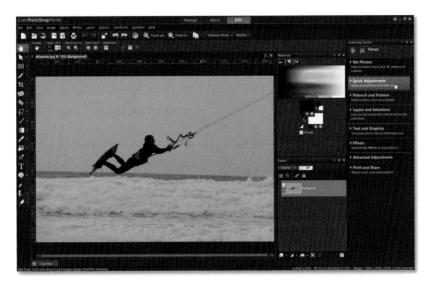

STEP 1 It's often not until you get to look at your photos on screen that you realize the horizon isn't level. Deliberate tilting of the camera to create a dynamic angle is one thing; a horizon that runs downhill, whether due to a tilted camera or skewed scanning, is generally to be avoided and can easily be fixed. Use the Organizer to open the offending image and click the Adjust button on the home page of the Learning Center.

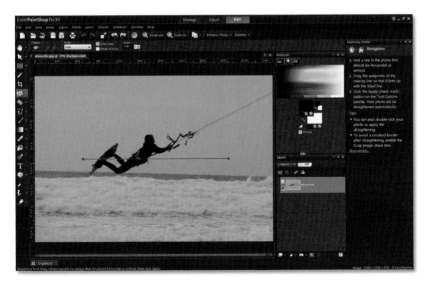

STEP 2 Select Straighten from the Adjust page in the Learning Center. The Straighten tool is automatically selected for you (it's the sixth tool from the top of the Tools toolbar) and a line appears in the center of your image.

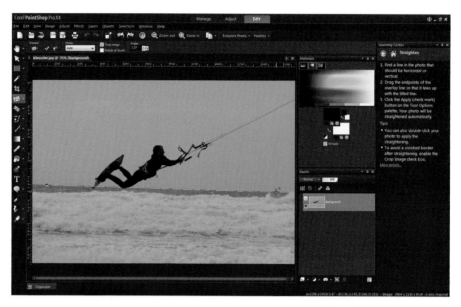

STEP 3 The panel in the Learning Center tells you exactly what you need to do to straighten the image. Move the endpoints of the line until it lines up with a horizontal or vertical line in the image – in this case the horizon.

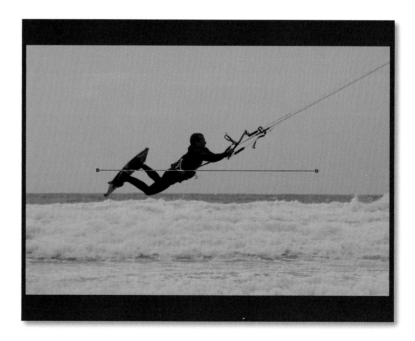

STEP 4 Then click the Apply button, or double-click the photo to apply the straightening. Bear in mind that when you straighten a photo like this the edges are cropped and the more straightening is required the more of the edges you'll lose.

Perspective Correction

STEP 1 As well as straightforward editing tasks like opening and straightening images, the Learning Center can help you with more advanced techniques. The Perspective Correction tool can be used to straighten 'converging verticals' – the tendency for tall buildings to appear to be falling backwards when you tilt the camera upwards. Start by opening the problem photo and selecting the Adjust button on the Learning Center home page.

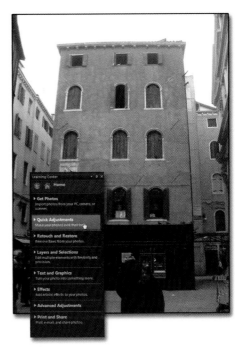

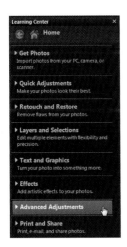

STEP 2 Click the Advanced Adjustments page on the Learning Center home page, followed by the Perspective Correction button. The Perspective Correction tool is selected and a rectangular box appears in the center of the image window.

STEP 3 Follow the instructions in the Learning Center to align the box with the edges of the building. If the building shape is irregular and you find alignment difficult, enter a number of around four to eight in the Grid Lines box in the Tool Options palette. This applies a grid to the perspective rectangle, making it easier to align it with what should be vertical features on the building.

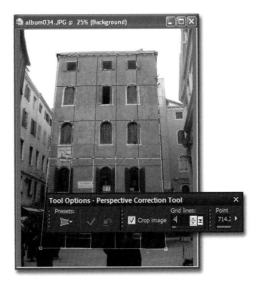

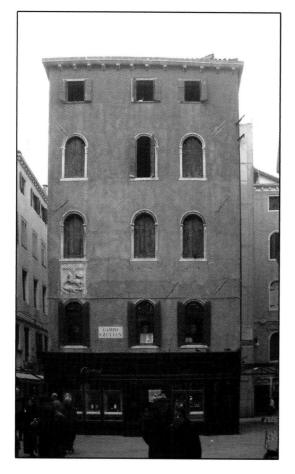

STEP 4 Click the Apply button to correct the perspective distortion. If you check the Crop Image box the edges of the photo will be cropped to remove the white space that appears as a result.

Tip

Select the Crop tool, click the Presents button on the Options palette and select one of the preset crop sizes from the pull-down menu. You can save your own crop settings to this list, enabling you to quickly apply custom crop settings to any number of images.

Cropping Pictures

After a while you'll find you can do without the Learning Center for simple and even more advanced editing tasks. Most pictures need cropping for aesthetic reasons and there are very few pictures that can't be improved by removing some of the detail around the outside to focus attention on the central subject. You might also want to crop a picture to change its proportions for printing, for example, so that it will fit a 4 × 6 inch or 5 × 7 inch frame, or a space on a web page.

STEP 1 Open a picture and choose the Crop tool from the Tools toolbar. Adjust the crop area size or position. The image area outside the crop rectangle is shaded.

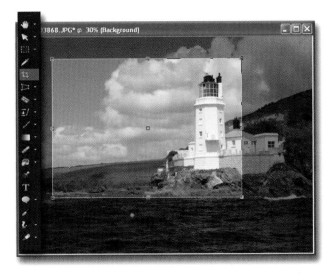

STEP 2 Click inside the crop area and drag to reposition it. You can constrain the crop area to its existing proportions by holding down the Shift key. If you're cropping for a standard sized photo frame choose a preset from the floating toolbar.

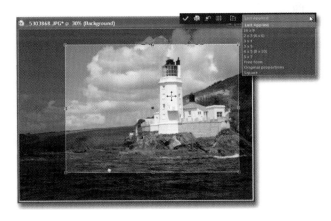

STEP 3 When you're satisfied with the area you've chosen double-click in the crop area, or click the Apply button (the green check mark) on the Tool Options palette to crop the image. The inside section of the marquee remains while the image contents outside the crop area are discarded. If it is not right, choose 'Edit > Undo' or Ctrl+Z.

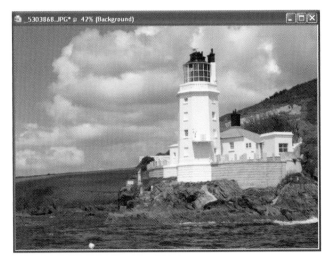

If you know the dimensions that the picture is to be cropped to, click the 'Specify Print Size' checkbox and enter the dimensions in the Width/Height and Units fields provided. The crop area automatically appears in the correct proportions for the desired crop. If you have many photos to be cropped for, say, a web gallery, this is a very productive tool. Click-drag any of the corner 'handles' or edges to expand or contract the crop dimensions while maintaining proportions.

You can also snap the Crop tool to a previously made selection in the image, its layer opaqueness or a layer's merged opaqueness. Once the cropped image is saved, the discarded area cannot be recovered. As a general rule you should click File > Save As to save a copy and make sure you have the originals safely backed up!

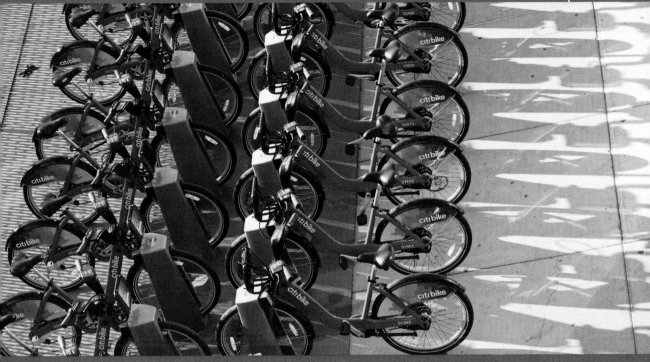

The Manage Workspace
Organizing Your Photos

What's Covered in this Chapter

- This chapter explains what the Manage workspace is and how you can use it to organize and manage your photos. As well as the image itself, a photo file contains text metadata, some metadata are recorded by the camera; other details can be added in Corel PaintShop Pro X6.

- In this chapter, I'll show you how to use the existing metadata in your photos and how to add captions, ratings, and keyword tags. You'll learn how to search for images using this information and how to turn searches into Smart Collections. The Manage workspace can be used to organize and edit Camera RAW files, and I'll show you how that's done. Next I'll show you how you can use recently introduced features in PaintShop Pro to search for people you know in your photo library and to organize photos according to their location and display them on a map. Finally, the step-by-step projects demonstrate how to caption, rate and tag photos, using the Organizer to apply a series of image edits to multiple photos, how to display photos on a map and finally creating a Share My Trip project.

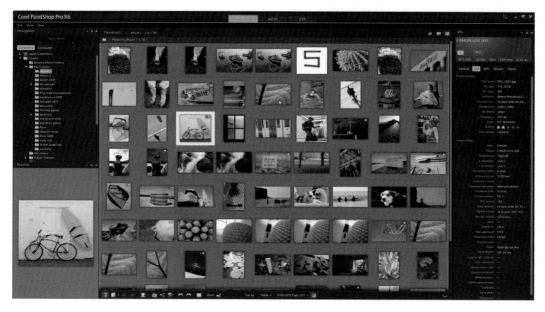

FIG 2.1 The default view of the Manage workspace is Thumbnail mode, which arranges the Navigation palette, Info palette and Preview palette around a central thumbnail area.

PaintShop Pro X6's Manage workspace is where you keep track of all your photos, organize them into collections, rate them and apply caption, keyword and other metadata. You can open images from the Manage workspace into the Adjust or Edit workspaces and you can view and prepare Camera Raw images.

When you first open the Manage workspace what you see will most likely look like Figure 2.1. In Thumbnail mode the Manage Workspace is arranged over four areas; the Organizer palette in the middle is flanked on the left by the Navigation palette and, below it, the Preview palette. On the right you'll find the Info palette arranged in five tabs for General information, EXIF data, IPTC data, People and Places.

Below the Organizer, at the bottom of the screen, the Organizer toolbar has controls for, among other things, grouping similar thumbnails, sharing photos, sorting thumbnails, rotating them, changing their size and printing a contact sheet. If you've upgraded from PaintShop Photo Pro X3 and are looking for the Search field, it's moved from the Organizer palette to the top of the Navigation palette. Its function is the same, though, you can use it to search image metadata, for example, to locate an image from its caption or keyword tags.

To get a better look at an individual image switch to Preview mode by clicking the Preview icon, the middle one in the row of buttons on the top right corner of the Organizer palette. Do that, and the Preview window is resized to fill the main area in the middle of the screen with the Organizer palette appearing as a strip along the bottom.

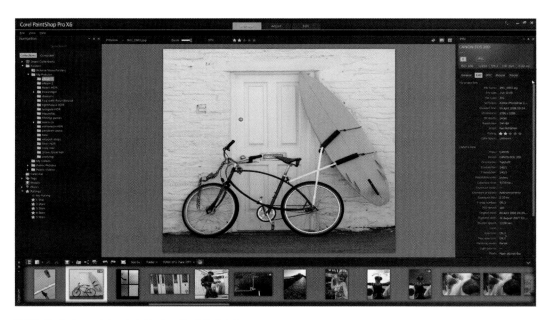

FIG 2.2 Use Preview mode to get a better view of individual photos.

The Manage workspace is customizable and you can change the layout to better suit the way you like to work. It's currently in Preview mode, which is good if you want to get a look at each of your photos; for more of an overview switch back to Thumbnail mode by clicking the Thumbnail mode button at the top right next to the Preview mode button. You can switch back to Preview mode at any time by pressing the Preview mode button.

You can further customize the workspace in both Preview and Thumbnail view by changing the size of the panels and windows by dragging the boundaries between them. Hover over the line dividing two panels until the cursor changes to a double-bar with a double-headed arrow and drag to expand one panel and contract the other.

The Navigation Palette

Take a closer look at the Navigation palette and you'll see that it has two tabs. Collections – the Collections tab – shows the structure of folders on your computer, but this isn't always the best, or easiest way to organize your photos. The Collections tab allows you to arrange your images in a way that isn't tied to the way you keep them on your hard drive – it's not bound by the folder and filename conventions used by windows.

Using the Computer Tab

If it isn't already selected, click the Computer tab at the top of the Navigation palette to display a Windows Explorer-style list of all of the disk drives and

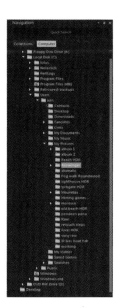

FIG 2.3 The Computer tab on the Navigation palette shows the contents of the hard drives and folders on your PC. It shows you everything, and if you're used to navigating folders in windows you'll quickly find what you're looking for, but all that other stuff mostly just gets in the way.

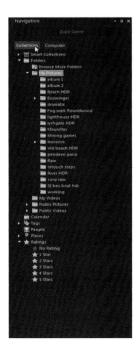

FIG 2.4 The Collections tab provides a much less cluttered way to view and organize your photos because it shows only those folders you choose, in other words only those containing photos and video.

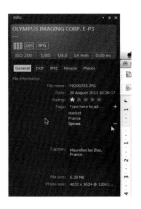

FIG 2.5 The Info palette panel is on the right of the Organizer in the Manage workspace.

folders on your PC. Click the triangle symbol next to a drive or folder to expand the list and reveal its contents. The thumbnail panel remains empty until you click on a folder that contains images or video.

You can organize your images using only the Computer tab of the Navigation palette, locating folders of pictures on your computer and carrying out all of the Manage functions, such as captioning and rating, described later, but then you'd be missing out one of the Manage workspace's best features. The problem with the Computer tab is that it shows you all of the disks and folders on your PC, whether they contain photos or not. Most people keep all of their photos in one place and all that other stuff – folders containing applications, text documents, spreadsheets, stuff downloaded from websites, your personal finances – all just gets in the way. The Collections tab lets you concentrate only on the folders containing your photos and videos.

The other really useful thing the Collections tab can do is group together photos on the basis of their content, rather than where they happen to be on your hard drive.

Using the Collections Tab

Click the Collections tab at the top of the Navigation palette and you'll see a list that contains several items, each of which can be expanded by clicking the triangle to the left of it. For now, click the triangle icon to expand the folders list. What you see here will depend to an extent on your version of Windows. Windows 7 users will see four folders My Pictures, My Videos, Public Pictures and Public Videos.

There's one other item in the list which looks like a folder, but isn't. Click the Browse More folders button and a dialog box opens which you can use to search for folders on your hard disk and add them to the Folders list. If you select a folder containing sub-folders, all the sub-folders are added too. So, if you keep all of your photos in a folder on your hard drive called 'Pictures' which contains sub-folders like 'Summer holiday 2013' and 'Joe and Anna's wedding' just select the Pictures folder and everything else will be added automatically neatly arranged in sub-folders just like on your hard drive.

I'll come back to the Collections tab of the Navigation palette after we've taken a look at some other aspects of the Manage workspace including how to add captions, keywords and other metadata to your photos.

Using the Info Palette

The Info palette displays metadata – information about your photos – which you can edit and add to. Adding metadata like caption information and keywords tells you and others more about your images than the picture data alone can and it also helps when it comes to finding particular photos, computers being much more adept at recognizing words than pictures.

As we saw in the last chapter, the Info Palette has five tabs – General, EXIF, IPTC, People and Places. First, let's take a look at what you can do on the General tab.

Adding a Rating

Near the top of the Info palette, below the file name and date, you'll see a Rating section with five stars. If you haven't rated any of your images the stars will appear greyed. Hover over them with your mouse and they turn gold, click on one of the stars to apply that rating to the selected image. That's all there is to it. If you change your mind, just click on the same star to remove the rating or one of the others to change it.

As you'll discover in the section about searching and Smart Collections, rating your images is one of the best ways to sort them, allowing you to quickly locate your best shots. It's quick and easy to do and the rewards are more than worth the effort.

Adding Keyword Tags

Underneath the Ratings section is the Tags section which is where you assign keywords to your images. To add a new tag to an image, type the tag in the top field, then click the Add Tag button to the right and it will appear in the tag list below. To add further tags just keep typing them in and adding them to the list.

Tip

The best way to apply ratings is to use Quick Review. Double-click the first thumbnail in a tray to launch Quick Review, click to set rating, click the next button and continue. You can speed the process even more using keyboard shortcuts – Press Ctrl plus the number of stars you want to assign.

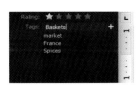

FIG 2.6 To add a tag to a photo, select the thumbnail, type the keyword into the tag field then press return or click the add tag button to the right.

Is there an easier way to add keywords than typing them individually for each and every image? Yes there is. Each time you add a keyword to a photo it is added to the tag list in the Collections tab of the Navigation palette. Once you've added a few keywords, click the triangle next to tags in the Collections tab of the Navigation palette to expand the keyword list – you'll see all of the keywords you just added in addition to every keyword tag you've ever previously added to a photo.

To add these tags to other images first select the images in the Thumbnail panel then drag and drop them onto the keyword you want to apply.

The way to get all your keywording done quickly, without it turning into a tedious chore, is to start with the most generic keywords and work down to more specific ones. For example, let's say you've spent a day at the beach with your family. You'll want to add the tag 'beach', to most, if not all of those shots, so select the first thumbnail, then press Control-A to select them all and drag them onto the word beach in the tags list.

A lot of your photos are of the sandcastle competition so Control-click to select those thumbnails and drag them onto the Sandcastle tag, then onto the competition tag. Remember, to get these words into the Tag list you'll first need to apply them to a single image by adding them in the Tags section of the General Info panel.

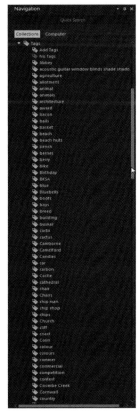

FIG 2.7 Every image tag is added to the Tag list in the Collections tab of the Navigation palette. Click the triangle icon next to Tags to expand it and see them all.

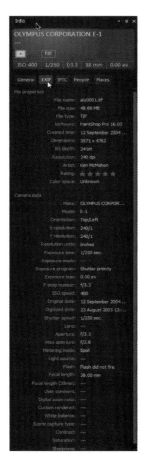

FIG 2.8 The EXIF section of the Info palette is divided into two sub-sections: File properties and Camera data. The EXIF section shown here displays camera make and model, exposure details and other metadata recorded by the camera at exposure time.

Keep on going in this fashion, selecting and tagging batches of images with common keywords – family members and so on. Eventually, you'll be dealing with small groups and single images which you can keyword tag from the Info palette.

Once all your photos are tagged, finding photos that contain a particular tag is easy, just select the tag from the list in the Navigation palette and all of the photos tagged with that word are displayed in the Thumbnails panel.

Adding a Caption

Like keyword tagging, captions can be applied to batches of photos. Shift or Control-click to select the photos you want to caption, then type the text into the Caption field in the General Info panel. If you can't be bothered to individually caption your images, give them all a more general caption – 'Beach trip, Cornwall, UK, August 2013' for example. You can always go back and edit them later if you have time.

The EXIF Tab

The Info palette's EXIF tab is divided into two sections. The top section displays the file properties and below it is the camera data recorded at the time the shot was taken. There's quite a lot of information on this tab and if you're in Preview mode you won't be able to see all of it because the Organize palette extends across the width of the screen. You could close the Organizer palette by clicking its close button (or pressing Shift F9), but there's a better way to manage your screen space.

If you're not already in Preview mode, then click the preview button at the top right of the screen. Now go to the title bar of the Organizer palette on the left and click the pushpin just below the close icon. When you do this the Organizer palette will disappear, but only temporarily. Look closely and you'll see the Organizer palette title tab is still there and, if you roll over it, it will reappear. You can auto-hide or 'rollup' other palettes in the same way by either clicking the pushpin icon (click it again to turn off the feature) or clicking the button below the pushpin and selecting Auto Hide from the palette menu.

Now you have a better view of the Info palette, but you'll probably still need to scroll to see all of the camera data.

EXIF data can tell you a lot of things including the date and time the image was taken, the camera model, exposure settings, the lens focal length, the exposure mode and whether a flash was used. Generally, EXIF data isn't editable – there's no reason you'd want to change it.

IPTC

Unlike EXIF, the IPTC section of the advanced Info panel contains information that is added after the event by the photographer or others. IPTC stands for International Press Telecommunications Council, which is the body that defined the standard. The IPTC standard for this kind of information was developed so that newspaper picture desks, stock photo libraries and other organizations dealing with lots of photos from lots of different sources would find it easier to manage them. But that doesn't mean IPTC data isn't useful to everyone else.

If you've added captions to your photos you'll notice that they appear in the Description IPTC field, where you can edit them. Your changes will be updated in the Caption field of the General Info panel – it's the same information, it just appears in two different places with a different label.

Other IPTC fields that are useful include Author and Credit, which you can use to state your ownership as the photographer and to add a copyright notice – useful if you apply to competitions or send your images for potential use in publications.

Earlier we looked at how to add folders of photos to the Collections tab of the Navigation palette. Then we saw how you can add keywords and other metadata to the existing metadata recorded by your camera and stored with each individual image file. Now we'll see how all this organization pays off by making it easy to quickly locate your photos and organize them into meaningful collections.

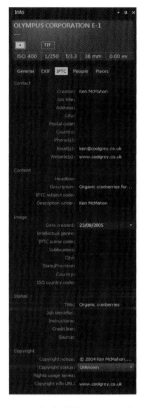

FIG 2.9 Use the IPTC sub-section of Advanced info to add and edit caption (description), title and author credits.

Searching and Smart Collections

Click the triangle icon next to the Smart Collections item at the top of the Collections tab on the Navigation palette to reveal the list of existing Smart Collections. Click the Smart Selection called 'Last 12 Months' and provided you've catalogued a folder of recent images (see Using the Collections Tab section earlier), the Thumbnails panel will display all of the shots taken during the last 12 months.

Using Search and Advanced Searching

We'll come back to Smart collections in a minute. There's another way to search for photos using the metadata they contain. As I mentioned earlier in this chapter the Navigation palette has a Quick search field. Type anything in here and the Organizer will show you thumbnails of all the images that contain what you type in any of the metadata fields or the filenames of your images. Before using search, select All Photos from the Collections tab to search all of your catalogued images. Alternatively you can search within a folder – either in the Collections tab or in the Computer tab.

For more advanced search options, select 'Add Smart Collection' – the first item under Smart Collections on the Collections tab – to open the Smart collection dialog. Use the left pull-down menu to select the search criteria; you can search by image name, caption, date, size, file type, keyword tag, edited date or rating. The next pull-down menu

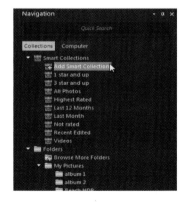

FIG 2.10 Smart collections are saved searches. The Organizer has a few preset ones including 'last 12 months' which displays all the photos you've taken in, that's right, the last year.

defines how the search engine matches the search term. Normally you'll set this to 'contains' but 'starts with' and 'ends with' can be useful, or you might want to search for images that don't contain a particular search term. Next, type your search term into the field on the right.

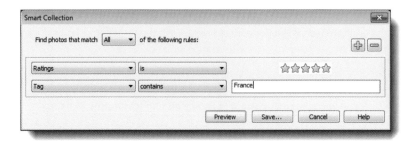

FIG 2.11 Using the Smart Collection dialog you can search for images that match all or any of multiple search criteria.

If you want to search for more than one term, click the plus icon to add another line. For example, you might want to search for images that contain the keyword 'beach', that were taken after 1 January 2013. In this case the first line of your advanced search would read 'Tag contains beach' and the second line would read 'Image date is after 01/01/2013'.

There's one final thing you need to consider before applying the search criteria. The pull-down menu at the top of the Smart Collection dialog has two settings. The default position is 'Find photos that match All of the following rules'. This means that if you select multiple criteria, like our beach example, only photos that comply with all of them will be displayed, i.e. they must contain the tag 'beach' and be taken after 01.01.13. Changing this to 'Find photos that match Any of the following rules' means that only one of your criteria need be matched for images to be displayed. With 'Any' selected, all photos tagged with the keyword beach will be displayed, regardless of when they were taken. Likewise, all photos taken after 01.01.13 will be displayed, even if they aren't tagged with the beach keyword.

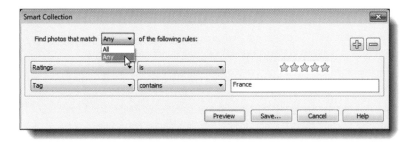

FIG 2.12 Searching multiple criteria using find any results in a wider range of images that match any of the search criteria.

Saving Searches as Smart Collections

When you've entered your search criteria and rules click the preview button to see all of the images that match. Click the Save button and enter a name to save your advanced search to the Smart Collections list in the Collections tab of the Navigation palette. Now you can access the same search simply by clicking its name in the Smart Collections list. You can also duplicate and edit existing Smart Collections.

Earlier versions of PaintShop pro came with a ready-made Smart Collection called 'highest rated' which displayed all images with a five-star rating. For reasons best known to themselves Corel have dropped it from PaintShop Pro X6, but it's easy enough to do yourself (maybe that's the reason).

First, click Add Smart Collection then choose Ratings from the left pull-down menu in the Smart Collection dialog. Leave the middle menu set to 'is' and click the fifth star to set the rating to 5. Click the save button and call the Smart Collection 'Highest Rated' or '5 Star photos' and click save. That's it!

I find these ratings-based Smart Collections really useful. Here's how to make another one, using a duplicated of the 5-star Smart Collection, that shows all your 3-star and higher rated shots.

First right-click the 'Highest Rated' (or whatever you decided to call it) Smart Collection in the Collections tab, select Duplicate from the contextual menu and enter '3 star and up' in the Save as a Smart Collection dialog. Click OK to add the new Smart Collection to the list.

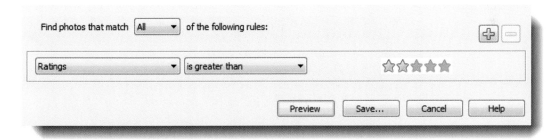

FIG 2.13 You can duplicate and edit Smart Collections to create new ones. In this case the Highest Rated Smart collection has been edited to produce a more useful 'Rated 3 stars and above' one.

Now right-click your new 'Rated 3 star and above' Smart Collection and select Edit from the contextual menu. The Smart Collection dialog shows 'Rating is 5 stars' – the setup for the Highest Rated Smart Collection which we duplicated. Change it to Rating is greater than 3 stars and click the save button – you'll be prompted with another dialog containing the name of the Smart Collection, as you've already renamed it just click save. Now when you select the Rated 3 star and above Smart Selection you'll see all images that have a 3 star or higher rating.

Smart Selections are live – whenever you catalogue new folders of images by adding them to the Collections tab your Smart Collections will automatically update to include them. So from now on any new images that you assign a 3 star or higher rating to will appear when you choose the Rated 3 star and above Smart Selection.

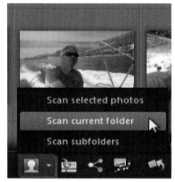

Searching for People

If you're looking for people in your photos PaintShop Pro has some specialist tools for the job that can help you organize and find people photos more easily. Essentially, tagging photos with the names of people is the same as tagging an image with any other word, except that PaintShop Pro can recognize faces so, once you've introduced it to everyone you know, it can automatically tag people and add them to a collection.

FIG 2.14 To start searching for people in a folder of photos, navigate to it then choose Scan current folder from the Find People button on the Organizer toolbar.

To run face recognition first switch to the Manage workspace and select a folder of images, then click the Find people button on the Organizer toolbar; it's the one that looks like a silhouette of a head. From the pop-up menu choose Scan current folder. If you like you can run Face recognition on a selection of pictures or on sub-folders within a parent folder, but beware of selecting more than, say, a few hundred photos at a time as the face recognition algorithm can take a while.

Once Find people has done its stuff the Organizer will display thumbnails of all the faces PaintShop Pro has recognized in the images in your selected folder. Of course it doesn't know who they are yet, but it has cleverly

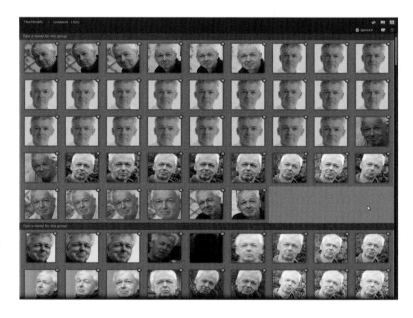

FIG 2.15 Find People scans all the images in a folder and groups faces it thinks are all the same person. It's done pretty well with me, but you occasionally find a mix of people and sometimes even objects grouped together. It's fairly easy to put right though.

organized them into ones that it thinks look the same. (Actually, it's not as clever as all that and you'll probably find that it's identified numerous things, clocks, parking meters, flowers, you name it, that aren't faces at all.) It's easy to get rid of these, along with any photos that are of faces, but not the same one as the others in the group. When all you're left with is photos of a single individual type their name in the space above where it says 'Type a name for this group'.

Repeat the process, deleting unwanted images and naming each group until they're all done. If there are too many to do in one go don't worry. Take a look at the Collections tab in the Navigation palette and you'll notice that a new entry has been added under the people heading for each of the people you identified. There's also an Unnamed group which is the one you've been working on in the Organizer palette. If you've had enough of identifying people for now just scroll back up to the top of the Navigation palette and select your original folder, you can come back to the Unnamed collection anytime and carry on with identifying groups of faces.

But let's stick with it for now. It may be that a group contains a bunch of faces that all belong to the same person but there's one that doesn't fit, it could be a relative or someone else, but it doesn't belong. You click the close button on the top right of the thumbnail to delete it from the group, but what if it's someone you want to identify? With any luck that person will appear in another group of their own but, even if they don't, you can still identify them. Once you've closed the thumbnail, click the Ignored button (with the trash can icon) at the top right of the Organizer palette.

The window that pops up contains all the faces that you've yet to identify. To identify one of them select it, then click the New Person button at the bottom of the window (even if it isn't a new person, but one you've identified before). In the pop-up window you can enter a name for the new person, or if it's someone you've previously identified just select them from the list. If you've done this before and have a long list of existing people, just type the first few letters of their name and PaintShop Pro will filter the list, showing only those that match what you've typed. Click OK to return to the Ignored window where you can identify other people or delete the clocks and parking meters.

To review all of the photos of a particular person, select the collection labelled with their name in the Navigation palette. If you subsequently discover a picture of someone who shouldn't be there, it's easy to delete or move photos between people collections. Just right-click the thumbnail and select one of the 'Move Person' options from the contextual menu.

Tip

To increase the accuracy of face recognition, find ten clear photos (head and shoulders portraits work best) of anyone you regularly take photos of and run face recognition on those, before letting it loose on other photos in your library.

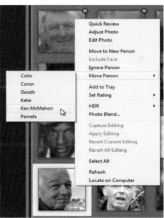

FIG 2.16 Right-click on any thumbnail in one of the people groups to move it to another one or ignore it.

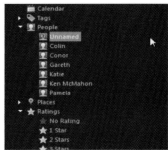

FIG 2.17 The people you've identified appear in the Collections tab of the Navigation palette, click on their name to display all photos they appear in.

Working with Places

As I briefly mentioned in Chapter 1, PaintShop Pro X6 has a range of tools for adding location data to your photos and using it to display them on a map. This geopositional data can also be used to search for photos, for example, to find all the pictures you took on your Italian holiday, or all the photos you've taken of the Tower of London.

The easiest way to work with location data is if your camera has a built-in GPS receiver, it automatically adds it to your photos. That way, when you bring them into PaintShop pro the data is already there for the program to work with. These days, more and more cameras coming onto the market are GPS equipped. Many recent models also have built-in Wi-Fi, so that even if they don't have GPS you can use a smartphone app to keep track of your position (using your phone's GPS) and add the data to your photos at the push of a button. So if you're planning on upgrading your camera look out for one that has built-in GPS and/or Wi-Fi.

Even if your images lack positional co-ordinates you can add them pretty easily in PaintShop Pro. And once they're added you can display the location of your photos on a Google map, to easily find all the photos you've taken in a particular spot, and to create a map-based interactive slideshow of your photos. See the Step-by-Step project at the end of this chapter for practical help with how to do that.

Working with Camera Raw Images

PaintShop Pro X6 supports Camera Raw Image file formats for a wide range of camera manufacturers and models. As new models are released Corel Updates the application to provide support for them, so even if your camera is a recent model, the chances are it will be supported. To check, go to corel.force.com and select your version of PaintShop Pro using the pull-down menus. Then type RAW into the search box and choose 'Supported RAW Formatted Cameras In PaintShop Pro X6' from the results or choose the appropriate result if you're using an earlier version of the program.

What are Camera RAW files and why should you use them? Camera RAW is a proprietary format that's available on most DSLRs, mirrorless compact system cameras and some advanced compacts. If you're not using RAW, your camera processes the information collected by the sensor and saves it as an RGB image file with JPEG compression (see Chapter 10 – Working with the Web – for more detail about how JPEG compression works). As well as compressing the file, in the process of converting the RAW file to a JPEG a lot of the original image data is discarded. By shooting and recording the RAW data, then doing the conversion yourself in PaintShop Pro X6, you can make your own decisions about how best to perform the conversion and get a better quality image than if you'd left it to your camera.

One of the main advantages of shooting and processing RAW files is that you can import them into PaintShop Pro X6 for editing as 16-bit RGB files – retaining all of the bit data for each pixel that the camera was capable of recording. When you shoot JPEG images the files are automatically down sampled to 8 bits per pixel, giving you much less scope when it comes to making tonal and color corrections and other edits.

The downside to this is that, with more bits per pixel and no JPEG compression applied, RAW files are much larger than JPEGs and eat up your memory card and hard disk space more quickly. With the falling cost of storage, this isn't the big issue it used to be though. And, when you've finished editing, you can always down sample files to 8 bits per pixel (select Image>Decrease Color Depth>RGB – 8 bits/channel), just remember to keep a backup of your original RAW files.

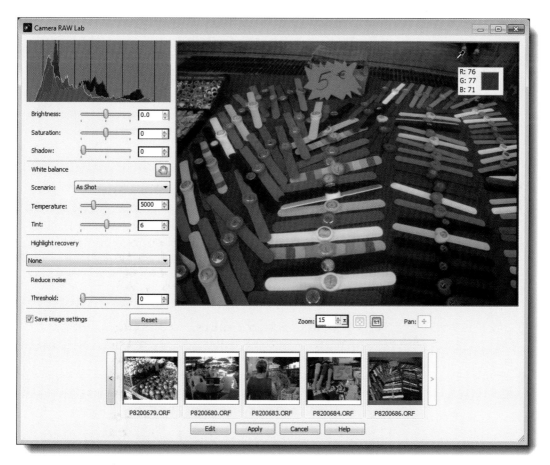

FIG 2.18 Select RAW thumbnails in the Organizer and hit the Edit tab (or right-click and select Edit photo) to open them into Camera RAW Lab. Several files can be opened into the lab for editing at the same time.

The Organizer displays thumbnails for supported RAW files. Camera RAW files are Processed by PaintShop Pro X6 in the Camera RAW Lab, to open a file into the RAW lab, select it and click the Edit tab. To process more than one image at a time, shift- or control-click to select several thumbnails, right-click and select Edit photo from the contextual menu.

The Camera RAW Lab window displays a preview image at the top, to get a better look maximize the window. It's important to understand that what you're looking at is an RGB interpretation of the RAW data. By adjusting the controls in Camera RAW Lab you can interpret the data differently to produce different results, finally outputting an RGB file for editing in the Full Editor or saving the settings to a 'sidecar' file that's associated with the original RAW file.

Two things about this approach are radically different to the way you might be used to working with image files. First, you can't make changes to and save RAW files, because RAW files are in effect locked. Because the data in a RAW file isn't in RGB format, it can't be edited in the conventional way. Instead, any changes you apply in the Camera RAW Lab are saved in the database and applied when you next open the RAW file in the Camera RAW Lab.

The second thing is that these changes in interpretation aren't destructive in the same way that editing an RGB file can be. You're not manipulating pixels, but re-interpreting the information in the RAW file to produce a different outcome. When you're happy with that interpretation you can output the file in RGB format for further editing in PaintShop Pro X6 or simply export it in any RGB format such as TIFF, JPEG or PSPIMAGE.

So let's take a look at the controls in the Camera RAW Lab. Below the histogram on the right you'll find four panels with controls for adjusting tonality and saturation, white balance, highlight recovery and noise reduction.

The brightness slider is used to rescue under- or over-exposed photos. It should be obvious from the preview if your photo is under- or over-exposed but the histogram can help you make a diagnosis as well as tell you how much correction is needed. Drag the brightness slider to the right to fix under-exposed shots and to the left to correct over-exposure.

Remember what I said earlier about Camera RAW Lab interpreting the data in you RAW files and how that's not the same thing as applying similar adjustments in the Edit workspace? Not only will these changes in Camera RAW Lab produce better results, you have a lot more scope for correction. The brightness slider extends to plus or minus 3, which means you can effectively correct up to three stops of under- or over-exposure – more than you could hope to achieve working on an 8-bit JPEG file in the Edit workspace.

The saturation slider works in much the same way as for RGB files; it's good for making small changes to saturation, but you don't want to go too far with it. The shadow slider can be used to add contrast to slightly over-exposed or flat shots that are lacking solid blacks.

Next are the white balance controls. Ordinarily white balance is applied in the camera – all you need to do is set the white balance to automatic or one of the available presets. But, as we've seen, none of this in-camera processing occurs when you shoot RAW and the white balance can be applied later. This is hugely advantageous as it allows you to easily remove color casts caused by incorrect setting of the white balance or the camera's auto white balance getting it wrong – it happens.

There are three white balance controls. A drop-down menu provides presets, one of which is the camera's 'As shot' white balance setting. Others include common lighting setups like Daylight, Tungsten, flash and fluorescent lighting. More control is provided via two sliders below. The main one sets the color temperature – you can enter it numerically in the adjoining field. Dragging it to the left, or entering a lower value makes the image cooler or more blue; in the opposite direction the image becomes warmer or more yellow.

If you know anything about color temperature this may seem a little counter intuitive. On the Kelvin scale used to represent color temperature the higher the color temperature the bluer the light, so how come setting a higher color temperature makes the image warmer? The answer is that the setting represents the color temperature of the prevailing lighting conditions when the photo was taken. By dragging the slider to a higher color temperature you're telling Camera RAW Lab the light used to create the image was cooler (more blue) than the currently specified setting, and therefore the result is a warmer (more yellow) image.

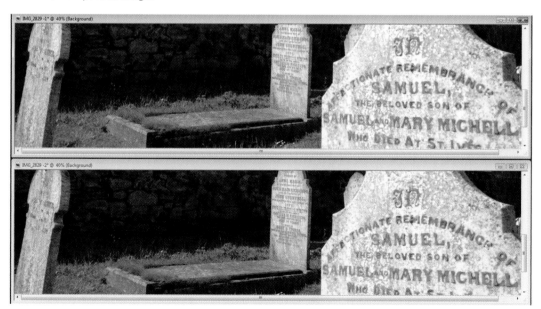

FIG 2.19 These two images show the same RAW file saved to RGB using different White balance settings in Camera RAW Lab. The one on top was saved with the 'as shot' white balance of 7770, the one below with the white balance adjusted to 12,500.

The tint slider below the temperature sliders is used to eliminate green/ magenta casts. Drag it to the right to add green (remove magenta) and to the left to add magenta (remove green).

The next panel down provides noise reduction controls. This has been simplified from the two slider setup in PaintShop Photo Pro X3. Now there's just one slider labelled threshold which goes from 0 to 100. The higher the setting the more noise filtering is applied, but beware. Beyond a certain point you'll start to lose fine detail in your image. Used sensibly though, these controls in the Camera RAW Lab, however, can give you a head start removing some of the digital noise from high ISO shots.

When you're happy with your adjustments you can either click apply to save them to the database (they'll be there the next time you open the RAW file in Camera RAW Lab) or click Edit to open the image as an RGB file in the Edit workspace.

Step-by-Step Projects

Managing Metadata

Captioning, Rating and Tagging Photos

Whenever you download a card of photos to your PC, it's always a good idea to rate them and add keyword tags and a caption. Don't put this off! If you do, you'll probably never get around to it and you'll be missing out on one of PaintShop Pro X6's most useful features. Tagging and captioning your photos will make them much easier to find in future.

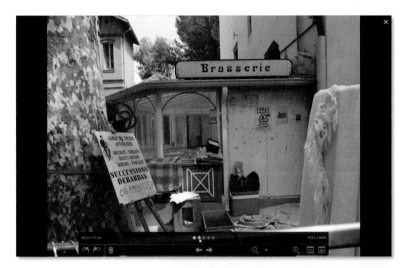

STEP 1 If you're not already in the Manage workspace click the Manage tab at the top of the screen and use the Navigation palette to locate the folder containing your photos. If you're in Preview mode click the Thumbnail mode button at the top right. Double-click the first thumbnail to enter Quick Review mode.

STEP 2 This is the Quick Review workspace, if you can't see the tool panel at the bottom move your mouse around and it will appear (it disappears after a few seconds of activity to give you a clear view of the photo). Apply a star rating to the photo by clicking one of the star buttons in the center of the tool panel, then advance to the next photo either by clicking the next button under the star rating or by pressing the right arrow on your keyboard. I find it easiest to have one hand on the keyboard navigating back and forth through the photos and the other on the mouse (or trackpad) to apply ratings.

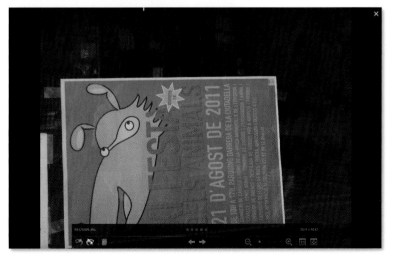

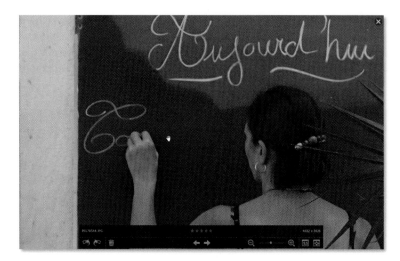

STEP 3 Keep on going until you've rated every single photo. Use the rotate buttons on the left to rotate photos and delete them. There are buttons on the right to zoom in to 100% view and back out to fit in window, but if you want a closer look, for example to check the focus, just click once to zoom in. While zoomed in you can move around by clicking and dragging, then zoom out again with a single click.

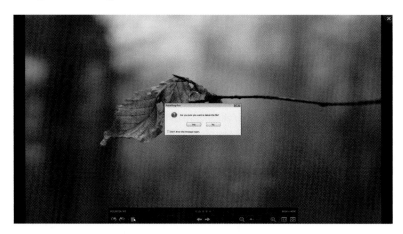

STEP 4 Every time you hit the delete button a warning appears asking you if you really want to delete the photo, which can get a bit tedious, particularly if you want to delete a lot of shots. In PaintShop Pro X6 you can turn it off (which makes deleting photos a lot easier, but clearly carries its own dangers. Once you've done this you don't get any second chance, though you can fish accidentally deleted images out of the Recycle bin in an emergency) simply by checking the box labelled 'don't show this message again'. In older versions of the program there's no checkbox, but you can still get rid of the warning. From the file menu select Preferences>General Program Preferences and select Warnings from the list on the left. Now uncheck the box that says WARNING – Confirm before deleting a file.

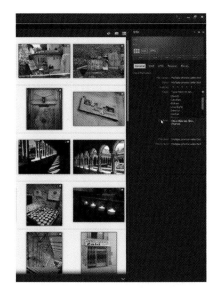

STEP 5 When you've rated the last image hit escape or click the close icon top right to exit Quick Review. Now it's time to caption every shot. You could go through captioning every shot individually, but that would take time and, in any case, many of your shots will probably share the same caption, or at least part of it. This folder of photos was mostly shot in and around the village of Maurellas Las Illas in southern France, so that's what we'll add as a caption. Back in the Manage workspace click on any thumbnail then press Ctrl-A to select all. In the Caption field of the General tab on the Info palette, type your caption, in this case 'Maurellas las Illas, France.' and hit return. It may take a short while to caption an entire folder of photos.

STEP 6 Some of these shots were taken in the nearby town of Ceret, so I'm going to recaption them. Click the first thumbnail

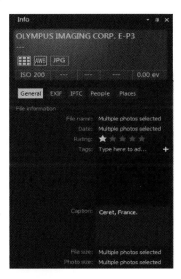

and Ctrl-click subsequent ones to add them to the selection. Then simply overwrite the caption field with the new caption, in this case 'Ceret, France.'. Likewise make group selections of other images you want to recaption. It's often a case of just adding to the caption to make it more specific, e.g. 'Shop, Maurellas las Illas, France.' or 'Street market, Ceret, France.'. Eventually, you'll get to amending captions for individual images – 'Harry buying sunflowers in the street market, Ceret, France.'. Even if you don't have patience for these individual captions, you'll have no problem locating the photos (or all your photos of street markets, or Harry) by typing the relevant search term into the search field at the top of the Navigation palette.

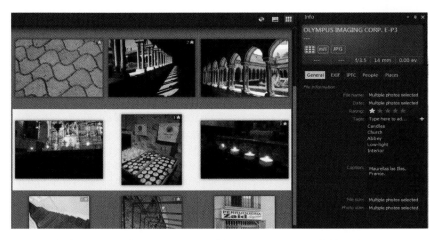

STEP 7 The final step in the process is to add some tags to your folder of images. As with captioning there are some tags that you'll want to add to lots

of photos. There are two ways you can do this. The first is by multiple selecting thumbnails, as we did for the captioning, and typing the keyword into the tags field in the General tab of the Info palette (above the caption field). Here, I've selected three thumbnails and added the word 'candles'. Click the plus sign (or press Enter) at the right of the tag field to add the tag, then enter any other tags you want and add them in the same way. Here I've added Church, Abbey, interior and Low-light.

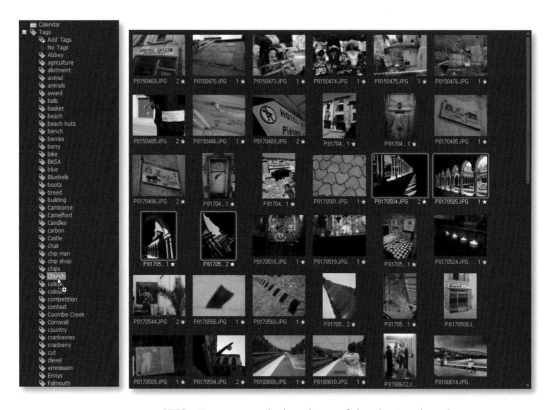

STEP 8 I've got several other photos of churches I took on this trip, some in the same location, but they don't have candles and they're not all low-light interior shots. I could just select these and add the Church or Abbey keyword in the same way, but there's an easier way that ensures I use the exact same keyword as before and don't mis-type it or change the capitalization. Click the triangle button next to Tags in the Navigation palette to expand the list of tags. Here you'll see all the keywords you've ever added to photos including the ones we added in the previous step. To add the Church keyword to several new thumbnails Ctrl-click to select them then drag them onto the Church keyword in the Tag list in the Navigation palette.

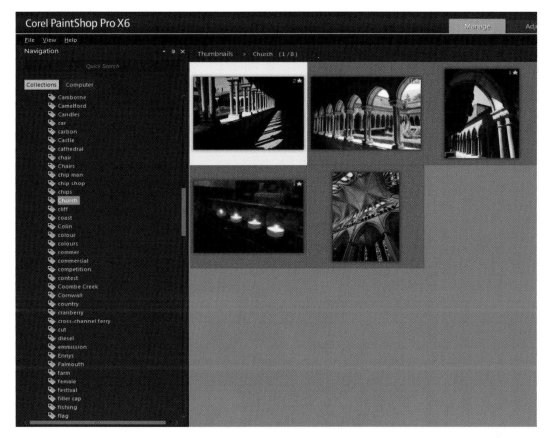

STEP 9 Continue to add keyword tags to images as described in the previous two steps. If you want to see all the shots tagged with a particular keyword just select it from the Tag list. And to check for any photos that haven't been tagged click No tags at the top of the Tag list. With your images rated captioned and keyword tagged you now have several ways in which you can organize, select and search for them.

Using the Organizer to Apply a Series of Image Edits to Multiple Photos

One of PaintShop Photo Pro's really useful features is the ability to capture a whole editing session from one image and apply it to many others. This feature is particularly useful for applying images edits to Camera RAW edits, but can be applied to any image that you've already edited in PaintShop Pro.

When dealing with RGB files, you can only capture and apply an edit list from photos that have been edited during your current session (the changes don't need to have been saved though). PaintShop Pro X6 keeps lists of all the edits you make to images (it uses these list for the undo command), but once you exit the program, the lists are deleted.

If you recall, when you make changes to a camera RAW file they're not saved to the RAW file itself, but as a list of edits in the database. This means that those lists are always available to PaintShop Pro (it applies them each time you open the program and view thumbnails for RAW files in the Organizer) and that means the current session limitation doesn't apply to RAW files; you can capture the settings you applied to them in Camera RAW Lab at any time and apply them to as many other RAW files as you like.

STEP 1 Select a RAW thumbnail in the organizer in the Manage workspace that you've previously edited in Camera RAW Lab and click the Capture Editing button on the Organizer toolbar.

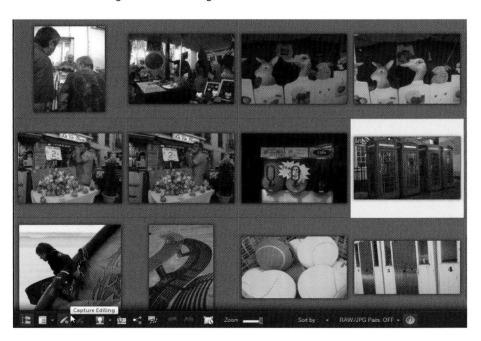

STEP 2 Now select all the other RAW image thumbnails that you want to apply the same settings to and click the Apply editing button. If you have selected more than a handful of images, it may take a short while for them all to be processed. You'll be warned that this can't be undone, and for RGB files this is the case, so make sure you have backups! For RAW files though, all you're doing is changing the Settings that determine how the RAW data in the original file is interpreted. And you could always open up one of the changed files, reset everything back the way it was, then capture that file's editing and re-apply it to the others to get back to where you started.

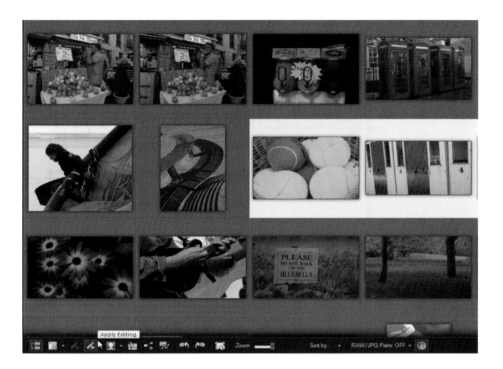

STEP 3 That's it! It really is that simple. I probably don't need to reiterate that all you've done is changed the Raw settings that are applied when you create an RGB file. To do that you'll need to right-click and select Convert RAW from the menu.

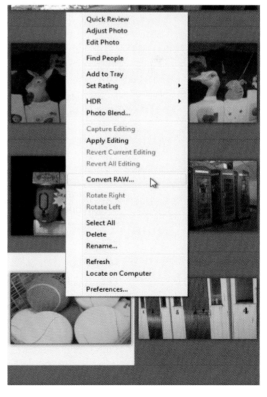

Displaying Photos on a Map

PaintShop Pro X6 has several features that make use of location data in photos. It can show you all the photos that were taken in a particular spot and can display a map showing the precise location of all the shots you took on your travels.

To make use of these features your photos must obviously be tagged with location data – the latitude and longitude positional co-ordinates that indicate the spot where they were taken. If you're lucky enough to have a camera with a built-in GPS or one that can link to your smartphone and get the GPS data from it, then there's nothing else you need to do. That information will be imported along with the other EXIF data in your images.

But even if you don't have a GPS-equipped camera you can still use PaintShop Pro's Places and Map features, you just need to add the information manually. That's easier than it sounds and this step-by-step project explains exactly how to do it.

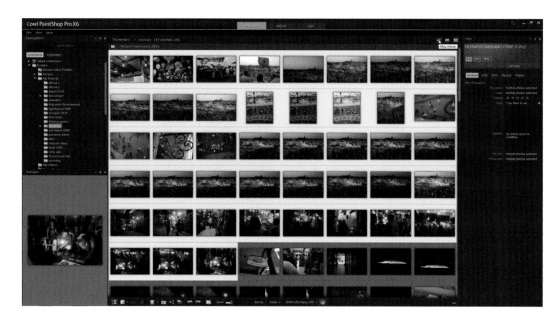

STEP 1 Select thumbnail view in the Manage workspace and navigate to the folder containing your images in the Navigation palette. Click an image thumbnail to select it and shift- or Ctrl-click to select any others that were taken in the same place. The information you're going to add will pinpoint their precise location, you can edit it later but you'll find it easier if you select a batch of images that were all taken within, say, a few hundred yards of each other. If all the photos were taken in the same place you don't need to select any, the location data will be applied to all of them. When you're ready, click the Map mode button at the top of the Organizer palette.

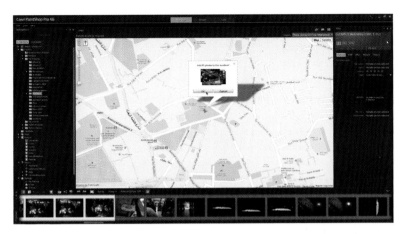

STEP 2 In the Search box at the top right of the Map window, type the name of the location where your photos were taken. Try and be as precise as possible, the search drop-down menu will list locations that match what you have typed it, when the correct match appears select it. The map zooms in to your selected location and a dialog box appears asking you to confirm that you want to add the selected photos, click OK. If you've selected more than a handful of images it may take a little while for the data to be written.

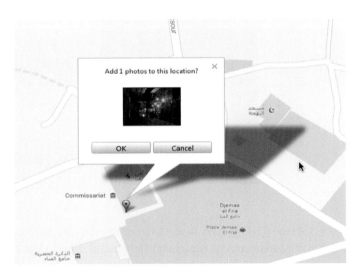

STEP 3 A marker for each of your selected images is now added to the map (each thumbnail also gets a marker badge to show it has been geotagged). At the moment, you can only see one map marker, because they're all on top of each other. Click on one image in the Organizer palette to select it then drag the marker to position it more precisely. In my example, here, all of these shots were taken in Djemaa El Fna, Marrakech, Morocco, but I spent a couple of hours wandering around taking photos in different places. When you reposition a marker, click OK in the dialog box to confirm you want to move it.

STEP 4 If you can't pinpoint the location of a photo from the map, click the Satellite view button at the top right, you may be able to get a better idea from the satellite image. PaintShop Pro uses Google maps, so in areas that support it you can use Streetview to accurately locate the exact spot you took a photo from. Streetview isn't available in Marrakesh, but I managed to find the spot on a remote rural street in Southern France where I took this shot of a notice fixed to a tree by identifying the blue garage door in the background.

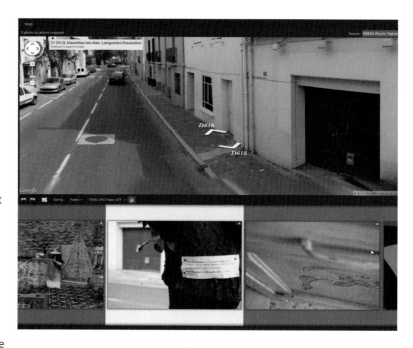

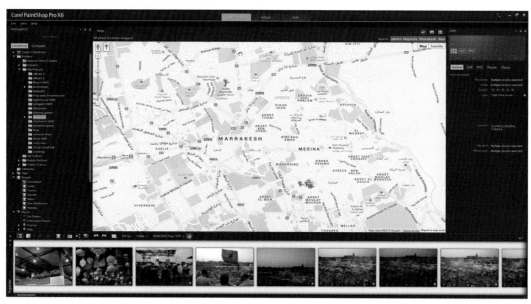

STEP 5 When you've tagged all of your photos, select the original folder in the Navigation palette, then select all (Ctrl-A) and you'll see a marker for each photo on the map. Click the marker and the Organizer palette displays thumbnails of the photos that were taken there. The Places section in the Navigation palette also provides a hierarchical list of the photo locations. By selecting these I can quickly display photos for any of the places I visited in Marrakesh or all of Marrakesh or all of Morocco.

STEP 6 Return to thumbnail view and select one of the places you've recently tagged – I've chosen Marrakesh. All of my Marrakesh images are displayed automatically sorted by place (you can change the sort order from the sort by pop-up menu on the Organizer toolbar). You can still see the map and the positional info for any image in this view by selecting the Places tab on the Info palette.

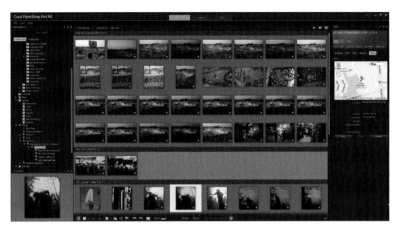

Creating a Share My Trip project

With all of the photos from a trip tagged with positional data, you can create a web slideshow that displays them superimposed on a map. If you have a Dropbox and Facebook account PaintShop Pro will upload the slideshow files to your Dropbox folder and post a link to them on Facebook.

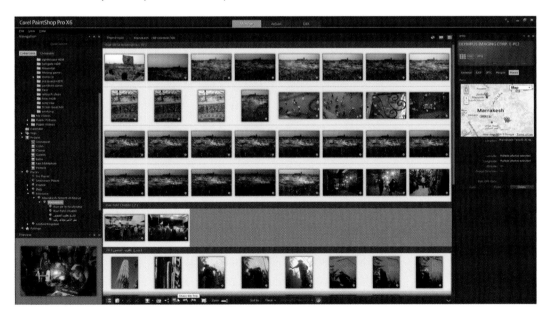

STEP 1 Start by selecting a folder of geotagged images in the Manage workspace – here I've used the Marrakesh images I geotagged in the previous project – and selecting all. Then click the Share My Trip button on the Organizer toolbar. If you haven't used Share My Trip before, a Getting started window will give you some details about how it works, when you've read it click the close button.

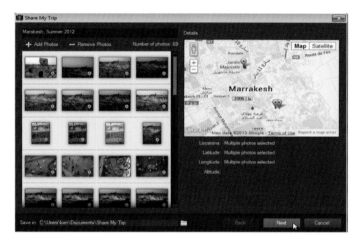

STEP 2 Type a title for your trip in the title field of the Share My Trip window. The project will be saved to your Documents folder unless you choose somewhere else by clicking the folder icon next to the Save in field at the bottom of the window. Next press Ctrl-A to select all of the thumbnails and click the Next button.

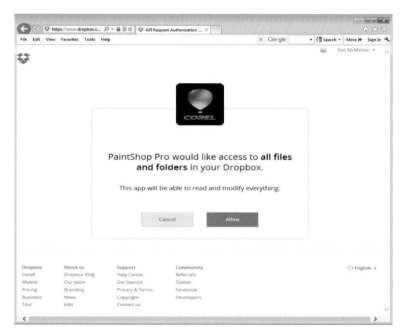

STEP 3 Depending on how many photos are in your trip, it will take a little while for PaintShop Pro to create the map. When it's done you can choose to have PaintShop Pro upload the HTML slideshow files to your public Dropbox folder and post a link to it on Facebook. Unless you do this the only place the slideshow will be viewable is from your computer. Check the box labelled 'Yes, upload my photo map to a public Dropbox folder' and a browser window will open for you to login and authorize access to your Dropbox account for PaintShop Pro.

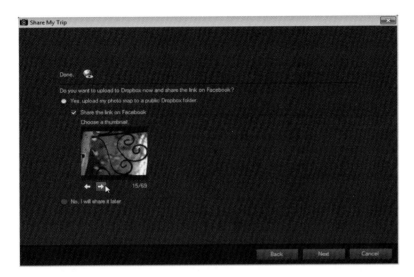

STEP 4 Now check the box to share the link on Facebook. Once again a browser window will open so that you can login and authorize access to your account. Once you've done that use the arrow keys to choose a thumbnail for the slideshow and click the next button.

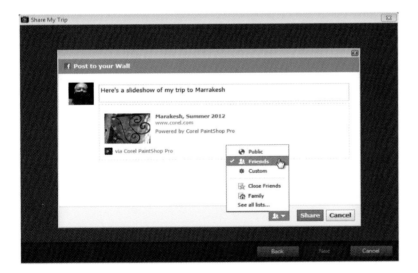

STEP 5 PaintShop Pro will now create the project files and start uploading them to your Dropbox folder. Depending on how many photos there are and the speed of your Internet connection, this may take a little while. When it's finished you'll be asked to log back into Facebook and you can then add a message to your post and choose privacy settings. Once that's done, the finish dialog box gives you the option to delete the local files and open a browser window to view your Facebook post.

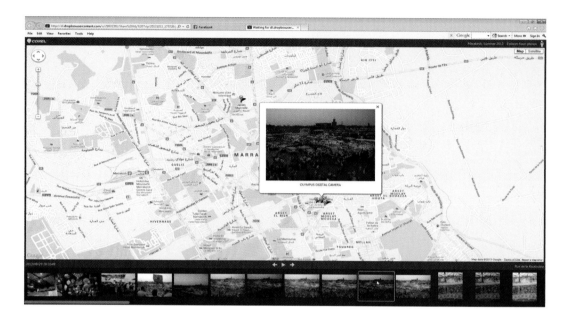

STEP 6 That's it, you're done, following the link from your Facebook post will take you to the Web slideshow hosted from a public Dropbox folder. You don't have to go via Facebook, just copy the url from the browser address bar then you can e-mail it to friends. Click on a map pin to display the photo taken at that location, scroll through using the navigation buttons and select a thumbnail from the film strip at the bottom.

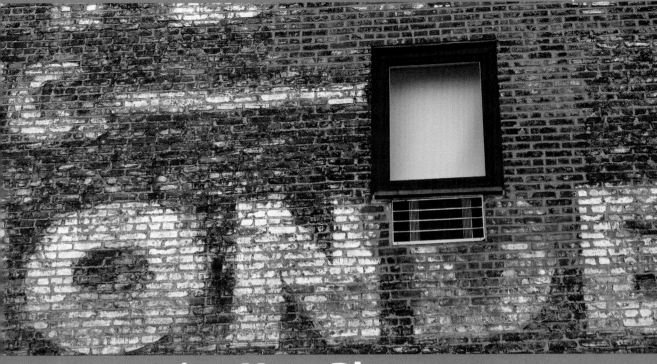

CHAPTER 3

Improving Your Photos
Basic Editing

What's Covered in this Chapter

- This chapter explains how to use PaintShop Pro X6's tools to improve digital photos that suffer from common problems like incorrect exposure, or are simply a bit dull and lifeless and need polishing up. PaintShop Pro X6 has a selection of tools like Smart Photo Fix and Color Balance which do most of the work for you and make it easy to get good results with very little effort. You'd have read in Chapter 1 that there are two workspaces designed for this kind of work. We'll begin by looking at practical things you can do to improve your photos using the Adjust workspace before moving on to explain in detail what kind of tools are available in the Edit workspace and how to make the best use of them. Later in the chapter we'll look at some of the more advanced tools for enhancing image quality like Hue/Saturation/Lightness, Levels, Histogram Adjustment, the Unsharp Mask filter and High Pass Sharpen filter.

- There are so many tools in PaintShop Pro X6 that it's sometimes difficult to know where to start, but if you work through this chapter, you'll discover one of its biggest strengths; you can start with the simple tools like Smart

Photo Fix and, if you can't get good results, move on to the more advanced tools that target specific exposure and color problems.

- It's not all about fixing pictures. Tools like Hue/Saturation/Lightness, Curves and the Hue Map can be used creatively to replace colors and this chapter also shows you how to do this.
- Sharpening digital photos is something that can hugely improve picture quality, but there's more to it than simply whacking on the Unsharp Mask filter. Toward the end of the chapter, I'll show you how to do it properly and, for those who want to squeeze every last drop of sharpness out of their photos without introducing other problems like noise and haloing, there's a step-by-step project that covers advanced sharpening using the High Pass Sharpen filter.
- Another step-by-step project goes into detail on how to use Smart Photo Fix. Although this is covered comprehensively in the chapter, it's such a useful tool that I thought a hands-on walk-through would be a big help if you haven't used this tool before.

Adjust or Edit?

PaintShop Pro X6 has a bewilderingly large array of tools for fixing up photos, so many in fact, that it can be a problem knowing where to start. If that's the case, then the short answer is probably the Adjust workspace, it contains all the tools you need to sort out most of the common problems that affect digital photos from bad exposure to red-eye removal.

Using the Adjust Workspace

To get started, if you're not already in the Adjust workspace, enter it by selecting the Adjust tab at the top of the screen and select an image to adjust from the Organizer palette. The Smart Photo Fix panel appears in the Adjust palette on the left with four sliders to control Brightness, Shadows, Highlights and Saturation.

Smart Photo Fix

The first thing to do is ignore the sliders and click the Suggest settings button at the top of the Smart Photo Fix panel. This almost always results in an improvement to the image, but there may be more that you can do. You'll notice that the sliders have moved with the suggested settings, now's your chance to tweak them to see if you can improve on the suggested settings.

With all these adjustments you need to be careful not to overdo it, particularly when you're altering the tonal qualities of an image as we are here. The brightness slider, for example, can be used to compensate for a small degree of over- or under-exposure, but nothing like the degree to which you can adjust Camera RAW files as discussed in Chapter 2. Keep an eye on the

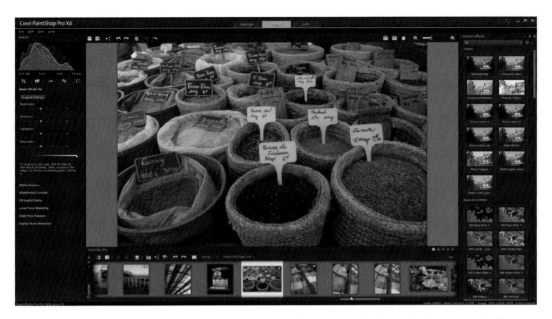

FIG 3.1 With Smart Photo Fix, start by clicking the Suggest settings button, more often than not it will result in a marked improvement and at the very least it will provide you with a result you can improve on using the sliders.

histogram when you're making these changes. Generally you're looking for a graph that just extends to both ends of the *x*-axis. For more help on understanding the histogram and using it to guide your adjustments, see page 72 later in the chapter.

When you use the brightness slider you affect the value of every pixel in the image – from the darkest shadows to the brightest highlights. The Shadows and Highlights sliders only affect pixels in their respective tonal ranges. These sliders can be used to make further changes to an incorrectly exposed photo or to add contrast to a flat one. Dragging either slider left darkens pixels and right lightens them. So to make the shadows a bit deeper you'd drag the shadows slider to the left, and you'd do the same thing with the highlights slider to recover blown highlights.

Tip

At any stage in the process you can use the Undo and Redo buttons on the Adjust toolbar to get a before and after view of the last change you made.

The saturation slider controls the vibrancy of the colors. If the color is looking a bit dull and washed out you can give it a boost by dragging the slider to the right and vice versa if the colors look over-saturated and unnatural. If the color saturation looks fine, but the colors themselves don't look quite right, maybe the entire image has a predominant color cast, or a sunlit evening doesn't look quite as warm and inviting as you remember it, position the cursor over the image and it will change to an eyedropper. Now find an area of the image that is, or should be neutral in color, black and whites are usually the better option, but greys work just as well. Click on that part of the image to add a color sampler and you should see an immediate change in the overall color of the image. If you've selected well, the change will be an improvement,

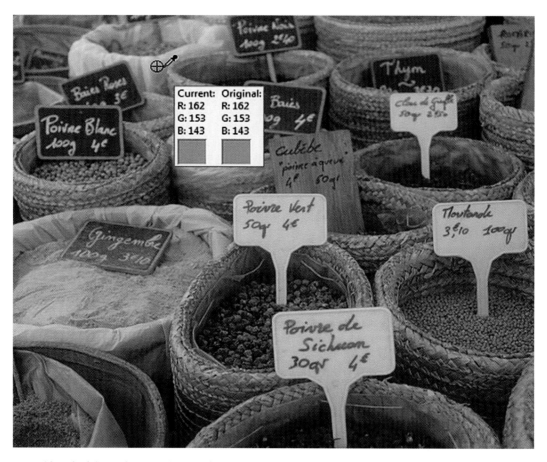

FIG 3.2 Adjust white balance and remove predominant color casts by placing samplers in the image using the eyedropper. You shouldn't need more than one or two sampling points.

if it isn't, don't worry, just click again on another neutral area to add another sampler.

You can add as many sampling points as you want, but two or three should be plenty. To delete a sampling point, just click in it with the eyedropper. As you hover over the image you'll see a color swatch with a numerical readout that tells you the before and after RGB (red, green and blue) values of the pixel beneath the eyedropper. The closer together these numbers are, the nearer to neutral the pixel already is (e.g. 0,0,0 is black, 255,255,255 is white and 128,128,128 is grey) and the less of a change you'll see if you add a color sampler. Clicking on a non-neutral pixel shifts the color of that pixel toward neutral and makes a similar adjustment to all other colors in the image. So if you click on a bluish pixel, it will become greyer and all of the colors in the photo will become less blue and more yellow (the opposite or 'complementary' color to blue). If you click on a yellow pixel the reverse will happen.

Now let's take a look at some of the other adjustments in the Adjust palette.

White Balance

White Balance provides a different way of doing what I've just been talking about – making a global adjustment to all the colors in a photo to remove a predominant cast. Instead of Smart Photo Fix's color samplers, there are two sliders, one labeled Cooler/Warmer and the other Purple/Green. If it makes it any easier you can think of the Cooler/Warmer slider as a Blue/Yellow slider. With these two sliders, you can add or remove pretty much any color cast from the image. More often than not, the Cooler/Warmer slider is the only one you'll need. You'll notice there's a numerical readout opposite both sliders. The Green/Purple one goes from −100 to 100 and the Cooler/Warmer slider goes from 9500 at the Cooler end to 2000 at the Warmer end. This is the color temperature – a numerical measure of the color of the light.

Brightness/Contrast

Brightness/Contrast is something that, at first sight, looks like a useful enough tool, but I'd recommend you treat it with caution. To see why, drag the Brightness slider to the right and watch what happens. Everything in the image gets brighter which is perhaps what you'd expect, but keep dragging and eventually everything turns pure white. Now you might think that as long as you keep the adjustments to a minimum, Brightness is OK, but the problem is it brightens all the pixels in a photo by the same amount when ordinarily you only want to brighten the darker ones. The result is that all the lighter pixels – the highlights in your photo – get blown out to pure white, and the detail is lost forever.

The same thing happens for contrast, only doubly so – you lose detail in the shadows and the highlights at the same time. Contrast can make for quite a dramatic effect, but if you're attempting to improve the tonal quality of your photos you're much better of sticking to the slider in Smart Photo Fix or venturing into the Edit workspace and using some of the tools described later in this chapter.

Fill Light/Clarity

Fill Light/Clarity was introduced in PaintShop Pro X4, and like all of these Adjust palette tools is also available in the Edit workspace. Fill light is specifically for adding light into the shadow regions of photos and is particularly useful for shots that are slightly under-exposed or where you should've used a fill flash, but didn't.

The Clarity half of this tool is more generally useful and in fact I'm not at all sure why Corel has lumped it in with Fill Light but there you are. What it does is difficult to explain, but easy to see so have a go with the slider and see what you think. Clarity increases local contrast; in other words, it takes a clump of pixels and lightens the bright ones and darkens the dark ones. It works in the same way as some sharpening filters only on larger groups of pixels and the

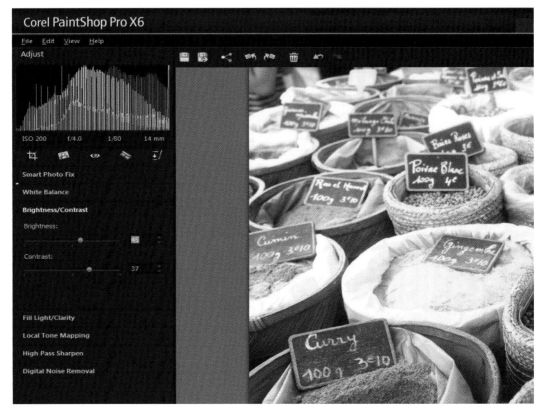

FIG 3.3 Treat Brightness/Contrast with caution, better still avoid it altogether, as it won't help improve the quality of your photos, no, not even the under-exposed ones.

effect, rather than to sharpen the image, is to make it 'pop'. Well, I did say it was difficult to explain, but it's something that will make the majority of your photos look better. It depends on the individual shot and it's down to your own personal judgment, but I'd say anywhere between 20 and 50 will give good results most of the time.

Local Tone Mapping

Even the Corel help file isn't of much help in describing what this does. Tone mapping is a technique used in HDR (High Dynamic Range) imaging that enables the huge tonal range of an HDR photo to be represented in an 8- or 16-bit RGB file. Local Tone Mapping as applied in the Adjust palette seems to make little positive difference to image quality, but it can be used as a special effect. If your camera has an effects mode, for example, Art filters on Olympus compact and system cameras or Creative Effects on Canon compacts, the Dramatic tone filters produce a similar result to what you'll get with Local Tone Mapping.

You can find a tutorial showing how to recreate the Dramatic filter effect on gopaintshoppro.co.uk.

High Pass Sharpen

High Pass Sharpen is a specialist sharpening technique that excels at sharpening image detail without exaggerating noise. There's a step-by-step project at the end of this chapter that demonstrates how to use it in the Edit workspace. If you just want to try it out here, first make sure to click the 1:1 button on the Adjust toolbar so you can see the results properly.

Digital Noise Removal

There's a full description of how to use the Digital Noise Removal filter in the Edit workspace in chapter 4 on page 113. Briefly, this filter reduces the impact of digital noise – the graininess inherent in digital photos taken with the camera set on high ISO sensitivities for low light conditions. The detail slider applies the noise reduction, so the further to the right you slide, the more noise filtration will be applied. The problem is that beyond a certain point, this will start to soften real image detail, so when this happens, you need to back off a little. You can restore detail back into the image by using the Correction Blend slider to blend the noise-filtered version with the original and finally apply some sharpening.

Using the Edit Workspace

The Edit workspace is the heart of PaintShop Pro X6. In earlier versions of the application, the Edit workspace was all you got, the Manage and Adjust workspaces have evolved over time to address the need for managing and applying straightforward adjustments to photos. So Edit is where you come to make more involved adjustments and to work on bigger projects.

The Edit workspace can look a little intimidating if you're new to it, but the Organizer palette running across the bottom of the screen should be familiar and the Learning Center, which I introduced in Chapter 1, is on the right. In Chapter 1, I also walked through what's on the various menus, the toolbars, the palettes and some of the more advanced editing tools.

What we're going to do next is take a more in-depth look at the tools available in the Edit workspace and how you can use them. Mostly, these tools are for the kinds of adjustments we've already looked at in the Adjust workspace, but they're more powerful and more versatile and therefore provide more scope both for improving photos and for creating something entirely new. But before we do that I first want to introduce the histogram. If it isn't already on the screen, you can display the histogram by pressing F7, or if you want to go the long way round, View>Palettes>Histogram.

Using the Histogram

The histogram is a graph of the values of all the pixels in the image. Dark pixels have low values and light pixels have high values. Black is 0, white is 255 and mid-grey is 128. So the histogram shows the distribution of pixels in the image from black to white with darker pixels on the left and light ones on the right.

When making tonal adjustment (in other words adjustments that only affect the brightness range of an image and not its color), it's useful to display just the greyscale histogram, you can do this using the histogram in the Edit workspace, just uncheck the boxes for the other channels. Unfortunately, the histogram in the Adjust workspace, which sits at the top of the Adjust palette, isn't so accommodating and shows separate charts for the RGB channels in the image. Even so, you can get a good idea of the tonal distribution by viewing the RGB charts as one.

The shape of the histogram depends on the nature of the subject, but generally speaking, it should show a reasonably even distribution from black to white. Typical problems like under- and over-exposure have very characteristic histograms. In an under-exposed image, there's a predominance of dark pixels and few, if any, white ones, so the histogram tends to be bunched down at the left-hand end. In over-exposed photos the histogram is bunched at the right-hand end, with no black or very dark pixels.

Another problem that is easily confirmed by a quick look at the histogram is lack of contrast. Images that lack contrast look flat and dull. They lack punch due to the absence of pure black and pure white pixels. The tonal range starts at light grey and ends at dark grey, and the histogram this time is all in the middle of the range with no pixels at either end.

In the Smart Photo Fix dialog box when you make an adjustment with the Brightness sliders, the histogram displays a pink overlay which shows you how the tonal distribution of pixels changes; the original histogram appears in grey. If you drag any of the sliders toward the right (brighter) direction, you'll see the histogram move the same way. Dragging the Shadows and Highlights sliders moves the histogram at the ends, whereas the Overall slider moves the whole thing, but the middle more than the edges.

The important thing to remember when making adjustments with the brightness sliders is not to let the histogram slip off either end of the chart – it should taper off just before reaching the end. If you allow pixels to drop off the end of the histogram, you are losing image detail – in the case of highlights remapping light grey pixels to pure white and, in the shadows, turning darker detail pure black. This applies to all dark and light colors which are represented by grey pixels in the RGB channels.

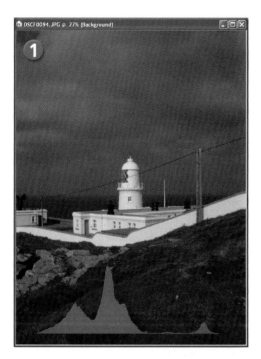
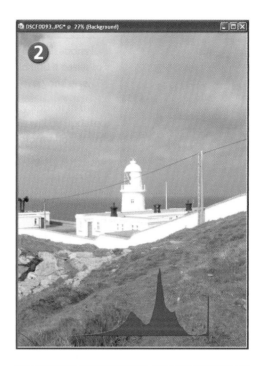
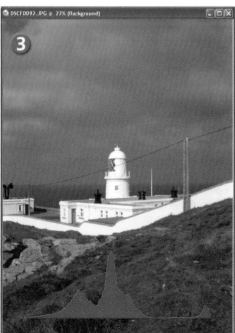
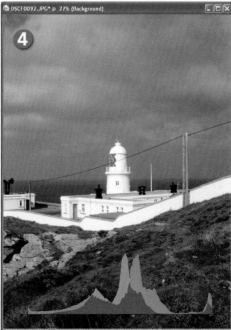

FIG 3.4 Understanding histograms will help you make the right decisions about tonal adjustments. (1) In under-exposed photos the graph is bunched down the left-hand side. (2) The histogram for over-exposed photos is squeezed up on the right-hand side. (3) The correct exposure shows most detail in the central area of the histogram, but the image lacks contrast. (4) Smart Photo Fix improves things by 'stretching' the histogram to produce true blacks and whites, but be careful: using these settings will lose some highlight detail in the lighthouse building -- note the clipped bunch of pixels on the far right of the histogram.

Tools for Correcting Color Problems

For most situations Smart Photo Fix provides all the tools you'll need to sort out exposure problems and remove unwanted color casts from your photos. But it's not the best way to deal with every problem, and it's always good to have alternatives. The following tools not only provide an alternative route to sorting out problem photos but also can be used creatively to introduce new color and tonal effects. Chapter 4 shows you how to introduce color into black and white images using some of these tools.

White Balance

To use PaintShop Pro X6's White Balance tool select Adjust>White Balance. You can check the 'Preview on Image' box to preview the results on the main image, but if you click the Preview triangle on the left you can see before and after previews which can be much more useful, particularly if you maximize the panel.

White Balance has a Basic and Advanced mode. In Basic mode it couldn't be simpler to use – you just drag the slider to the right to make photos warmer and to the left to make them cooler. If you simply want to neutralize a color cast, check the Smart White Balance box and set the slider in the center.

For more control over white balance, check the Advanced Options box. This divides the dialog box into two panels.

For PaintShop Pro X6 users, this just provides an additional set of sliders (the ones on top) which you can use to make further adjustments to the white balance. If you're using PaintShop Pro X4 or an earlier version, these sliders work a little differently (it's also called Color Balance, not White Balance in X4 and earlier versions). The tools in the Color Balance panel are used to identify the original conditions under which the photo was taken; you then use the sliders in the Enhance Color Balance panel to make further minor adjustments. This can be a little counter-intuitive if you're not used to it, because dragging the Temperature slider in the Color Balance panel toward warm actually makes the image cooler or more blue. This is because you're telling the program that the original lighting conditions were warmer than those depicted in the unadjusted image.

For example, if you set your camera's white balance for indoor use, and then go and take photos outdoors without resetting it, all of your pictures will have a blue cast. This is because daylight is much cooler (or more blue) than the artificial indoor light that you've set the camera up for.

In the Color Balance dialog, by dragging the White Balance Temperature slider toward cool, you're saying that the actual color temperature of the light this picture was taken in was much cooler than what the camera was set up for and recorded – and the blue cast is eliminated.

Tip

In the White Balance dialog box, clicking either side of the slider makes a fixed increment adjustment. The Color Temperature sliders increase or decrease by 100 and the Tint sliders go up or down by 10. Alternatively, you can enter a figure in the number field or use the toggle buttons to increase or decrease the amount by one.

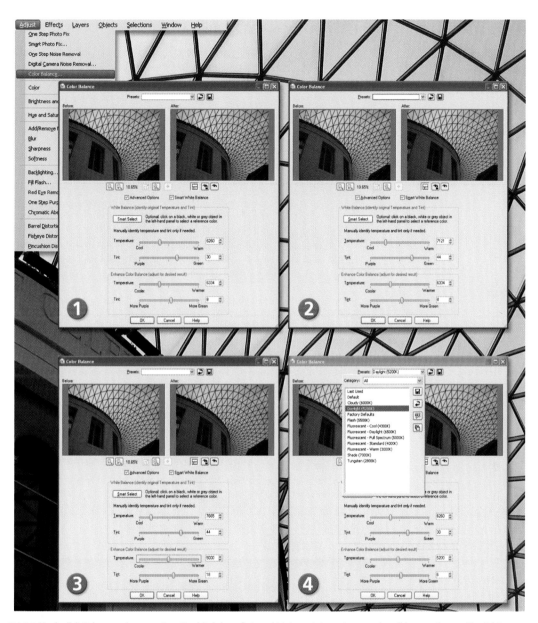

FIG 3.5 Nearly all digital cameras have an automatic white balance feature which in most circumstances works well to assess the prevailing lighting conditions. It's not foolproof however and in this instance has resulted in a blue/green cast. (1) When you select Adjust>White Balance, the image is automatically assessed and the preview thumbnail on the right shows you what the corrected image will look like. These settings are based on an automatically selected neutral area indicated by the cross-hair target. (2) To select a different neutral area click anywhere in the left thumbnail; keep trying different locations to see if you can improve the result. (3) You can nearly always improve things by making your own adjustments using the sliders – in this case to produce a more neutral, slightly warm result. (4) The Color Balance dialog is one of the few to offer a useful set of ready-made presets – just pick the one that most closely resembles the lighting conditions under which the photo was taken. Here, the Daylight (5200K) preset produces near perfect results.

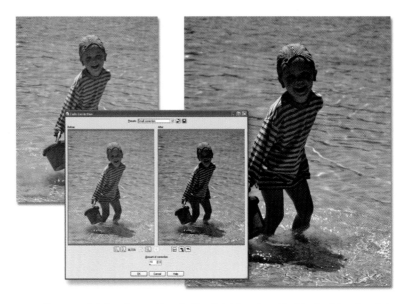

FIG 3.6 You can use Fade Correction on pictures that have faded through age, like this color slide, or those that just suffer from poor contrast.

There's another way to get rid of unwanted color casts in the White Balance dialog box and that's to use the Smart Select button. This works in a very similar fashion to the White Balance option in the Smart Photo Fix dialog box (don't confuse it with Smart Photo Fix in the Adjust workspace, this one's in the Edit workspace and you get to it by Adjust>Smart Photo Fix), except that you only get to place one target on a black, white or neutral grey area. This isn't as much of a limitation as it might seem as one sample is all you really need. If it doesn't produce the desired results, just click somewhere else in the image and carry on sampling until you hit somewhere that does. When you're happy that the color cast has been neutralized, you can use the sliders in the Enhance Color Balance panel to fine-tune the result.

Channel Mixer

Although it appears under the Adjust>Color menu, the Channel mixer isn't the best tool with which to make color changes to photos. The most practical use for the Channel mixer is to produce black and white images – this is covered in Chapter 4.

Fade Correction

The Fade Correction tool is intended for use on, you guessed it, faded photos. The inks and dyes used in photographic printing processes aren't permanent and, as anyone with prints more than a few years old will know, they tend to fade with age. Exposure to the air and light accelerates this process but, even if you keep your photos in a sealed box, after a few years, they won't look as good as the day they were printed.

The Fade Correction tool is a one-step solution to this problem. There's only one setting – use the Amount slider to vary how much correction is applied. Fade Correction boosts the saturation and makes a levels adjustment, so if you're confident about making those changes individually, you'll have more control using Smart Photo Fix, or Hue/Saturation/Lightness and any of the tonal adjustment tools. It'll take a little longer, but you'll have more control and obtain better results.

Red/Green/Blue

Red/Green/Blue allows you to add or subtract color from the individual RGB channels in the image. It works a little like the Channel mixer, only slightly more intuitively. The trick with Red/Green/Blue is to make sure all your adjustments add up to zero; otherwise you'll affect the brightness of the image. For example, if you add 20 to the red channel, you should subtract 10 from both the Blue and Green channels (or two other amounts that add up to 20).

Red/Green/Blue has a few useful presets, like 'Sun exposure', which produces a color cast simulating the warm tones of late afternoon sun. And you can of course create and save your own presets.

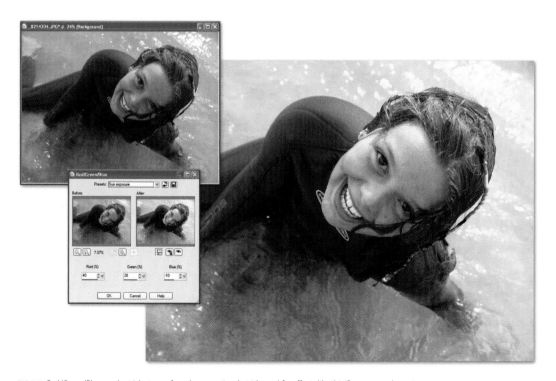

FIG 3.7 Red/Green/Blue can be tricky to use for color correcting, but it's good for effects like this 'Sun exposure' preset.

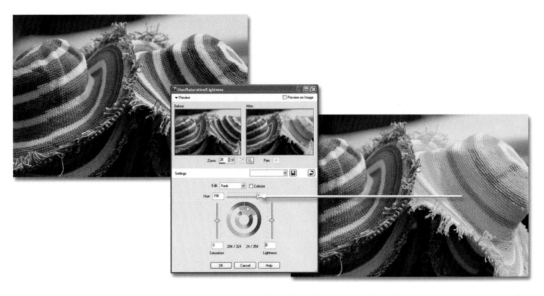

FIG 3.8 By matching a subject color with one of those displayed under the 'Master' drop-down menu and then shifting the Hue values you can radically change the color in one part of the picture while not affecting anything in the rest of the picture.

Hue/Saturation/Lightness

While it's simple enough to change contrast and color in a photo using the Histogram and Color Balance tools, not all picture-makers take the time to adjust the color hue and its intensity or 'saturation'.

PaintShop Photo Pro's Hue/Saturation/Lightness or 'HSL' tool ('Adjust>Hue and Saturation>Hue/Saturation/Lightness') is a feature that allows you to change specific color values within a picture. What this means, in English, is that you can choose the yellow values and shift them to blue. When this is done, all other colors shift the same amount. So reds shift to green, blues to yellow, and so on. The outer color circle in this dialog box represents the original color while the smaller inner color circle represents where that original color has been shifted to.

This tool can be used to remove slight color casts in a picture or to add specific color effects that you might not be able to achieve using one of the Color Balance tools. For my money, the real power in this feature is its ability to shift color values in individual color channels. On some pictures this works as if you have custom-made selections built into the picture.

For example, if it's a snap of a green-colored car, you'll be able to select 'Green' from the 'Master' drop-down menu and change the Hue values so that only the car color changes. How neat is that? If there are other green objects in the frame, these will also change color proportionally; while the selection concept works, it's important to note that it's color-specific, not pixel-specific. Options include 'Reds', 'Greens', 'Blues', 'Cyans', 'Magentas' and 'Yellows'.

What else can be done using this tool? While hue is an expression of color values within a picture, saturation refers to the intensity of those colors. If you worked through the Smart Photo Fix section a few pages back, you'll have already discovered saturation, so I'll just reiterate my earlier advice about overdoing it. Over-saturated colors not only look unnatural, but can cause problems when printing.

You can also use this dialog to change the lightness of the image – although there are plenty of other tools better suited for making tonal adjustments. Another neat effect is to colorize the picture by clicking the Colorize checkbox and increasing the Saturation slider. Colorize essentially applies an old-fashioned tinting effect to the picture; the higher the saturation, the stronger the tint. Click the 'Colorize' checkbox and move the Hue slider, noting how the color in the tint changes. Move the Saturation slider to increase or reduce the intensity.

If colorizing as a special effect is all you are after use the Colorize dialog ('Adjust>Hue and Saturation>Colorize'). This is faster and less complicated than the full-on HSL tool, plus it has the additional benefit of having vari-colored 'amount' sliders that display the part of the spectrum that the sample is taken from. This is a nice touch.

Hue Map

The Hue Map is another slightly off-center tool used to change specific colors within a picture. This is similar to applying a color change using the HSL tool on a specific channel, as just described. You can select a particular color,

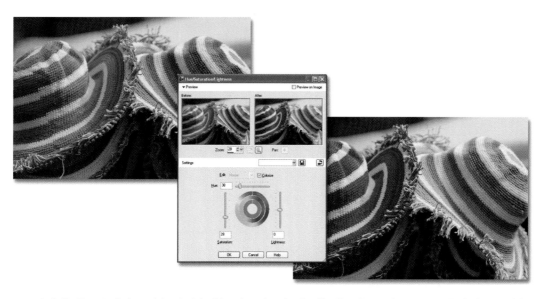

FIG 3.9 In the Hue/Saturation/Lightness dialog, check the Colorize box and watch as PaintShop Photo Pro tints the entire image. Use the Saturation slider to temper the effect.

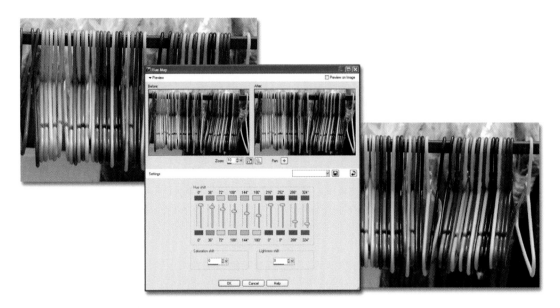

FIG 3.10 The Hue Map works like a graphic equalizer for colors. Use the sliders to change only colors in a specific band of the hue spectrum, here the blue hangers have been changed to red. Fine-tune the effect using the two fields at the base of the dialog for Saturation.

move the appropriate slider to choose another hue for that color only and check the results live.

Tools for Correcting Exposure Problems

On the Brightness and Contrast submenu of the Adjust menu, you'll find no fewer than ten tools for adjusting the tonal values in your pictures. Why so many? Well, many of these tools do the same thing in a slightly different fashion. As you become more experienced, you'll no doubt find your own personal favorite. For some people, Levels is the only way to make tonal adjustments to an image, others swear by Histogram Adjustment. There is at least one tonal adjustment tool that's probably best avoided, so we'll deal with that first.

Brightness/Contrast

This is the first option on the Adjust>Brightness and Contrast menu – give it a rearward glance every time you flash past it on your way to more useful tools. As we saw earlier, the problem with Brightness/Contrast is that it applies a blanket adjustment across the tonal range – there's little that's sophisticated or subtle about it.

When you drag the Brightness slider to the right, each and every pixel value is increased by the same amount and the result is that the highlights in your image quickly disappear. The same happens to the shadows when you go in the opposite direction. Let's waste no more time on it.

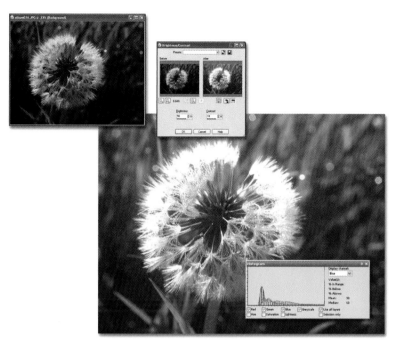

FIG 3.11 OK, this is the last word on Brightness/Contrast. A quick glance at the histogram reveals the damage – no more highlights and shadows turned to mush. You have been warned!

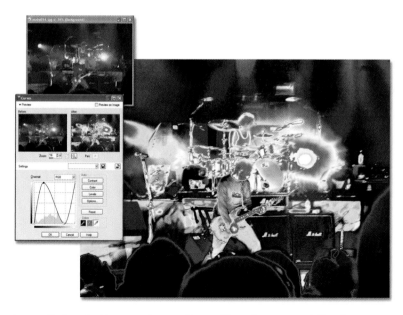

FIG 3.12 Use Curves for ultimate control over specific parts of the tonal range, or special effects. Create a solarization effect using an S-shaped curve or reverse the slope for a negative.

Fill Light/Clarity

Fill light/Clarity can be used to give a boost to slightly dull looking photos. Fill light boosts detail in the shadows if dragged to the right and darkens highlights if dragged to the left. Clarity applies a local contrast boost to photos which makes them 'pop'. The filter is a sort of hybrid that combines contrast adjustment and sharpening. If you're interested in the technical wherewithal, and this is guesswork on my part, Clarity applies the Unsharp mask filter with a high radius setting and a low amount.

Curves

In some ways, Curves is the most versatile of the tonal adjustment tools because it allows you to experiment with altering pixel values in any one part of the range without affecting the rest. The curve is also a simple concept to grasp. Input values are displayed on the horizontal axis and output values on the vertical axis, so initially the curve is in fact a straight diagonal line running upward from left to right at 45 degrees.

Dragging the top end of the line horizontally to the left has the same effect as dragging the Highlight Input slider in the Histogram Adjustment or Levels tool to the left. If you click in the center of the line, a control point is added and dragging this is akin to moving the Gamma slider in Histogram Adjustment or Levels.

But neither of those tools can match Curves when it comes to tweaking a narrow range of tones. By adding additional points to the curve and adjusting them, you can tweak the shadows while leaving the highlights untouched. You can also use Curves for extreme tonal effects. You can create a solarization effect (traditionally achieved in the darkroom by momentarily switching the lights on halfway through processing) by making the curve S-shaped.

Highlight/Midtone/Shadow

This could be quite a useful tool as it provides individual control over the highlights, midtones and shadows in your photos. However, it is complicated by the fact that, instead of pixel values, it uses percentages. It also has two different ways of applying the figures – an absolute and relative method, which makes it even more difficult to work out what's going on. There are other tools, namely Histogram Adjustment and Levels, that are more versatile, provide better feedback and are easier to use.

Histogram Adjustment

The Histogram Adjustment dialog box can be a little intimidating at first glance, but if you've read the earlier section on using the histogram, you'll already be well on your way to getting the most from this versatile tool.

Tip

You can apply any of these adjustments to selections. Make the selection first, save it, and then run the tone adjustment, as described.

As we discovered earlier, the histogram is a graphical representation of the tonal values of all of the pixels in an image. Black pixels appear on the far left, getting lighter as you move toward the right on the horizontal axis. The more pixels there are of a particular value, the higher the line appears at that point.

The three most useful controls in this dialog box are the triangles that appear beneath the histogram, which allow you to remap the black point, white point and gamma. To produce an image with good tonal distribution and contrast, you should drag the Highlight Input slider (the white triangle) to the right edge of the histogram and the black triangle to the left edge. Use the central Gamma slider to make overall adjustments to the brightness.

There are other controls, like the slider on the right that allows you to expand or compress the midtones for solarization-style effects, but Curves is better suited to making these kinds of adjustments.

Histogram Equalize and Histogram Stretch

These two are essentially one-step applications of specific histogram (or levels, or curves, depending on how you want to look at it) adjustments. Equalize is the least useful of the two as it averages out all the pixel values across the histogram (try pressing F7 to display the Histogram palette, then applying Histogram equalize and you'll see).

Histogram stretch automatically sets the black and white points to the values of the darkest and lightest pixels in the image. It's exactly the same as selecting Histogram Adjustment and dragging the triangle controls explained in the previous section to the ends of the histogram. As such, it's an excellent one-step contrast fix.

Levels

The controls in the Levels dialog box work in a similar way to those of the Histogram Adjustment tool. You can use the Output Levels controls to reduce contrast in the shadows and highlights. This is the best way to produce a 'knocked back' image tint for a panel on a website or printed publication that has text running over the top. By dragging the black Output Levels slider to the right, you can lighten the dark pixels in the image and still retain detail in the midtones and highlights.

Threshold

Threshold converts an image to pure black and white – what used to be called 'lineart'. Enter the value that determines whether pixels are converted to black or white in the Threshold dialog box. The default is 128 – any pixels darker than a midtone grey are turned black and any lighter are turned white. As with desaturation, threshold removes the color, but doesn't change the image mode, making it possible to add color back in and produce interesting graphic effects.

> **Tip**
>
> Though not all the tonal adjustment tools have their own histogram display (Levels being the prime example), the live Histogram palette can be used instead. Prior to selecting Levels (or Curves, or Highlights/ Midtones/Shadows) press F7 to display the Histogram palette. Now, when you click the Proof or Auto Proof button the Live Histogram palette will automatically update.

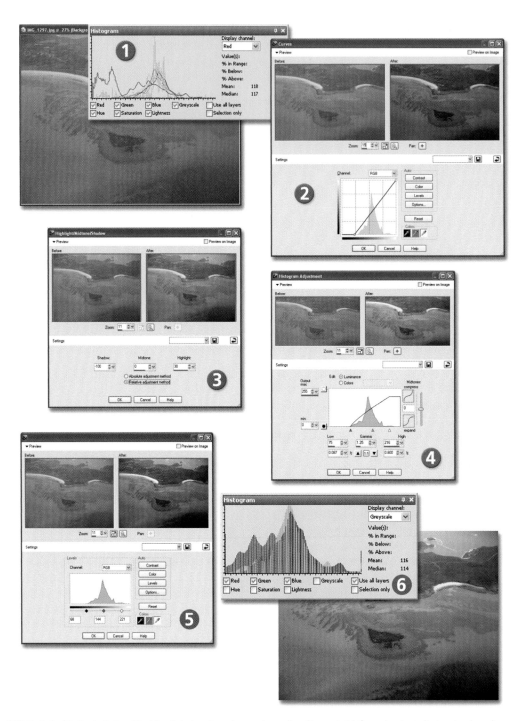

FIG 3.13 Each of the tonal adjustment tools has their strengths and any can be used to achieve a straightforward contrast adjustment as shown here. (1) Press F7 to display the Histogram palette and confirm the problem. (2) Curves. (3) Highlight/Midtone/Shadow. (4) Histogram Adjustment. (5) Levels. (6) The adjusted image with new histogram covering the entire tonal range.

Using Fill Flash and Backlighting

While the Histogram Adjustment tool provides ultimate control of image tonal values throughout the entire range, sometimes that can be its biggest drawback. Often you'll want to change tonal values in one part of the range – the shadows or the highlights. The difficulty with using the Histogram Adjustment tool in such circumstances is that, more often than not, while you can make considerable improvements in one part of the image it's at the cost of lost image detail elsewhere in the tonal range.

For example, in trying to get back shadow detail in under-exposed areas, you'll often find that you lose detail in the highlights. Likewise, attempting to restore detail in over-exposed areas, the sky for example, you'll find that shadow detail disappears into the darkness.

You can get around this problem by making careful feathered selections, but PaintShop Pro has two filters aimed at precisely this problem: the Fill Flash filter and the Backlighting filter.

The Fill Flash Filter

As its name suggests, the Fill Flash filter provides the digital equivalent of fill-in flash – a photographic technique that uses flash in daylight conditions to provide fill-in lighting for shadow detail.

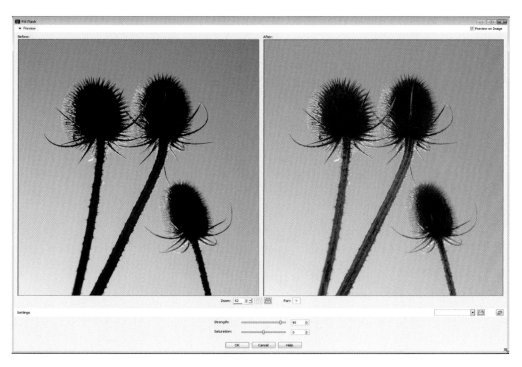

FIG 3.14 Use the Fill Flash filter to restore detail in shadow areas of strongly backlit subjects.

The kind of situation where you might use fill-in flash is where the subject is strongly backlit, for example in front of a window or on a beach. Typically, camera automatic metering systems select an average exposure setting for such situations, resulting in very dark shadows. The Fill Flash filter allows you to lighten the tones in the shadows while leaving the midtones and highlights unaffected.

To use Fill Flash click the Fill Flash button on the Photo toolbar or select Fill Flash from the Adjust menu. Maximize the Fill Flash dialog box, so you can see a generously sized before and after preview and use the Zoom tools so that most of the photo is in view. You can adjust the amount of fill flash applied by entering a value in the Strength field, or by using the slider just below it. The default setting of 40 works well with all but very under-exposed images. If you need to apply more than 60 keep an eye out for noise – a speckled grainy appearance in areas of flat color or tone. The Fill Flash filter also includes a Saturation slider which can be used to add or remove color.

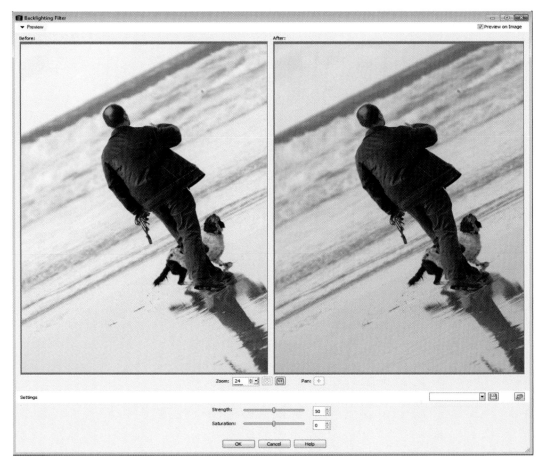

FIG 3.15 Use the Backlighting filter to restore burnt out highlights.

The Backlighting Filter

The Backlighting filter solves the opposite problem to Fill Flash. Where the camera has made a suitable exposure to capture good shadow detail in an image with a wide tonal range, the highlight detail will be over-exposed. This often happens to the sky detail on photos taken in the shade on bright sunny days. The Backlighting filter can help restore highlight detail without affecting shadow areas. Select the Backlighting filter by clicking its button on the Photo toolbar or from the Adjust menu (Adjust>Backlighting).

Making Photos (Appear) Sharper

Sounds too good to be true? While it's acceptable to change color, contrast or saturation in a digital file, changing the sharpness is a little trickier.

PaintShop Pro has several tools designed to make pictures appear sharper than when they were scanned or shot using a digital camera. For some this might seem a godsend, but it's important to note that you can never really change an out-of-focus picture to one that looks pin-sharp. Even well-focused digital shots can look a little soft, however, and that's something that can be fixed.

How does this magic work? Most sharpness tools act on picture contrast. You might have noticed this using the Histogram tools. A general contrast boost usually makes a picture appear sharper.

Unsharp Mask

PaintShop Pro has several sharpness filters. Clarify is a one-button filter used to add a quick bump in contrast and image sharpness. Most times this works well; however, for total control you have to use the perversely named Unsharp Mask filter. What this does is apply a selected contrast boost, at pixel level, to parts of the picture with varying lightness levels.

The reason that this is the best picture-sharpening tool is that it has three adjustable controls written into the equation: Radius, Strength and Clipping. Radius selects the number of pixels around the point of contrast difference. Strength controls the amount of contrast added to those pixels while Clipping affects the lightness of the chosen pixels.

One of the disadvantages in sharpening digital pictures is that the filter is non-discretionary; it has a habit of sharpening the bits you don't want to sharpen as well as the bits you do. This might include a model's skin as well as any digital noise, film grain or other electronic imperfections that have been added to the file along the way. So, the more it's sharpened, the more noticeable the imperfections (the digital noise) become. Help is at hand though, because the main reason for the dialog controls is to help in minimizing this inevitable noise increase.

- Too much Radius creates a nasty-looking whitish halo throughout the high-contrast sections of the picture.

87

- Too much Strength adds an equally fiendish grittiness that looks particularly bad once in print.
- Too much Clipping makes the picture appear soft, destroying the sharpness effect entirely.

Like all sophisticated photo-editing tools, unsharp masking requires practice to get right. There's no 'perfect' setting because some pictures need more sharpening than others.

The picture's end use also has a bearing on how you sharpen its pixels; inkjet prints and images destined for the web need less sharpening than those designed for commercial printing.

As a general rule start with:

- A Radius of one or two pixels.
- A Strength between 100 and 200.
- A Clipping value of 'zero'.

If nothing seems to improve in the picture with these settings, increase the Strength value. Then try increasing the Radius value (a bit at a time). If the Unsharp Mask effect is applied to a high-contrast picture, you'll need to dial-in a small Clipping value to soften its impact. The beauty of this is that you see what you are getting instantly and can make changes live before applying them to the full resolution version.

PaintShop Pro comes with two other no-brainer sharpen tools: the Sharpen and the Sharpen More filters. The Sharpen filter is a good place to start; it applies a preset contrast boost to a selected range of pixels. This might be enough to give most digital snaps a nice sharpen. For a stronger filter effect, try the Sharpen More filter. This is slightly more radical, though still by no means as radical as the Unsharp Mask filter can be. The good thing about these effects is that they are repeatable. If the effect isn't strong enough, repeat it using the keyboard shortcut 'Ctrl+Y' till it is.

High Pass Sharpening

As we've already mentioned, one of the problems with unsharp masking is that it can sharpen parts of the image you just don't want to sharpen. PaintShop Pro X6 includes a method of sharpening that doesn't suffer from these drawbacks because it confines sharpening only to edge detail and other high-contrast areas within an image.

High pass sharpening isn't new, but previously it was a complicated business that involved duplicating layers, applying a High Pass filter, or creating an edge mask and using Layer Blend modes. While all this was great fun, the new High Pass Sharpen filter makes things much easier. See the step-by-step work-through at the end of the chapter to find out how to get the best from High Pass Sharpen.

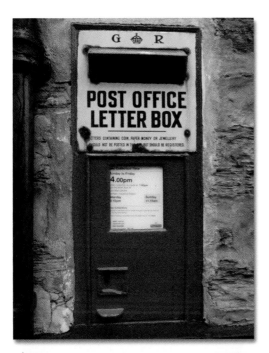

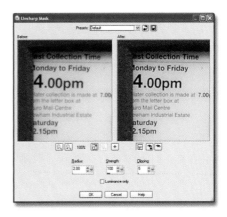

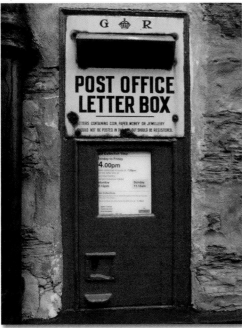

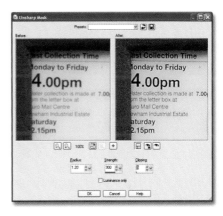

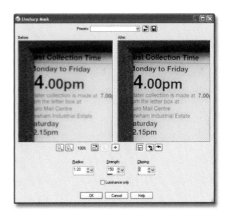

FIG 3.16 Different images require different Unsharp Mask settings, so a trial and revise approach is required. The trick is to increase overall sharpness without introducing sharpening 'artifacts'. Reducing the radius from its default setting of 2 and increasing the strength to 300 introduces unwanted white specks. You could eliminate these using the Clipping slider, but it's better just to reduce the Strength until they disappear. A final setting of Radius 1.20, Strength 150 and Clipping 5 results in a sharper image with minimal sharpening artifacts.

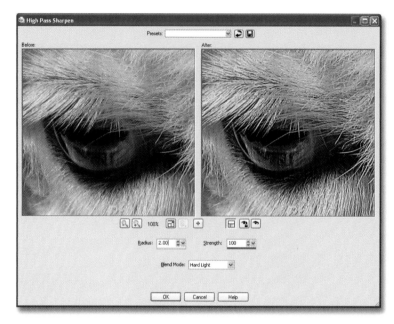

FIG 3.17 Use PaintShop Photo Pro's High Pass Sharpen filter to sharpen edge detail without exaggerating noise and other unwanted detail.

Tips for making digital files appear sharper:

- If using a digital camera, make sure that the picture is exposed correctly and that the focus is correct for the subject. It's possible to enlarge the image on the camera LCD screen to check this focus closely. If you think that there's a problem, reshoot.
- In Shutter (S) or Manual (M) shoot modes, pick a faster shutter speed (a higher number) to 'freeze' action, essential if the subject is fast-moving.
- Learn to use the AF lock in the camera. This works by half-depressing the shutter button that activates the AF system. Once the in-camera audio 'beep' confirmation sounds, you can then either press the shutter fully or reframe to position a subject off-center and then take the picture. The most obvious cause of out-of-focus snaps is from the subject not being in the camera's AF focusing area when the shutter button is pressed.
- Scans normally require unsharp masking to compensate for the scan process, which can make things appear slightly unsharp.
- Most scanner software comes with inbuilt Unsharp Mask filters to compensate for quality loss. Most will not be as good as PaintShop Pro's Sharpen tools. You might want to leave that feature switched 'Off' and sharpen the files using PSP later. It's always preferable to have an untouched 'Master' file on your hard drive. Once an effect like unsharp masking has been added to a file, it's impossible to remove.

- Use PaintShop Pro's Overview palette to move the view around the preview picture. Sharpening never has the same effect across all sections of a picture, so it pays to check the important bits up close.
- If you just don't have a clue where to start, try the Randomize tab. It's a good starting place and one that's likely to come up with an answer in a matter of a few clicks.

Adding Soft Focus Effects

In a digital file, regular blur filters never produce as nice a result as you'd get using film and real glass soft focus filter screwed to the front of a lens.

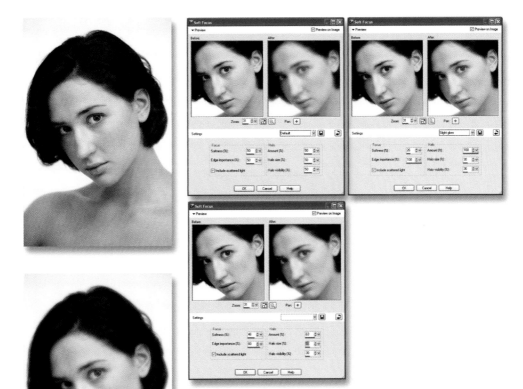

FIG 3.18 The Soft Focus filter has a range of possibilities. The default values may give an over-the-top result, particularly on low resolution images. The presets provide good results, though, and you can experiment with the sliders to get the exact effect you're after. *Nathan Blaney, iStockphoto 1790776.*

PaintShop Photo Pro addresses this problem with a Soft Focus filter. The difference between this and the straight 'blur everything' filter set (Average, Blur, Blur More, Gaussian Blur, Motion Blur, Radial Blur) is that the former applies more blur to the highlights than to the other tones. This produces an effect similar to the effect that you'd get using a regular glass photographic filter – only PaintShop Photo Pro offers a wealth of controls over how you can influence the way that the blur looks.

You can vary the overall softness of the filter, as well as the edge importance (edge sharpness), plus there are three controls for adjusting the blur halo (Amount, Size and Visibility).

Much time has been put into creating this filter and it works extremely well, emulating the precise look of a glass filter costing more than PaintShop Photo Pro itself. As with most filters, it's possible to try a combination of effects using the Randomize tab. You can also save a particular combination for use any other time via the Preset tab.

Step-by-Step Projects

Improving Your Photos Using Smart Photo Fix

Often, you can make big improvements to photos that lack contrast, look a bit washed out, are a little on the dark side or slightly sub-standard in some other way using One Step Photo Fix.

Sometimes, though, One Step Photo Fix doesn't result in a big improvement and you need to take matters into your own hands. If you don't feel confident about dealing directly with tools like Histogram Adjustment and Color Balance then Smart Photo Fix is the tool for you. We've looked in detail at using Smart Photo Fix in the Adjust workspace in Chapter 1, but you can also use it in the Edit workspace where it provides a little more control over some of the adjustments.

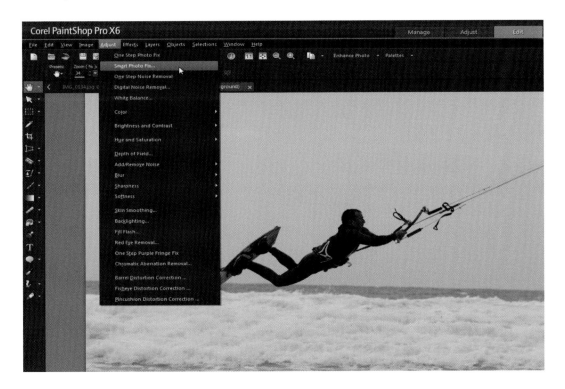

STEP 1 Open the photo you want to fix in the Edit workspace and select Smart Photo Fix from the Adjust menu.

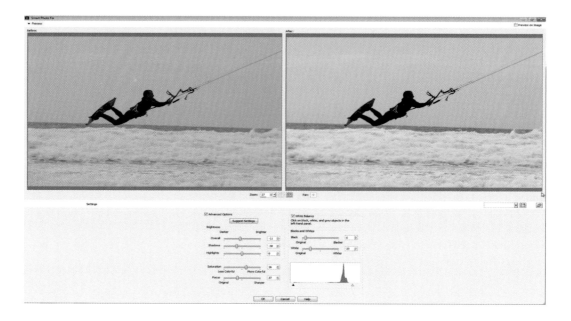

STEP 2 If it isn't already showing, click the Preview triangle to display the before and after views and maximize the Smart Photo Fix dialog box to fill the screen, you can also uncheck Preview on image. Then check the Advanced Options box to display the histogram, black and white point sliders and the Color Balance checkbox.

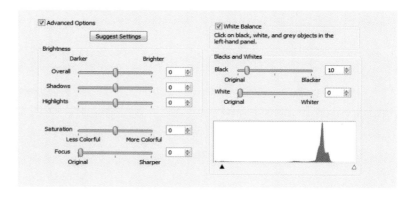

STEP 3 Select default from the preset menu to return all the settings to zero. The first job is to set the black and white point sliders, so that the darkest and lightest pixels in the photo reach either end of the histogram. Drag the Black slider to the right and watch the black triangle under the histogram – it too moves to the right as you drag the slider. Stop dragging when you reach the first peak or bump in the histogram – in this case there's a small group of pixels at around the 10 mark.

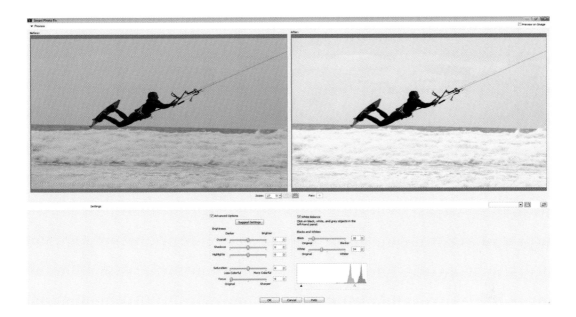

STEP 4 Now drag the White slider until the white triangle reaches the first bump or peak on the right side of the histogram – in this case there's a shallow plateau that starts at 34 – before the big peak nearer the middle. What you've just done is remap the darkest and lightest pixels in the photo to pure black and white. The new histogram is overlayed in red on the old grey one. You can see the improvement in the after preview, but if you're still not quite sure how you've managed this, take another look at 'Using the histogram' on page 72.

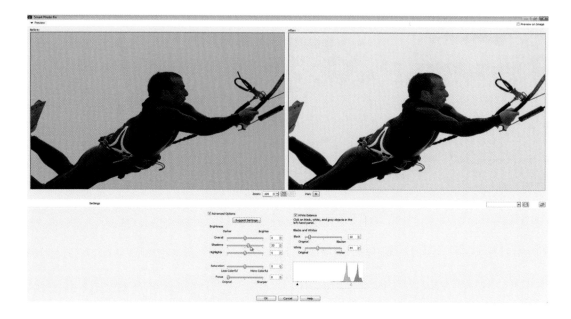

STEP 5 Often, adjusting the black and white sliders will be all that's needed, but the brightness controls can be used to add detail to the shadows and highlights and to brighten or darken the image overall. Click the 'Zoom image to 100%' button under the thumbnails and use the pan tool to center the kitesurfer. Drag the shadow slider to 20 to bring out the detail in his face and wetsuit.

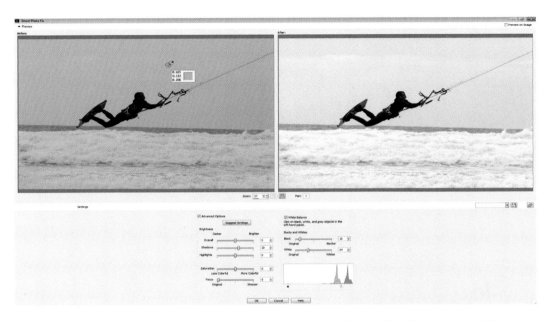

STEP 6 The next problem is the white balance. This photo looks much bluer than the actual conditions in which it was shot. Click the 'Fit image to window' button and correct the blue cast by checking the White Balance box and clicking with the eyedropper to place a color sampler on any part of the photo that should be neutral, i.e. Black, white or grey. Here, I've placed markers on the kitesurfer's black wetsuit and a cloud. If positioning a marker produces unexpected or undesirable results, click on the marker again to remove it.

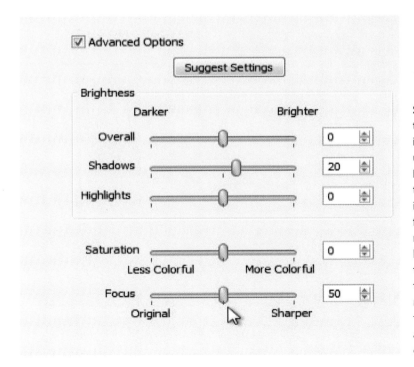

STEP 7 Before sharpening the photo, click the 'Zoom image to 100%' button under the thumbnails. Drag the Focus slider to the right to sharpen the image, but don't go too far or you'll exaggerate noise and make the photo look grainy. Finally, drag the saturation slider to the right, again, be careful not to over-do it, to give the color a bit of a boost and click OK to apply the changes.

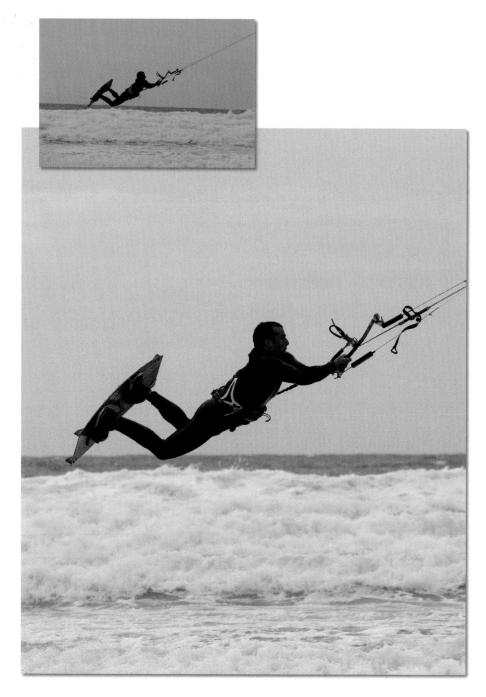

STEP 8 It doesn't end with Smart Photo Fix, there are lots of other simple things you can do to improve photos and give them more impact. Here I've used the crop tool to remove some of the background, change the aspect ratio and straighten the horizon.

Sharpening Photos Using the High Pass Sharpen Filter

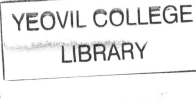

YEOVIL COLLEGE
LIBRARY

The High Pass Sharpen filter is a real lifesaver with certain kinds of images. While Unsharp Mask does a fantastic job 90% of the time, as we've seen, it's indiscriminate and can create problems, or at least make existing ones more obvious.

The kinds of photos you should avoid unsharp masking include:

- Those taken on a high ISO setting (400 and above) which will, depending on how good your camera is, display at least some visible noise.
- Photos that were badly exposed and have had a large tonal correction applied using Smart Photo Fix, Histogram Adjustment or one of the other tonal adjustment tools.
- Photos with high JPEG compression applied, either because they were taken using a low-quality camera setting or have subsequently been recompressed using a low-quality JPEG setting.
- Photos that are well exposed, of a high quality and fine in every other respect, but have large areas of flat color, such as an expanse of clear blue sky.

For all of these images and anything else that fails to come up shining using the Unsharp Mask filter, follow these steps.

STEP 1 Open the image to be sharpened in the Edit workspace. If you plan on using 'Preview on Image' to preview the effect then first make sure to zoom in to 100% view (keyboard shortcut Ctrl+Alt+N). Always view sharpening adjustments at 100% magnification as it's the only way you can really see what's happening to the individual pixels in the image.

STEP 2 Select Adjust>Sharpness>High Pass Sharpen to open the High Pass Sharpen dialog box and use the Pan button to select a representative part of the image. To preview the sharpening in the image window, check the 'Preview on Image' box, having first zoomed to 100% view as described in step 1.

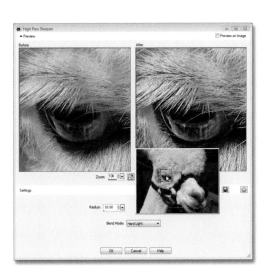

STEP 3 The High Pass Sharpen dialog box has three settings – Radius, Strength and Blend Mode. The default values for these are 10, 70 and Hard Light, respectively. The Radius setting determines the distance within which the filter looks for dissimilar pixels to sharpen. A larger Radius value will result in more of the image being sharpened, a smaller one will sharpen less. With zero Radius none of the image is sharpened. Use the Pan button to find part of the image you don't want sharpened (the sky, or out-of-focus background) and adjust the Radius to a value just below that at which you can see a change.

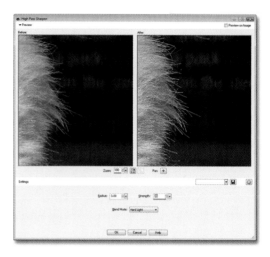

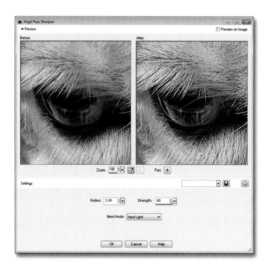

STEP 4 Now use the Pan button to center a part of the image that's representative of what you want to sharpen. If necessary adjust the Amount slider to increase or decrease the amount of sharpening applied.

STEP 5 The Hard Light blend mode produces the most dramatic sharpening. To reduce the effect change the blend mode to Overlay and for even gentler sharpening use the Soft Light blend mode.

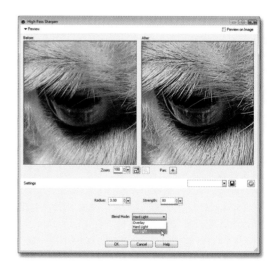

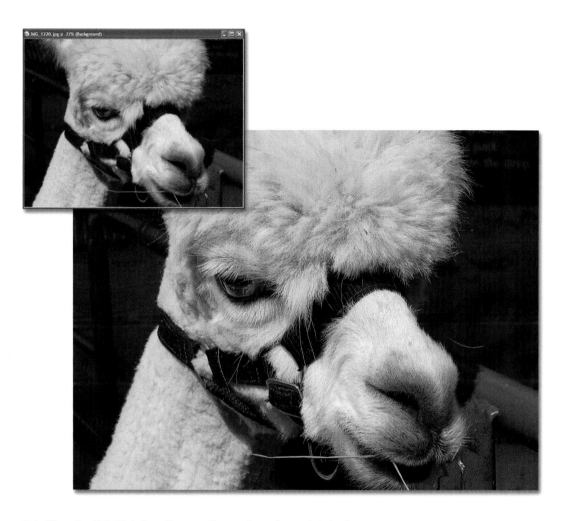

PaintShop Pro X6's High Pass Sharpen filter makes a fantastic job of sharpening edge detail in images like this, without affecting out of focus areas or compounding common digital image problems like noise.

Tip

Remember that sharpen filters work by increasing image contrast and when you increase contrast you may inadvertently lose highlight and shadow detail from your photos. When using sharpening filters always keep one eye on the Histogram palette (keyboard shortcut F7) to make sure you are not 'clipping' the ends of the tonal range.

Using Camera RAW Lab to Restore Detail in Over-Exposed Photos

This shot of a horse's head is over-exposed by around a stop. If you'd shot this as a jpeg, you might be able to recover the lost highlight detail in the front of the horse's head and the sky in the background, but with only eight bits per channel of pixel information, the chances are the image would begin to look harsh and contrasty before you recovered as much detail as you'd like.

Making the exposure corrections in Camera Raw Lab gives you much more scope – you can recover more detail without causing the kind of image degradation that editing pixels inevitably results in. Remember, what we're doing here is simply interpreting the raw data to give us a more acceptable starting point. Once the corrections have been made, you can output the image as a 16-bit RGB file. Then, there's nothing to stop you making further improvements in the Editor workspace. With a rock-solid 16-bit RGB file, you'll still be in a better position to make further improvements than you would have been with a 8-bit jpeg from the camera.

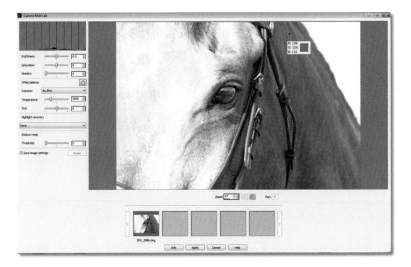

STEP 1 Select the Raw file thumbnail in the Manage workspace, then select the Edit workspace tab to open the file in Camera RAW Lab and click the maximize button at the top right to fill the screen. This is your first chance to get a look at the image as interpreted using Camera RAW Lab's default settings. As well as suffering from over-exposure the white balance is on the cool side, both problems easily dealt with in Camera RAW Lab.

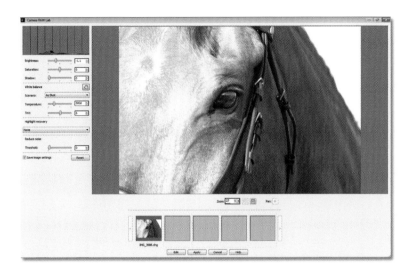

STEP 2 First deal with the exposure by dragging the Brightness slider to the left. In this case we've dragged it to −1.0 – effectively reducing the exposure by one stop. It doesn't matter if you can't drag the slider to precisely 1.0, but if you do want more precise control use the nudge buttons on the exposure numeric field next to the slider.

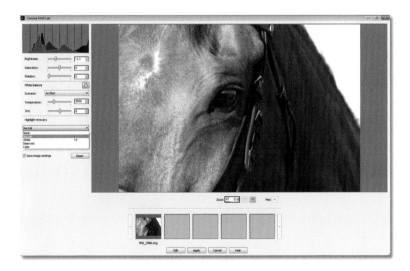

STEP 3 The exposure is looking a little better, but the highlights are still blown out. PaintShop Pro X6's Camera Raw Lab has a Highlight recovery tool to deal with this and it's extremely effective. Select Normal from the Highlight Recovery pull-down menu to restore the highlight detail.

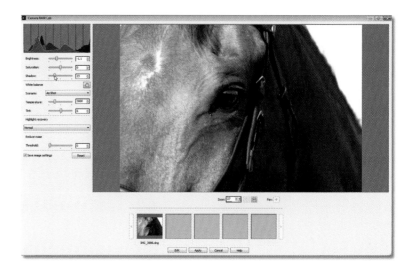

STEP 4 The exposure is looking better, but now the shot looks dull and murky. To increase contrast in the shadows, drag the Shadow slider to the right. As you drag, the preview will update and you need to make a visual assessment of how much Shadow to apply. You want to increase contrast in the shadows without losing any detail. Here we're aiming to make the horse's bridle black without losing detail in the neck and eye.

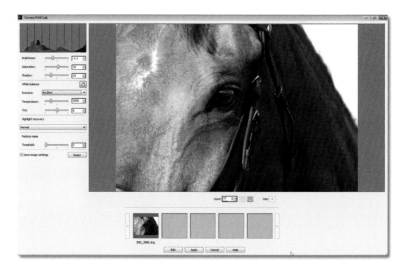

STEP 5 Increasing the contrast in the shadows has improved things, but the shot still looks a bit flat. Drag the Saturation slider to the right to increase the saturation a little. Don't overdo it, small movements of the Saturation slider have quite a large effect. Use the nudge buttons for precise control. Around 15 on the Saturation is enough to give the color a bit of a boost.

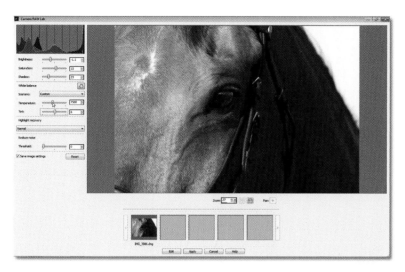

STEP 6 Now we can address the color cast. The 'As Shot' white balance is 5000, but produces too cool a result – notice the blue highlight running down the horse's neck at the back. Selecting one of the presets – for example Daylight or Cloudy – won't help as these are both lower and will result in more blue (see the section on white balance earlier in this chapter for a description of how this works). The simplest way to deal with most color casts is simply to drag the Temperature slider while assessing the result in the preview window. Because this shot was taken quite late in the evening, the light was getting very blue and the color temperature setting required to eliminate the cast and produce a more natural looking result is around 7500.

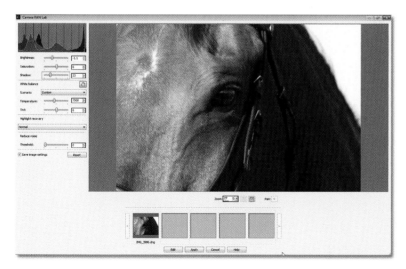

STEP 7 Notice how changing the white balance has increased the saturation of the yellows and browns? Our earlier saturation adjustment is now looking a bit over the top. Use the nudge buttons to knock the saturation back a little – to around 6 should do it.

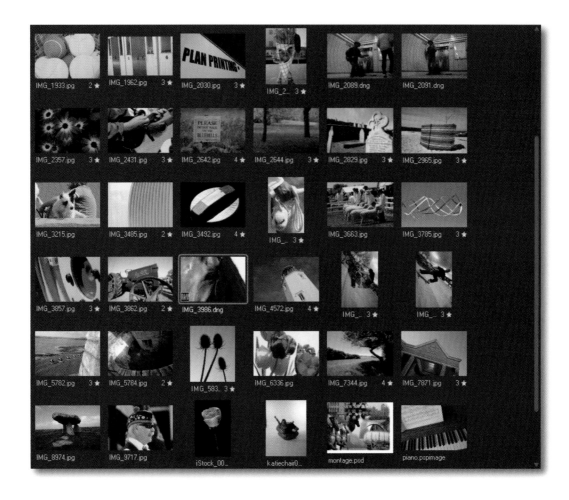

STEP 8 If you don't want to edit the image in PaintShop Photo Pro, clicking the Apply button will close Camera RAW Lab. If you take a look at the thumbnail in the Organizer, you'll see that it has been updated to reflect the changes you just made and has a small RAW badge to indicate it has been edited. These changes are stored in the PaintShop Pro X6 database.

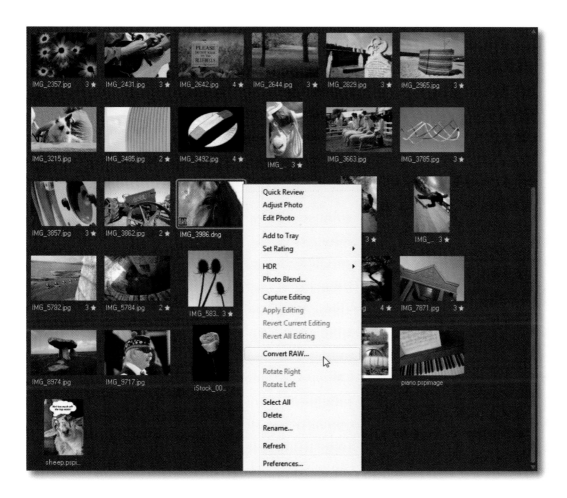

STEP 9 To export the RAW image to an RGB file without opening it again in Camera RAW Lab, select it in the Organizer and click the Convert RAW button on the Organizer toolbar. Select an image type and choose a location on your hard drive where you want the image saved. The modify button allows you to add text or sequence numbers to the file name for batch conversion.

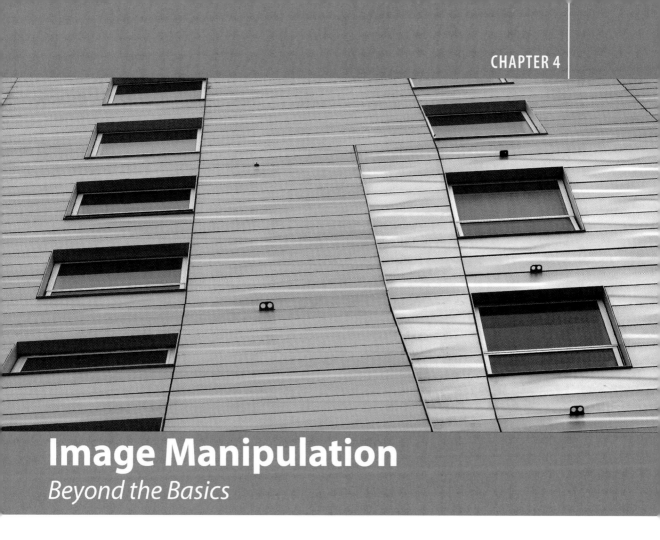

CHAPTER 4

Image Manipulation
Beyond the Basics

What's Covered in this Chapter

- So far we've looked at what PaintShop Pro X6 has to offer in terms of features and tools for organizing and editing your photos and covered some of the basics of image editing. We've also looked at how to fix photos that have a problem with brightness or color.
- This chapter is subtitled 'Beyond the Basics' because we're going to look at some more complex features than the 'one-step' fixes and tonal and color adjustment tools covered in the previous chapters.
- The chapter begins by looking at some of the methods for removing scratches and blemishes from your photos. This is a particular problem with scans of prints, slides and negatives and also when using digital SLRs which can get dust on the sensor leading to blotchy photos.
- The same techniques can be usefully applied to removing other things that you don't want in your photos such as lamp posts, trees and people you're no longer on speaking terms with. You'll learn how to become an expert retoucher with the Clone tool and about some other tools for fixing damaged photos.

- As in the last chapter, it's not all about fixing things. Later on in the chapter you'll discover how to produce black and white photos from color originals using Black and White Film photo effects and how to produce tints and color overlay effects to add extra depth and tone to black and white photos.
- Digital noise can be a real problem when shooting in low light conditions using a high ISO setting on your camera. PaintShop Pro X6 has one of the best tools around for dealing with this problem and I'll go into detail on how to get the most from it. Paradoxically, I'll also show you how to add noise to your photos to create atmospheric grain effects.
- Finally, there's a brief introduction to PaintShop Pro's Scripting features. Scripts are one of PaintShop Pro's most powerful features, allowing you to automatically record and apply a sequence of editing steps to any number of photos.
- The step-by-step projects at the end of the chapter guide you through the process of restoring badly damaged photos and applying a hand-colored effect to black and white pictures.
- No matter how careful you might be when scanning film or prints, dirt always gets in the way and inevitably ends up on the scan. PaintShop Pro has a good range of filter-based tools designed for cleaning up or removing these problem areas, however bad they might appear. Dirt isn't only a problem with scanned photos. If you use an older digital SLR (many recent models vibrate the sensor to remove dust) you may have noticed slight dark blotches on your photos. These are caused by small particles of dust which find their way into the camera body and settle on the sensor. Eventually, you will need to clean the sensor, or have it done for you, but in the meantime you can use the techniques described below to fix the problem.

Removing Scratches and Blemishes from Scans

You might never realize quite how dirty scans can be unless they are magnified to a size that reveals the mess. If you only enlarge your snaps to about 6 inches × 4 inches, the worst dust blemishes may never become apparent. If you print to 20 inches × 16 inches, however, you might get a shock when you see the dirt and surface scratch marks picked up by the scanner!

The first thing to do is rescan the print or negative. Clean the flatbed scanner's glass platen, the place where the print is positioned. Use a mild window cleaner and a soft, lint-free cloth (i.e. linen). Finger grease, however minimal, is a great dust attractant so don't forget to gently wipe the surface of the print as well. If scanning film, use an appropriate film-cleaning solution and soft cloth.

Once the scan is made, open the file in PaintShop Pro and enlarge the file to between 200% and 400%. Do you see dust specks that weren't there in the original? They probably were there, but were just too small to be noticed. If you

Tip

Don't use filters to remove large blemishes; they aren't that effective and will degrade the overall picture quality. Use the Clone or Scratch Remover tool instead.

are planning to enlarge and print to A3, or bigger, you might need to run one, or more, of PaintShop Pro's clean-up filters over the file to improve the quality.

Here's how: open the picture and crop to suit. Many scanners are more than generous with their flatbed scan areas, adding extra 'real estate' to the edges of the print or transparency. Select the Crop tool from the Tools toolbar, and when the Crop Box appears, drag it to the required dimensions and click the Apply button. (To maintain the aspect ratio use the 'Maintain aspect ratio' checkbox in the tool's Options palette.)

Assess the damage. Enlarge the file to 400% or 500% by clicking on the picture with the Zoom tool (keyboard shortcut 'Z'; left-click or push your mouse wheel forward with your index finger to zoom in on the affected area) and, using the Pan tool (keyboard shortcut 'A' – it sits over the Zoom tool), move the picture around the screen for a closer inspection. Increase or decrease the magnification according to the amount of detail you might want to retouch. If it's a high resolution scan (i.e. scanned for A2 output), you'll have to zoom in on the image further, say up to 400%, to see the same (scratch) detail as if it were scanned to A4 and magnified only to 200%.

A quick way to remove dust spots blanket fashion is to run a filter over the entire picture. Zoom to 100% view and select the Automatic Small Scratch Removal filter from the Adjust > Add/Remove Noise menu ('Adjust > Add/ Remove Noise > Automatic Small Scratch Removal'). To preview the effect check the 'Preview on Image' checkbox in the filter dialog box. Most filters and effects have this option and, though it takes a while longer to display, you get a much clearer picture of the result than with the dialog box thumbnail previews.

Try the default settings first. The reason there are many variants is to cover the multiple quality situations scanning introduces. Note that there are checkboxes for 'light' and 'dark' scratches, a contrast inhibitor (move the sliders to the center to limit the contrast range), as well as three filter strength settings. It's important to remember that, with this, and most of PaintShop Pro's other filter-based tools, the dialog window offers multiple options so that you can customize all actions to suit whatever image you have open. If the filter effect doesn't work fully first time, try another combination.

Scratch Removal filters apply their effects globally. For difficult or large blemishes, use a scratch removal tool locally first. This is a more effective technique because you can limit the filter's softening action to a small area of the scan only. There is no point in softening the entire picture to remove one or two scratches.

Click the small triangle next to the Clone Brush and choose the Scratch Remover tool from the fly-out. Drag the cursor over the blemish to remove or soften it. PaintShop Pro clones/blurs out the damaged pixels. This is quite a fast tool to use and, like most of the tools in PaintShop Pro, it has a preset save function allowing you to create your own custom scratch remove brushes.

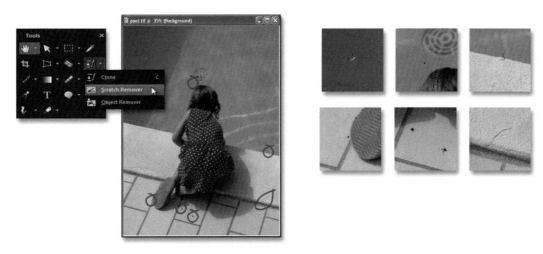

FIG 4.1 Color negatives and transparencies are among the worst culprits for attracting dirt and scratches. Although they may look OK to the naked eye, the high degree of scanning enlargement necessary to produce a decent-sized digital image also enlarges the dirt. A global filter won't do the job – you will need to individually retouch these marks out with the Scratch Remover and Clone tools. The same applies for blotches caused by dust on the sensor of a digital SLR.

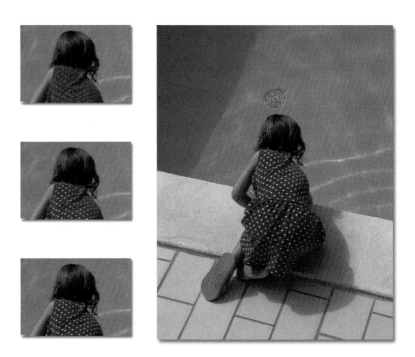

FIG 4.2 The Salt and Pepper (*top*), Median (*middle*) and the Edge Preserving Smooth (*bottom*) filters can be used for removing dust or subtly softening skin blemishes, but the filter strength required to remove larger spots and scratches results in unacceptable loss of overall image quality. The best result (*right*) is achieved by repeated application of the Scratch Removal and Clone tools.

Once satisfied that PaintShop Pro has removed/diffused enough of the small scratches to make the scan appear credible, save the file under another name before continuing with further editing (always keep the original file untouched, where possible).

Other smoothing filters to try:

Salt and Pepper filter.

Despeckle filter.

Median filter.

Edge Preserving Smooth filter.

(All of which are found on the 'Adjust > Add/Remove Noise' menu.)

Controlling Digital Noise

Photos taken with a digital camera all suffer, to a greater or lesser extent, from a phenomenon called 'digital noise', which gives digital photos a speckled, grainy appearance. Noise is generated by a camera's electronic circuitry, mostly when the electrical current generated by the image sensor is amplified before being digitally sampled.

If you've owned a film camera, you'll be familiar with film grain – clumps of silver in a photographic emulsion that become visible when enlarged – and you'll also be aware that fast films – those with higher sensitivity to light – exhibit more grain than slow ones.

With digital cameras it's the same story; if you set your camera to a higher ISO rating, to capture images in low light conditions, the digital noise becomes worse. Depending on your camera, you may not notice noise on images taken at an ISO setting of 200 or lower, but at settings above 400 ISO, particularly at larger image sizes, noise can become very intrusive.

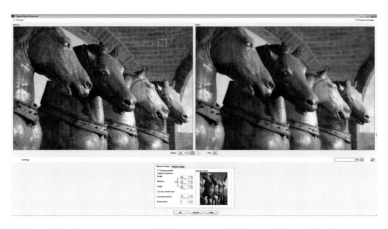

FIG 4.3 The Digital Noise Removal filter allows you to remove noise from some areas of the image while protecting others.

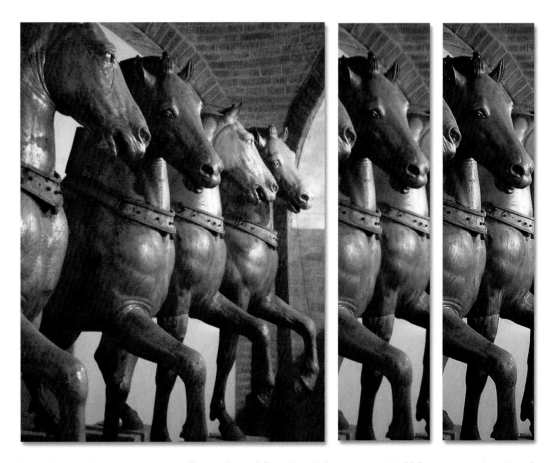

FIG 4.4 Noise-wise, this is about as bad as it gets. The original image (left) was shot with the camera set to 1600 ISO. The center section shows the results of the DNR filter on the default settings, and on the right, the same settings with 70% sharpen.

Digital noise can also occur as a result of long exposures – shots taken at night are often prone to noise because of the high ISO setting used, combined with long exposures.

In some circumstances you can live with noise. Like film grain it can provide a gritty atmospheric realism. Mostly though, it's something you'd rather do without. You can't get rid of noise entirely, but you can reduce it. Before version 9, PaintShop Pro users had to rely on techniques using the Salt and Pepper, Median, Texture Preserving Smooth and other filters on the Adjust > Add/Remove Noise menu. Now we have the Digital Noise Removal filter, which, for the sake of brevity, I'll call the DNR filter.

Select Adjust > Digital Noise Removal, or click the DNR button on the Photo toolbar. The DNR filter provides a quite sophisticated dialog box with the usual before and after preview windows and two tabbed panels labeled Remove Noise and Protect Image. Maximize the dialog box to get the biggest preview possible so that you can see the noise and what the filter is doing to the image detail. Use the Pan tool (it appears automatically in most of the filter dialog boxes when you mouse over the right-hand [after] preview) to select a representative area of the image.

In the Noise Correction pane, the three input boxes and sliders control the degree of noise removal for small, medium and large noise artifacts. Clicking the Link Detail Sizes box locks these three together, maintaining the relationship between them – so if you increase one of them by, say 5, they all increase by 5.

In practice, you'll get better results by using a higher value in the small field than in the other two, but much depends on the image and you'll need to experiment. When you apply the DNR filter it combines the corrected image with the original one and the value in the Correction Blend field determines the proportions of the two. 100 is all corrected image and no original. By lowering this value you lessen the degree to which the correction is effective, but also minimize overall loss of image detail. Finally, you can sharpen, which will help restore detail softened by the noise reduction process.

On the right of the Remove Noise tab there's a thumbnail preview with, initially, two cross-hair targets on it. These are the sampling regions; they appear in the before preview window as rectangular marquees with resize handles. You can move and resize the existing sampling regions (by clicking and dragging them) and create new ones (by clicking and dragging anywhere in the left preview window). Try to sample image areas where noise is particularly bad, or that are representative of noise in large areas of the picture. Careful sampling will help the DNR filter to distinguish noise from genuine image detail.

Another way to protect parts of the image from the unwanted attention of the DNR filter is to use the Protect Image tab, where you can select a range of colors from within the image that you don't want processed by the filter.

Tip

You can save DCNR filter settings as a preset and easily reapply them to other images taken on the same camera with the same ISO settings.

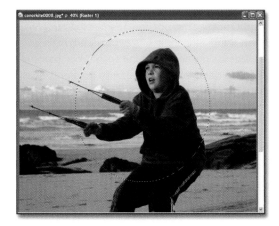 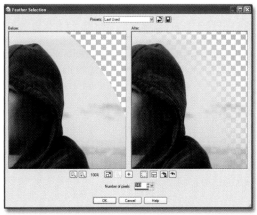

FIG 4.5 *(Left)* Adding noise can transform a photo into something quite special. Here I have drawn an elliptical selection. *(Right)* The next stage is to apply a feather to this selection to soften the edges (in this example, by 143 pixels).

115

The simplest way to use this feature is to Ctrl-drag the area you want to protect in the left preview window.

PaintShop Pro also has a filter that is ideally suited for adding noise (Add Noise). Why add noise to a digital photo? For several reasons.

All retouching, whether you are using a filter effect or a specific retouching tool (like the Clone or Scratch Remover tools), smooths out textures. This is an excellent result for portraits, glamour, fashion and any other applications where flattery pays.

But if one area of the picture has had too much retouching, it will look smoother than the rest of the image. Add noise to the retouched section to make it appear more like the rest of the photo rather than attempt to smooth

FIG 4.6 Use Levels to brighten the center of the picture (i.e. the bit that's selected), then press Ctrl+D to select none and add the grain effect to the entire image using the Add Noise. The final stage involves adding a blur effect using the Radial Blur filter in Zoom mode. You can restrict the effect to the outside of the image – keeping the center sharp either using the filter's Protect center controls, or by making a selection.

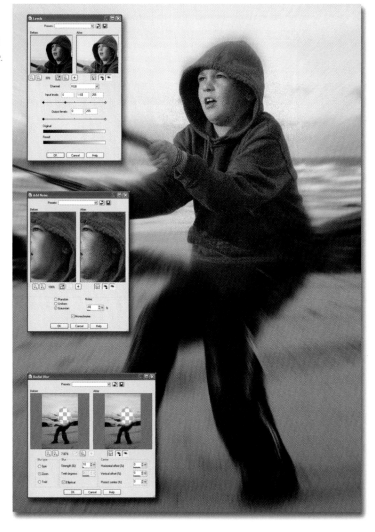

out the entire picture. You can also add noise to increase the grittiness and overall impact in a picture (see Fig 4.6). There are several ways to do this:

- Add noise to the retouched section using one of the textures from the Materials palette.
- Copy the background layer, make sure that the new layer is selected and use PaintShop Pro's Add Noise filter to add a suitable quantity of noise to match the rest of the image. Then, using the Eraser tool, rub out the bits of the top layer that have had no retouching done to them.
- Apply noise using a selection.

Retouching Using the Clone Brush

The Clone Brush is possibly the most useful of all PaintShop Pro's retouching tools because it can be used for repairing damaged pictures and for improving photos with distracting background, or other unwanted detail. Learn how to use this tool with skill and it'll open up potential you never thought possible with your current photo-retouching skills.

There's no big mystery to the Clone Brush. What it does is simply to copy one part of a picture into the clipboard or temporary memory (this is called the 'Source') and paste it over another part of the picture (called the 'Target'). You can feather the edge of the clone brush and adjust its opacity to make your changes blend in.

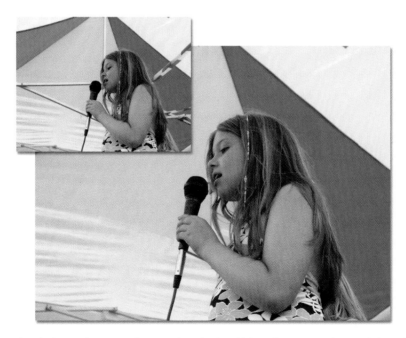

FIG 4.7 The Clone tool can do a lot more than remove a few spots and scratches from old photos. Use it to remove distracting background detail, unwanted objects and even people from your pictures.

Cloning in Practice

Choose the Clone Brush from the Tools toolbar (keyboard shortcut 'C'). This is shared with the Scratch Remover and Object Remover tools so you might have to click the latter's icon and reselect 'Clone' from the fly-out menu. Make sure that the Tool Options palette is also open by right-clicking on the Menu bar and choosing 'Tool Options' from the palette's sub-menu. Pressing F4 toggles the Tool Options palette on and off.

To make the Clone Brush work properly you must select a Source area. First off, find a spot in the picture that is tonally close to the tone in the section to be replaced. There's no point in trying to copy a dark patch over a light patch. The light patch goes dark with the copied pixels and ends up looking unconvincing.

Move the brush over this area and right-click once with the mouse. This sets the Source point and copies the pixels that are under the brush. Move the brush to the target section of the picture, left-click and drag to paint. This pastes or 'clones' the copied pixels over the damaged pixels. You should see the target section disappear or, at least, reduce in intensity.

The Clone Brush has several options designed to fine-tune the brush performance. These include Size, Step, Density, Thickness, Rotation, Opacity and Blend mode. The most important controls to try first are the brush Size, Hardness, its Opacity and, finally, the Blend mode.

Tip

To replace larger sections of an image with background detail try making a feathered-edged selection and copying and pasting it.

Setting brush size is important. If there are huge scratches, large fade spots or ripped sections in the picture, choose a brush size that's smaller than the damaged areas. Do this because building up the repair gently is preferable to trying to do it with a single brush stroke, and besides, there might not be enough of the Source area to copy from. Several smaller brush strokes always produce a smoother finish and inevitably a more convincing result.

Change the brush size during the retouching operation as well as the Source area. Many novices copy-and-paste with such enthusiasm that they don't notice the tell-tale step-and-repeat tracks left across the print surface because they have not reselected the Source area. This is something to be avoided. Moving the Clone Source point often is the best way of avoiding these tell-tale marks and (usually) produces a more convincing retouched result.

The Options palette also offers an Opacity setting. This affects the brightness of the pixels copied from the Source area. Effectively, this slows the retouching process noticeably as you end up by trying to cover damaged areas with less dense pixels (reduced opacity). Several mouse-clicks might have to be made to achieve the same as one set at 100% opacity. However, it's nearly always better to reduce the opacity to get a smoother tonal result.

Another control to experiment with is the Blend mode. Blend modes, which I discuss in detail in Chapter 5, influence the way copied pixels react with the underlying, original, pixels. For example, click the default 'Normal' drop-down

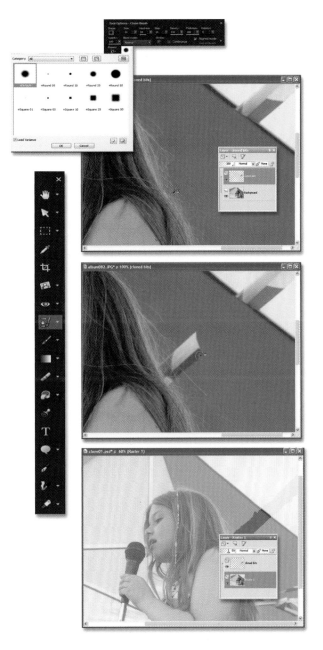

FIG 4.8 The Clone tool Options palette provides a wealth of brush presets and other settings so that you can adapt the tool to the job in hand. Before you do anything, create a new Raster layer to clone into, keeping all your changes in one place and keeping the original unmarked. Make sure to check the 'Use All Layers' box on the Options palette so that you can clone from one layer to another. Start with a small brush and use lots of small strokes so that if you make a mistake you can easily undo. Change brush size frequently to match the area being cloned and experiment with brush Hardness, Opacity and Blend mode to get the best result. Here, the background layer opacity has been reduced so you can more clearly see the cloning on top. If you're not happy with your first effort, just erase the cloned sections from the 'cloned bits' layer and start again.

menu in the Options palette and try cloning using Burn (darken), Dodge (lighten) or the Color Blend mode.

Other tools for fixing up damaged pictures:

   Scratch Remover tool (to remove blemishes locally).

   Small Scratch Remover tool (to remove small blemishes only).

Clarify filter (to make a picture sharper and clearer).

Fade Correction (to rejuvenate contrast and color).

Histogram Adjustment tool (to increase the contrast).

Makeover tool.

Other Tools to Try

Like many of PaintShop Pro's tools, the Dodge and Burn Brushes perform the digital equivalent of a conventional darkroom technique. During print-making, areas of the paper exposed under the enlarger are held back, or given additional exposure using masking tools. In this way it's possible to bring out detail in parts of the print that would otherwise be over- or under-exposed.

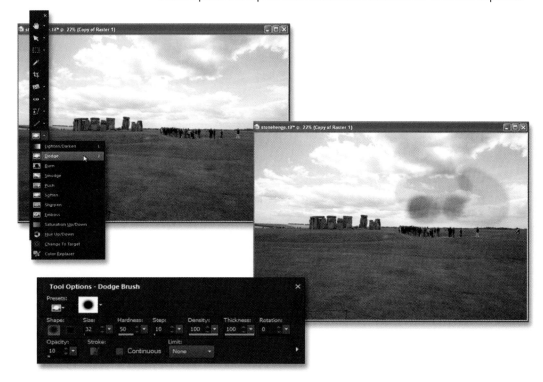

FIG 4.9   The Dodge and Burn tools provide, in the form of a brush, the power to add (or subtract) exposure to a photo. Before using any retouching tool, duplicate the background layer and call it 'retouching' and make all your changes to this new layer. That way you can compare before and after versions by toggling the layer visibility; you can also go back to the original should things go badly wrong. The secret to successful burning (and dodging) lies in the Tool Options palette. Too much burning produces these tell-tale dark smudges. Use a large, soft-edged brush and reduce the opacity so that each brush stroke makes only a small difference. Then gradually build up the effect using multiple strokes. Just press Ctrl+Z to undo if something doesn't look right.

The Dodge and Burn Brushes do exactly the same thing. Dodge lightens the pixels to which it's applied and the Burn Brush darkens them – the equivalent of giving more exposure under the enlarger. You need to be careful not to overdo it with these tools, or your intervention will become obvious.

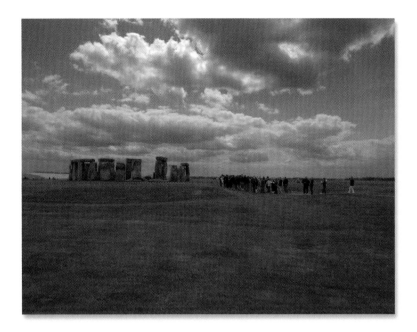

FIG 4.10 This is what the Burn tool can do for a photo — completely transform an image that would have otherwise perhaps found its way to the trash bin, but is now something worth showing to others.

With each application of the tool the effect becomes more obvious. It's a good idea to duplicate the background layer before using the Dodge and Burn Brushes and apply the changes to the copy. Use large, soft-edged brushes and reduced opacity settings to avoid burning hard-edged holes. You can use the left and right buttons to switch between Dodge and Burn, but I wouldn't recommend this; if you've over-burned an area, undo, or use the History palette to get back the detail.

Creating Black and White Pictures

Despite the fact that digital photography makes it no more difficult or expensive to shoot in color than black and white, monochrome images are proving as popular as ever. For some subjects removing the color altogether produces an aesthetically desirable result and digital image processing makes it easier than ever to produce toning effects like sepia, split toning and cross-processing that, in the days of chemical processing, were messy, time-consuming and often produced hit and miss results.

One of the simplest ways to produce black and white photos is to set your camera to Black and White mode but, other than in exceptional circumstances, I'd advise against this. Shooting color in the camera and converting the images to black and white, as we shall see, gives you a much greater degree of control over the process and provides many more creative opportunities. It also gives you the option of keeping the color photo as well.

Tip

The Channel mixer produces the same effect as yellow, red, or other colored filters on the camera with black and white film; use it to create dramatic skies and other effects.

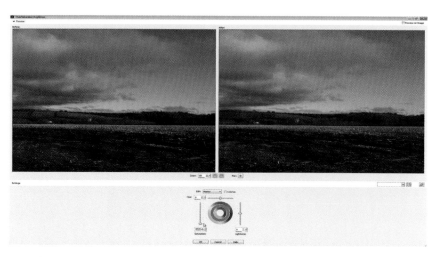

FIG 4.11 Converting a photo to greyscale using Image > Greyscale removes the color data which results in a smaller file size, but is irreversible. Use Hue/Saturation/Lightness to convert to black and white, but retain the color data should you want to reintroduce color to the image later.

PaintShop Pro X6 provides several methods of converting color images to black and white ones. These are:

Image > Greyscale. This converts the image to an 8-bit single-channel greyscale image and discards the color information. Once the image is saved in this mode there's no getting the color data back, so if you want to keep the color image, make sure to keep a back-up copy and choose File > Save As so you do not overwrite your original.

Adjust > Hue and Saturation > Hue/Saturation/Lightness. By dragging the Saturation slider all the way to zero in the Hue/Saturation/Lightness dialog box, you can completely desaturate the image. The difference between doing this and converting to greyscale is that, although you can no longer see it, the color information is still there. You can go back to Hue/Saturation/Lightness at any time and put the color back by dragging the slider in the opposite direction. You can also introduce new color in ways we'll look at shortly.

Effects > Photo Effect > Black and White Film. This filter can convert your photos to black and white and at the same time simulate colored filters placed over the lens to help differentiate color with similar grey tonal values. For example, when shooting black and white landscapes a yellow filter is commonly used to darken blue skies and help pick out cloud detail. Like Hue/Saturation/Lightness, using the Black and White Film effect retains the color channels in the file so you can add new color effects, but the effect isn't reversible – you can't get the original colors back once the file is saved.

Adjust > Color > Channel mixer. The Channel mixer works in a similar way to the Black and White Film effect, only it provides a lot more control. Whereas the Black and White Film effects are confined to a limited number of filters – Red, Green, Yellow, Orange and Blue – using the Channel mixer

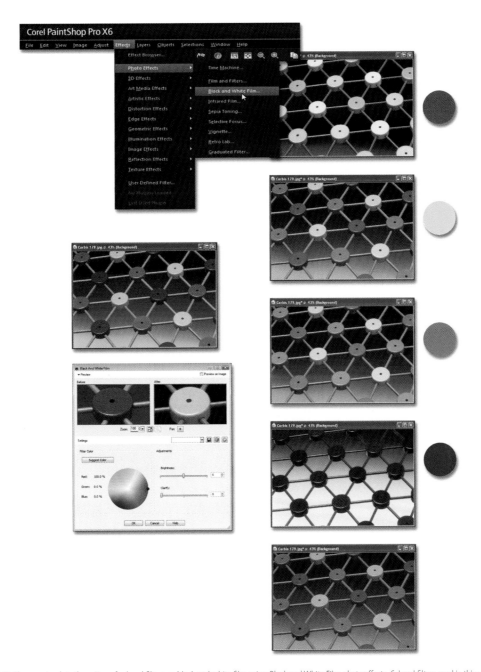

FIG 4.12 You can simulate the action of colored filters on black and white film using Black and White Film photo effects. Colored filters used in this way lighten the tone of same-colored objects and darken those with complementary colors. On this image, red lightens the red discs and darkens the blue background. Because of its proximity to yellow and orange, red also lightens the yellow and orange discs to a degree, but yellow and orange have a greater effect on their respective colors in the image. Blue has the reverse effect, lightening the blue background and darkening the discs. You can save commonly used filters like yellow, orange and red as presets. Bottom: You can also use the Photo Effects Sepia filter to apply a quick sepia tone to an image, but the Colorize option on the Hue/Saturation/Lightness dialog box provides more scope for color tinting of black and white photos.

to combine the data from the red, green and blue channels you can produce a widely variable range of tonal effects.

Tinting Black and White Photos

In the last section I described ways to use PaintShop Pro to convert a color picture to black and white. Now we'll take a look at how to color-tint a black and white photo. Why color-tint? Most black and white pictures reproduce only a limited tonal range: 256 tones to be exact. The addition of color, albeit in subtle amounts, produces a print apparently much richer in tonal scale.

This process is sometimes called a 'duotone'. Adding two colors to a black and white photo in the same fashion is called a 'tritone' and adding a third color makes this a 'quadtone'.

How It's Done

Tip

Color Balance and Hue/
Saturation/Lightness
are best applied as
Adjustment layers, so
that changes remain
editable and can be
removed later if required.
(See Chapter 5.)

Aside from using Effects > Photo Effects > Sepia Toning which, as we've seen, limits you to fairly crude applications of a single color, the simplest way to tone a black and white photo is using White Balance. Remember, you can only produce color effects like this (or in fact carry out any color editing, such as adding colored text) on an image that, though it may appear black and white, is an RGB color file. So, if you're starting with a full color image, desaturate it, as explained on the previous page. If it's a greyscale image convert it to an RGB one by selecting Image > Increase Color Depth > RGB – 8 bits/channel. Now open the White Balance dialog box by selecting Adjust > White Balance and uncheck the Advanced Options box to turn off the advanced controls if they are displayed. Now all you have to do is drag the slider to the right or left to make the image warmer or cooler. Warmer adds red and yellow to the image and Cooler adds blue. The further you drag the slider the more color is added. To add other colors to the image, check the Advanced Options box and use the More Purple/More Green slider.

You can add a wider range of tints to a photo using Adjust > Hue and Saturation > Colorize. This is actually pretty simple to use. First select a color using the Hue box on the left – the colors won't mean much to you so click the down arrow to display a color picker. Next, adjust the strength of the tint using the Saturation slider.

Tip

For an interesting effect
use a Hue/Saturation/
Lightness Adjustment
layer in Colorize mode
to apply a tint, then
reduce the layer opacity
to blend it with the
original color.

Again, if you click the down arrow you can work with a visual tint gradient rather than a number.

You can also use the Hue/Saturation/Lightness dialog box with the Colorize box checked to tint a monochrome photo. This works in pretty much the same way as the colorize method, using the Hue and Saturation sliders to set the tint color and strength. The Hue/Saturation/Lightness dialog box (as its name implies) also provides a Lightness slider.

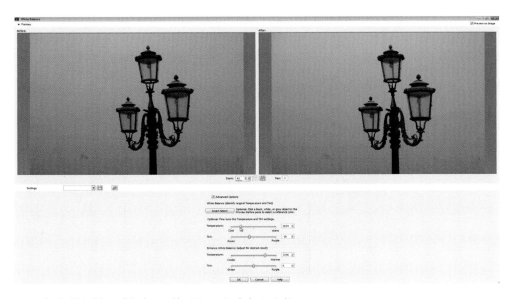

FIG 4.13 Use the White Balance dialog box to add a tint to previously desaturated images.

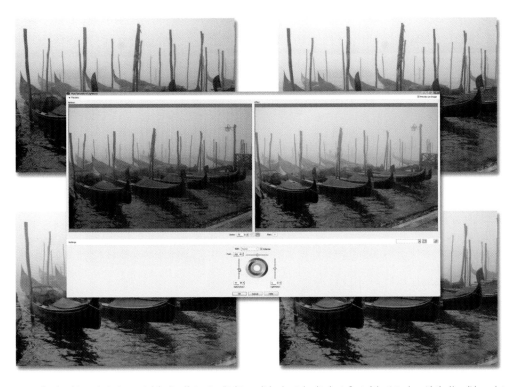

FIG 4.14 For the ultimate in tinting control the Hue/Saturation/Lightness dialog box is hard to beat. Control the tint color with the Hue slider and strength using the Saturation slider. You can also adjust image brightness using the Lightness slider, though adjustments of this kind are usually best left to Levels.

FIG 4.15 The Colorize command provides the best balance between control and ease of use. Just select your tint color using the Hue color picker, then adjust the strength using the Saturation slider.

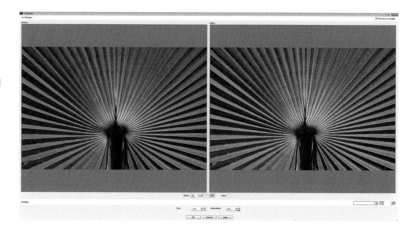

Whenever you're tinting images in this way it's a good idea to use an Adjustment layer, rather than applying color changes directly to the image. Using an Adjustment layer will allow you to easily make changes to the tint at a later stage in the editing process – for example, if you add some text and decide that a different colored tint would work better. You can even remove the tint altogether if you decide against it.

Adjustment layers also provide additional control over the effect. You can reduce the strength of the effect and blend it with the original using layer opacity and Blend modes. See Chapter 5 for more about how you can use Adjustment layers to edit images non-destructively.

Creating Color Overlay Effects

In the earlier editions of this book I devoted these pages to a technique that involved using the Color Balance tool to apply a multi-tone effect, using different colors for the image shadows, highlights and midtones. While PaintShop Pro's White Balance tool is now easier to use, it no longer lets you apply color changes individually to the highlight, midtone and shadow regions of a photo. But we're not going to let that get in the way of a good technique! Here's how to achieve the same effect using a layer property called Blend Range, which masks parts of a layer that fall within a tonal range that you specify.

Open the image you want to tint and duplicate the background layer twice by selecting it in the Layers palette, right-clicking it and selecting Duplicate from the context menu. Rename the new layers after the color you intend to use for the tints; here I've called them red and blue. Tint the layers using the colorize technique described on page 124.

Tip

Like Adjustment layers, the changes you make using Blend Ranges aren't permanent and you can go back and edit them at any stage. Try combining Blend Ranges with Blend modes to produce interesting graphic effects.

Double-click the top 'blue' layer in the Layers palette to open the Layer Properties dialog box and click the Blend Ranges tab. If it isn't already selected, choose Grey Channel from the Blend Channel pull-down menu and take a look at the two graduated bars underneath it. You can use these bars to control how pixels in the two layers are displayed. The top bar, labeled 'This layer' can be used to hide pixels on the upper (blue) layer using the four triangle-shaped buttons. Drag the buttons on the left to hide pixels in the shadows and those on the right to hide highlight pixels. By dragging the top and bottom triangles to different positions you can create a smooth transition between the layers, rather than have the color change abruptly.

The bottom slider essentially does the same thing in a different way. Think of it as forcing pixels on the layer below (in this case the blue layer) to show through the top (red) one. I find it keeps things simpler to ignore the Underlying Layer controls and just use the controls for the upper layer to choose which parts of the tonal range I want to appear in that color.

Using the Warp Tools

PaintShop Pro has several powerful brush tools that can be used to radically bend and distort the pixels in a photo. These are the Warp Brushes.

Why use a Warp Brush?

- To create zany, surreal pictorial effects.
- To increase eye size in a portrait (i.e. to enlarge a model's pupils for that wide-eyed look; it can also be used for reducing the size of other unsightly body parts like noses, if it's important).
- Straighten facial detail (i.e. a broken nose).
- To entertain your kids.

The Warp Brush works just like any other brush in PaintShop Pro in so far that you can run it over the picture and it applies a direct change. In this situation you have massive influence over how the pixels bend and warp under the brush. Some computing power is needed to make this work swiftly.

There are eight warp modes which can be combined or used individually. Brush effects are 'Push', 'Expand', 'Contract', 'Right Twirl', 'Left Twirl', 'Noise', 'Iron Out' and Unwarp.

If you don't like what this brush does, click the 'Cancel' tab. Other options include 'Brush Size', 'Hardness', 'Strength', 'Step' and 'Noise'. When you have finished the warping process, click the OK check mark to render the warping action. Warping can place heavy demands on your CPU, so if

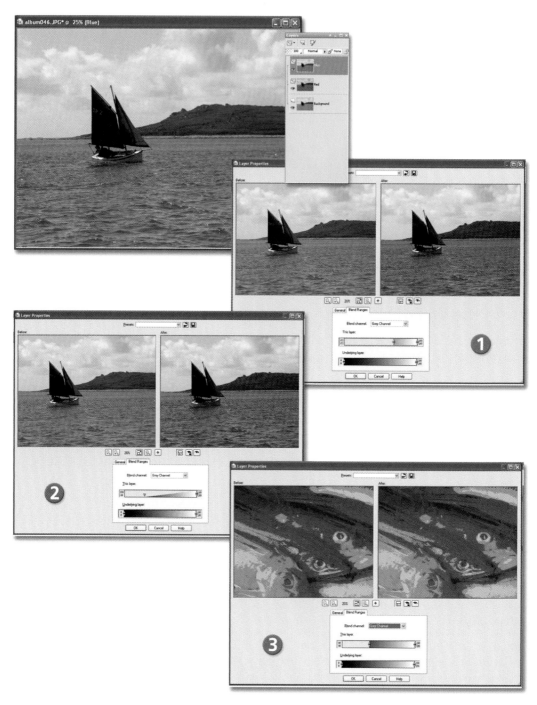

FIG 4.16 Use Blend Ranges to confine color tints to parts of the image like the highlights or shadows. (1) Confining the top blue layer to the highlights creates a hard-edged transition between red sea/land and blue sky. (2) Soften the transition by creating a 'ramp', allowing the red to bleed into the sky and vice versa. (3) You can use this technique on high-contrast images to produce two-color posterization effects.

You are working on a older PC, set Coarse Draft quality in the Tool Options palette. This doesn't affect the final result, so for best quality results, you should check the Best quality box, regardless of the Draft quality setting.

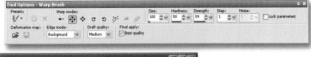

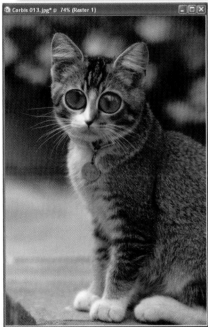

FIG 4.17 The Warp brush is perfect for making domestic pets look absurdly funny.

Scripting

Scripting is a powerful PaintShop Pro feature introduced back in version 8. It allows you to automatically combine several editing steps and apply them to another image. Say, for example, you have a whole folder of images and you want to do the same thing to each of them – open them, resize them, unsharp mask them, add a frame and save them. That's the kind of repetitive work that scripting was designed for. (PaintShop Pro's One Step Photo Fix is a script.)

Scripts are easy to create. The Scripting toolbar works a little like a VCR, with a record button that when pressed keeps track of everything you do and produces a script so that the same process can be applied with a single click to any other image. There's also a selection of pre-supplied scripts, including 'Border with drop shadow', 'Black and white sketch', 'EXIF captioning', 'Photo edges', 'Sepia frame', 'Simple caption', 'Vignette' and 'Watercolor'.

You can add scripts as buttons to toolbars, which makes them even easier to apply. Right-click on the toolbar and select Customize from the contextual menu, click the Scripts tab in the Customize dialog box and select the script you want to add from the pull-down menu. Choose an icon, click the Bind button and the Script button will appear in the Bound Scripts pane. Next, drag this icon from the Bound Scripts pane onto the Scripts toolbar. Now all you have to do to apply the script to any image is click the button.

Pre-written scripts are all very well, but what if you want a script to handle a repetitive task that doesn't appear on the Scripts toolbar drop-down list? Well, you can record your own, but you can also edit the existing scripts. PaintShop Pro's scripts are written in a scripting language called 'Python'. You don't need any special scripting knowledge to edit existing scripts, but if you're interested in finding out more about Python take a look at http://wiki.python.org/moin/BeginnersGuide.

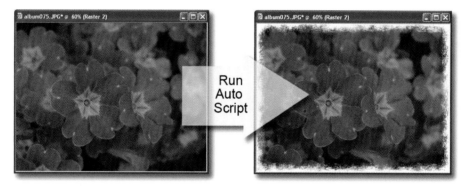

FIG 4.18 At a basic level, scripting allows users to run a pre-recorded action over an image (or images) in order to produce a quick – and predictable – result. Or you can record your own script and save it for use another time.

To edit a script click the Edit Script button on the Script toolbar. Some of the PaintShop Pro scripts provide editing tips. For example, the Thumbnail 150 script begins:

```
# if you want thumbnails generated at a different size just
change this to the desired value.
```

```
MaxThumbnailSize = 150
```

The # symbol at the beginning of the first line denotes a comment – what follows is ignored by the script interpreter – but its meaning is clear enough to anyone else.

PaintShop Pro X6 has an even easier way of creating scripts – called 'Quickscripts' – using the History palette. The History palette automatically records everything you do in PaintShop Pro. You can use the History palette as a super-undo feature. While selecting Undo from the Edit menu (or pressing Ctrl+Z) will take you back through recent editing in linear steps, the History palette can be used to selectively undo. You can, for example, undo the Lens Distortion filter effect you applied 10 minutes ago, but keep the cropping, Red-eye Removal and Automatic Color Balance subsequently applied.

To create a Quickscript select the steps you want to use by Shift-clicking (Ctrl-click to select non-contiguous steps) them in the History palette and click the Save Quickscript button. To apply the Quickscript to the current image click the Run Quickscript button. What could be simpler?

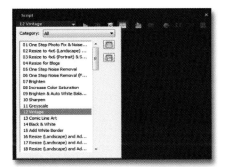
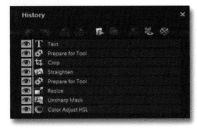
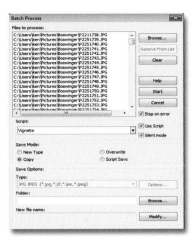

FIG 4.19 Use the Script toolbar (left) to select and apply scripts to the current image. You can create Quickscripts from the History palette (center). Combining scripts with Batch Processing (right) is the route to major effort-saving automation.

Clearly, scripts can save you a lot of legwork if you need to apply the same editing sequence to a large number of images. But you still have to open the image and click the button. It may not sound like hard work, but if you have to do it 300 times, or every time you download a batch of pictures from your digital camera, you'd be forgiven for considering it quite a chore. This is where Batch Processing comes in. Batch Processing can automatically apply editing commands to an entire folder of images. Combine Batch Processing with Scripting and you have some real image-editing power at your fingertips.

PaintShop Pro's Batch Processing feature grew out of a Batch Convert feature designed to allow you to convert a bunch of files from one format to another. It was extended to allow you to apply scripts and there's also a useful Batch Rename feature which you can use to change the anonymous file names of digital camera images to something more meaningful.

To open the Batch Process dialog box select File > Batch Process. Click the Browse button, navigate to the folder of images you want to process and click the Select All button. Before you do this make sure to back up the originals somewhere safe and work on a copy of the images so that, if something unexpected happens, you still have the originals to fall back on.

Check the Use Script box, select a script from the pull-down menu and check the Copy Radio button. This will save a copy of the processed image into the folder you specify in the Save Options pane. Click the Browse button and create a new folder called something like 'processed files' on your hard disk. The Save Mode pane provides other saving options. If you have included a Save As command in your script, check the Obey Script Radio button to use this rather than the Batch Process save instructions. If you check the Silent Mode box, Batch Process will run the selected script and apply the settings you used when you recorded it. If you leave the Silent Mode box unchecked, a dialog box will open at relevant points in the script for each processed image, requiring you to enter values.

When you're sure everything is correctly set, click the Start button, sit back and watch while PaintShop Pro does the hard work for you.

Step-by-Step Projects

Restoring Damaged Photos

Once you've mastered the retouching techniques demonstrated in this chapter and elsewhere in the book you'll be able to make improvements to digital photos that aren't quite 'right' as well as scanned pictures in need of restoration. With skilled use of the Clone Brush in combination with the other retouching tools there's little you won't be able to fix. This step-by-step project shows how to restore an old photo that's suffered quite bad damage, in this case more due to lack of care than the ageing process. Don't be put off attempting to restore old photos because they look past saving. Even very severe damage, such as tears, staining, fading and folds, can be reduced or eliminated altogether with the repeated application of the simple techniques shown here. And if your first efforts don't meet with much success, keep trying; retouching is one of those things that improves with practice.

Tip

A pressure-sensitive stylus and tablet makes retouching much easier. Use the Brush Variance palette to determine how the brush responds to stylus pressure. When you press harder, the brush can get bigger, or change opacity or thickness.

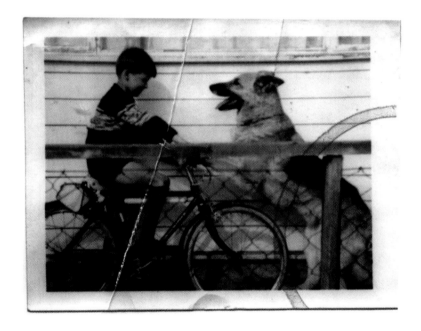

STEP 1 This photo is about 40 years old. It hasn't aged too badly, but it has a couple of serious fold marks, one running upwards from the dog's ear and another running vertically through the middle, as well as a nasty stain from a coffee cup. Overall the picture has accumulated some dirt and grubbiness, most noticeably in the white border area.

STEP 2 Even if the original is black and white, scan it as an RGB color image. The additional channels in an RGB image can bring out (or cover up) detail which will help in the retouching process. Scan at a high resolution so you can zoom in and work on small details; you can always downsample the photo later for printing or web use.

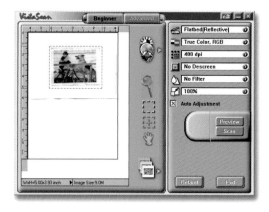

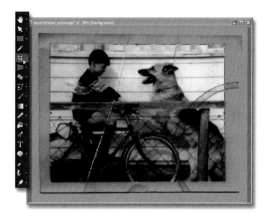

Step 3 Crop the picture to get rid of that grubby border. Depending on the shot, you can save yourself a great deal of work by cropping close and removing a lot of material that you might otherwise have to retouch, but here we want to keep everything other than the border.

STEP 4 From the Image menu select Split Channel > Split to RGB to separate the photo into its constituent red, green and blue channels. Select Tile Horizontally from the Window menu to compare the channels. Notice how the coffee stain isn't nearly so obvious on the red channel. This is the one we'll use for our retouching. Close the original scan and the green and blue channels and resave the red channel.

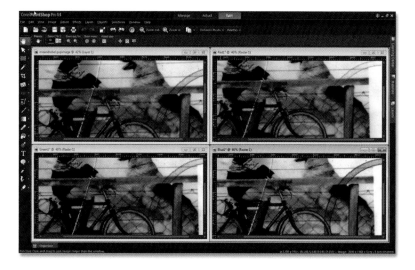

STEP 5 Click the New Raster layer button at the top of the Layers palette to create a new layer; call it 'retouching'. First we'll deal with the coffee stain. Sometimes it's easier to deal with big problems like this using copy and paste rather than the Clone Brush. Use the rectangular marquee with a feather setting of one and select an area just above the stain. It's a lucky coincidence that this selection is exactly the same, bar the stain, as the area below it, but you'd be surprised how often this happens.

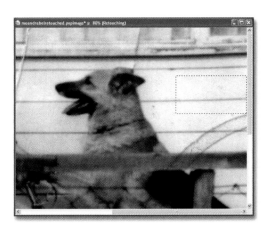

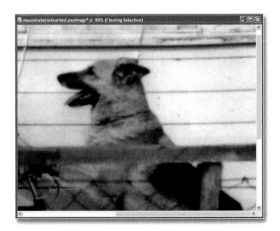

STEP 6 Select Copy Merged from the Edit > Copy Special menu followed by Paste As New Selection and position the pasted selection over the coffee stain, taking care to match the horizontal line of the wood cladding. Press Ctrl+Shift+F to defloat the selection. Repeat the process with different selections to cover as much of the stain as possible. Press Ctrl+D or choose Select None from the Selections menu.

STEP 7 Select the Clone Brush and set the size big enough to cover the width of the fold in one hit. Set the hardness to around 50 and make sure that Aligned mode and 'Use all layers' are both checked. Right-click with the brush just to one side of the fold to set the sampling point, then move onto the fold and left-click to clone. If your cloning isn't seamless try again from a slightly different start point. You'll need to experiment with the brush size, opacity and blend mode; you'll get better results using many short strokes, rather than one long one, and you'll also need to frequently reset the source point.

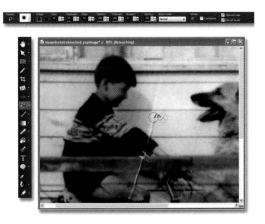

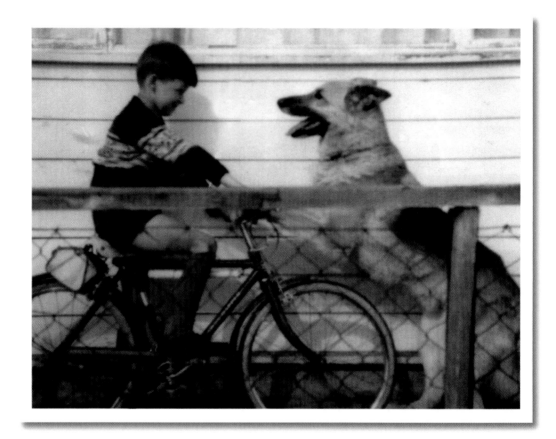

STEP 8 Continue with the Clone Brush down the length of the fold. Usually best results are achieved by sampling close to the area to be cloned as you will get a better match. Sometimes this will be to the left of the damaged area, sometimes to the right. Occasionally you may find there is no suitable material close by and you'll need to sample from a more remote location with similar detail. After cloning out the two fold lines I've gone back and removed the traces of the coffee stain from the area below the fence using the Clone tool. Picking the green channel, where the mark was least visible, meant that very little work was needed to remove the remaining traces. Finally I've added a nice clean white border.

Hand-Coloring Black and White Photos

In the days before color photography, a commonly used technique was to add color to black and white prints using inks and a small retouching brush. The aim of this process wasn't to create an exact facsimile of a scene in full color, but rather to add a little color detail to heighten the realism and add a little life to what otherwise may have appeared a little drab and austere.

If you've ever seen a hand-colored black and white print you'll know just how charming they can be. Using PaintShop Pro you can recreate this effect either to add a new dimension to archive family photos, or to produce an interesting new take on more recent digital images.

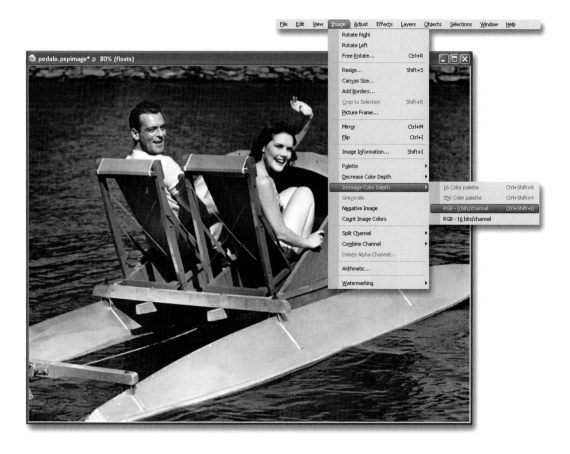

STEP 1 If you're starting off with a scanned black and white photo in greyscale mode you'll need to convert it to RGB by selecting Image > increase color depth > RGB – 8 bits/channel. If it's a color image, desaturate it using Hue/Saturation/Lightness as described earlier in the chapter.

Tip

You'll find it much easier to hand-color and carry out other retouching tasks using a pressure-sensitive tablet and stylus. It's much more natural to paint with a stylus than with a mouse, and PaintShop Pro's Brush tools respond to pressure – the harder you press, the more paint is deposited. Some styli even have an eraser on the end, so you can flip them over and rub out!

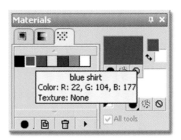

STEP 2 You'll get a more realistic result using a limited color palette. Using the Materials palette in Swatch mode, create up to six colors. Depending on the image you might, for example, choose a skin color, red to add color to lips and cheeks, one or two colors for items of clothing and another one or two swatches for other detail such as sky, a car or, as in this case, a pedalo. You might also find it helpful to name the swatches appropriately, for example, 'skin tones'.

STEP 3 Select the Paint Brush and choose one of your color swatches. Use the Tool Options palette to set the brush size, shape, hardness and other parameters. To a degree these will depend on the detail you are coloring, but generally, you'll find that soft-edged brushes with reduced opacity give good results. You might also try the Airbrush.

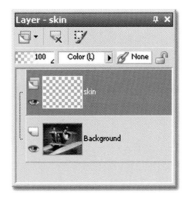

STEP 4 Create a new raster layer on which to add the color. There are two reasons for this. First, it's always a good idea to keep any retouching on a separate layer as it leaves the original untouched on the background layer and if things go drastically wrong you can always delete the retouching layer and start again. Second, it gives you a lot more control over your editing. You can change the opacity to fade the retouching and make it less obvious and use PaintShop Pro's Blend modes to produce a more natural look.

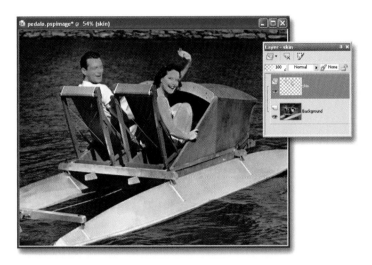

STEP 5 Making sure the new layer is selected, start to paint over the background image. At this stage the paint will go on thickly and may even completely obliterate the detail below, producing a crude and ugly result. Don't worry! Once you've applied a few strokes to a small area of the picture, stop painting.

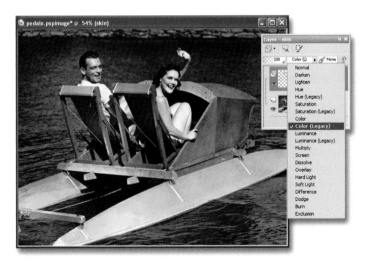

STEP 6 In the Layers palette change the Blend mode from Normal to Color (Legacy). Now, your brush strokes apply color to the image, but maintain the original tone, producing a more natural effect. As well as retaining the underlying detail, you'll notice that the color varies from your original swatch, depending on how light or dark the underlying pixels are.

Tip

When you change the Layer Blend mode to Color (Legacy), the paint that you've applied with the Brush tool adopts the tonal characteristics of the underlying (grey) pixels. Dark pixels pick up darker color and vice versa. It pays to be realistic in your choice of colors. If your subject is wearing a dark shirt, you won't be able to paint it light blue. If colors don't come out as expected, try using the Hue/Saturation/Lightness controls to change the color of the paint layer – another good reason for keeping each color tint on a separate layer.

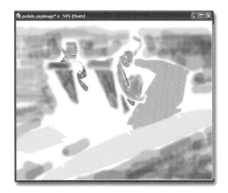

STEP 7 When you've finished painting all of the image detail in one of your palette colors, for example all the skin tones, create another new layer and continue painting in the next color. You could put all your colors onto one layer, but using a different layer for each color gives you more control over the finished result. Suppose, when you are nearing completion, everything looks OK, but the skin tones look a bit over the top, like everyone's had a bit too much sun. By reducing the opacity of the skin tones layer you can correct this problem without affecting the other colors.

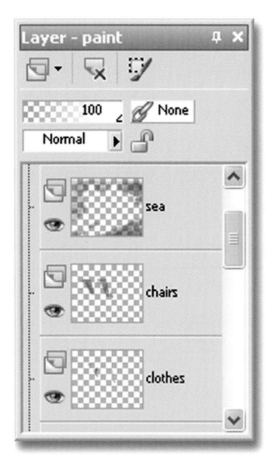

STEP 8 The great thing about hand-coloring is you don't have to be a great artist or even incredibly accurate, as this screen of all the paint layers at 100% opacity in Normal mode shows!

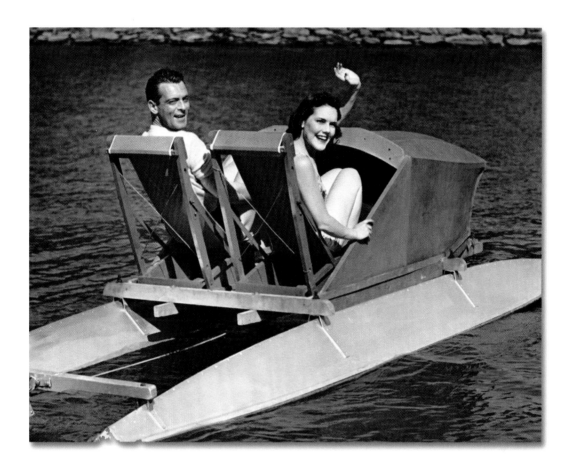

The final result.

Creating a Dramatic Tone Effect

If you've bought a new camera recently it more than likely has a shooting mode that applies effects filters. These have become increasingly popular and these days you find them not just on point-and-shoot compacts, but on more advanced cameras as well. When I first tried an Olympus PEN Micro four thirds compact system camera, I was really impressed with its Art filter effects and in particular with the Dramatic tone effect which made otherwise quite banal and forgettable shots look, well, a lot more dramatic! Here's an example showing the effect alongside the 'straight' shot without the effect applied.

Dramatic tone was clearly popular with other photographers, as it, or something like it, soon started to appear on models from other manufacturers. Here it turns a fairly ordinary shot of a moped into something much more graphic. If you don't have a camera with effects filters, you can't take advantage of the Dramatic Tone filter, or can you? How hard can this effect be to create in PaintShop Pro I thought. The answer? Pretty easy as it happens. The Dramatic Tone art filter looks like it applies a local contrast enhancement in combination with some kind of faux HDR effect. It turns out you can get a remarkably similar effect to the Olympus one using a Local Tone Mapping adjustment in PaintShop Pro X6.

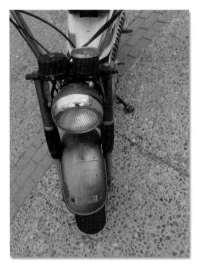 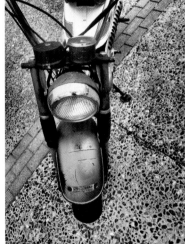

STEP 1 To apply the Local Tone mapping adjustment as an adjustment layer open your image and, with the background layer selected, click the New Adjustment Layer button on the Layers palette and select Local Tone Mapping.

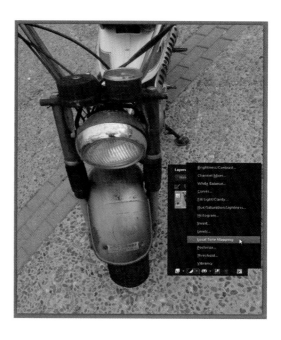

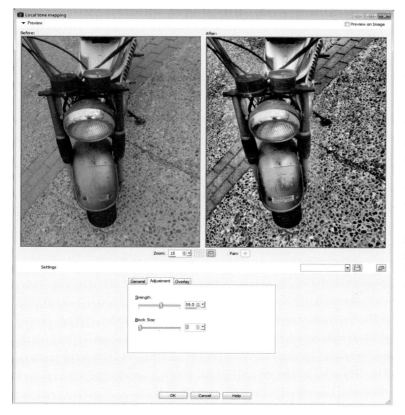

STEP 2 Maximize the dialog box, uncheck Preview on image, click the Fit to window button to get decent sized before and after thumbnails and select the Adjustment tab. You really have to ladle it on with this adjustment to get close to the Dramatic Tone look of the Olympus filter. The strength needs to be around 50–60, but keep the block size small, here I've used the minimum setting of 8. When you're done, click the OK button.

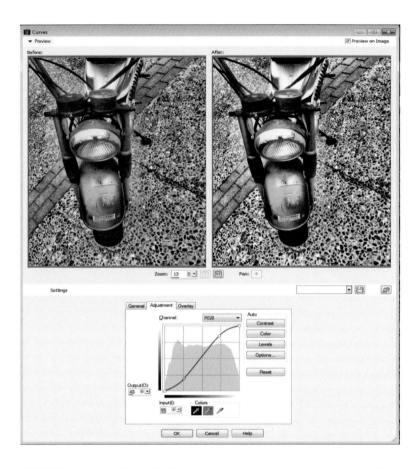

STEP 3 We're almost there, it's that simple, but there's a couple of things still to do to get this result even closer to the genuine Olympus one. I want to exaggerate the contrast a little more. Do this using a Curves adjustment layer. Here, I've made the curve S-shaped to increase the contrast without losing too much detail in the shadows or highlights.

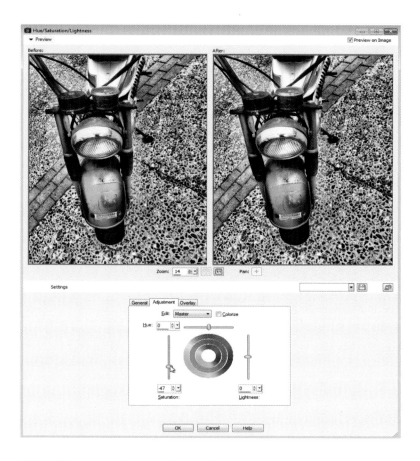

STEP 4 The curves adjustment has resulted in some heavily saturated colors which are at odds with the slightly desaturated look of the Olympus Dramatic tone filter, so the final adjustment, once again applied as an adjustment layer, is a Hue/Saturation/Lightness adjustment. I've reduced the saturation to around −50 to match the look of the Olympus filter.

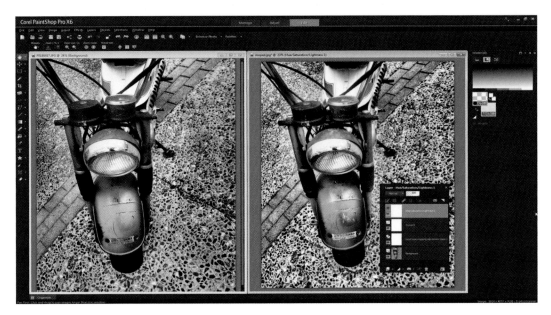

So here's the comparison. On the left, the original Dramatic Tone art filter applied in-camera on the Olympus E-P3 and on the right my attempt to create the same effect on the 'straight' version in PaintShop Pro X6. It's pretty close, but although I was trying to replicate an existing effect, there's nothing to stop you experimenting. If you like this effect, but you don't own an Olympus it's a good alternative and it doesn't take a lot of work to produce.

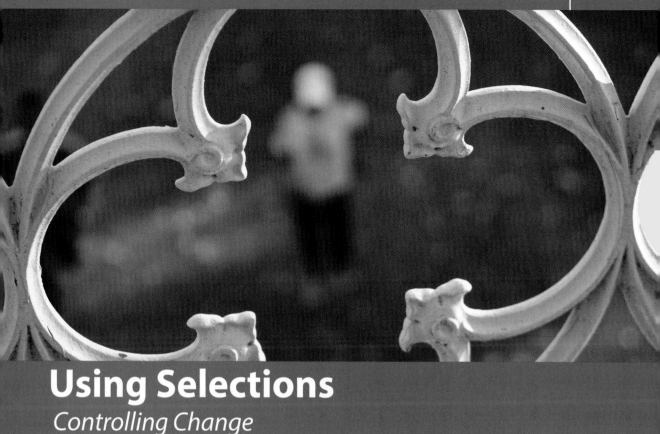

CHAPTER 5

Using Selections
Controlling Change

- This is a short chapter, but it covers crucial techniques that will take your photo editing skills way beyond what we've covered up to now. This chapter is all about selections and how to make them. Selections and their close relatives mask layers and alpha channels, allow you to confine changes to a part of the image – a bit like using a stencil.

- PaintShop Pro X6 has more than 20 selection tools, ranging from easy to use tools that do nearly all of the work for you to more hands-on tools that require a little more skill and input, but are useful for difficult subjects. PaintShop Pro X6 introduces two new selection tools that make grabbing parts of an image easier than ever. The new Smart Selection Brush allows you to paint the element you want to select and has an uncanny knack for knowing where the edges are. Likewise, the Auto Selection tool starts with a rectangular selection but shrink wraps the selection marquee to precisely fit the edges of the object you want.

- Beyond that are the Geometric selection tools, the Freehand Selection tool and the Magic Wand as well as specialist tools like the Object Extractor and

Background Eraser. The keys to successful selection are knowing which tool to use for particular selection tasks, how to set the tool options so that you get exactly what you want – nothing more and nothing less – and, if you don't get quite what you want, how to add to and subtract from existing selections.

- The selection tools can take you only so far. For one thing, they're not permanent so if you want to close your photo and come back to work on it later, you'll need to save your selection, this is where alpha channels and mask layers come in. As well allowing you to make selections permanent, alpha channels and mask layers can be worked on with PaintShop Pro's brush tools. Masks produced in this way can show or hide anything in your photos, even things with indistinct edges, like fur, hair, clouds and water. Once the mask is made you can use it as the basis for selectively applying filters, making tonal and color changes or anything else. This chapter introduces alpha channels and mask layers, in Chapter 6; you'll learn some more advanced masking techniques using layers.
- The step-by-step project at the end of the chapter shows you how to use some of the techniques you'll learn here to replace a dull sky with something more dramatic.

Tip

As with many other aspects of photo editing, making selections, particularly with the Freehand Selection tool is much easier with a graphics tablet and stylus than with a mouse.

Understanding Selections: Adding Creative Power

PaintShop Pro has several tools that allow the isolation of specific areas within the picture based on certain selection criteria such as color, tonality, contrast or simply by drawing around it. You have to distinguish the best selection tool, or tools, to use for the picture in question. For example, sometimes it's possible with one mouse-click to get a good, clean selection around an object. Sometimes it is not so easy because the photo might be multi-colored or irregular in tone. In this case you'd use a combination of selection tools to successfully 'grab' the object cleanly. PaintShop Pro also has a number of tools that you can use to clean up these selections once started. These are called Selection Modification tools.

There's no point in making a job more difficult than it needs to be, so the approach with selections is to try the quickest and simplest tools first, if they don't get the results you need you can move on and try something different. After a while you'll develop a knack for knowing what's straightforward and what isn't from a selection standpoint. Likewise, in this chapter we'll first look at the quick and easy selection tools and graduate on to the more complex ones.

PaintShop Pro's Selection tools can be broadly categorized as follows:

- The easiest to use tools are the new Smart Selection Brush and Auto Selection tools.
- Next up is the Magic Wand tool. This finds pixels either of a similar contrast, color, brightness or opacity within the picture.

- The Freehand Selection tool has edge-seeking ('magnetic'), point-to-point (polygonal line), smart-edge (linear 'magnetic') or just freehand characteristics.
- The Geometric Marquee selection comes in rectangular, square, circular, star, triangular and ten other preset shapes.
- Finally, the Object Extractor, Background Eraser and Smart Carver are specialist tools for cutting out and removing elements form an image.

Bear in mind that the ToolOptions palette has more refining controls for some of the tools mentioned. Controls include a Tolerance level, Blend mode, Anti-aliasing, Smoothing, Feathering and Match mode.

The Smart Selection Brush and Auto Selection Tool

Faced with the task of making a selection, the first tool you should reach for is PaintShop Pro X6's new Smart Selection Brush. It makes little difference if you're an old hand or a newbie, the Smart Selection Brush really is aptly named and can save you a lot of painstaking manual work. In fact it's so smart and at the same time so easy to use, it requires very little explanation.

The Smart Selection Brush (Fig 5.1) is on the selection tool fly-out of the Tools toolbar; to select it click the triangle next to the current selection tool and choose it from the fly-out – it's the fourth one down and its icon is a wand with a green star at the tip. Take a look at the Tool options palette to get an idea of how you can modify the brush, there are options for size and feather and a mode pull-down. The default mode is Add which means that each time you use the brush it adds to an existing selection to make it bigger.

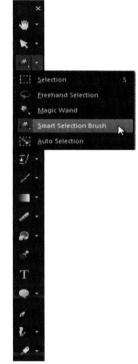

FIG 5.1 The Smart Selection Brush is on the selection tools fly-out of the Tools toolbar.

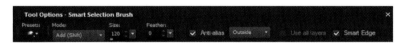

FIG 5.2 Make sure that Smart Edge is checked in the tool options palette (and Use all layers if you're working on a multi-layered image and what you want to select spans more than one layer).

On the right of the Tool options palette you'll see a checkbox labelled Smart Edge, (Fig 5.2) make sure it's checked then click and drag with the brush on a part of your image that you want to select. Notice how the selection isn't confined to where you paint, but extends right up to edges of the thing you're trying to select? That's the Smart bit, PaintShop Pro automatically detects the edge of the element your painting and fits the selection to it. If you haven't got the whole thing with your first brush stroke just continue painting, with each brush stroke the Smart Edge continues to do its work, adding to the selection on the basis of the area you paint. Eventually you should be able to get the entire element selected in this way.

149

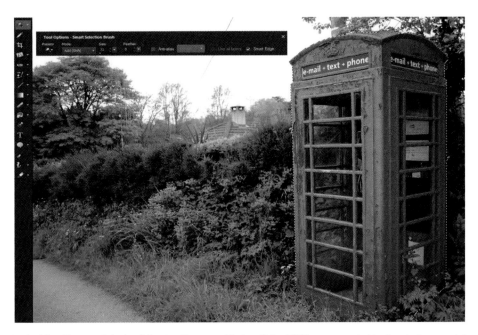

FIG 5.3 You should be able to get a fairly close fit first time. Use two modifier keys (Ctrl and Shift) to remove and add to the selection as needed and don't forget to zoom in and alter the brush size for more control.

Depending on the boundary between the element you want to select and the background, the Smart Selection Brush may have more or less success in making an accurate selection. If it's picked up bits of the background in addition to what you wanted, just change the mode from Add to Remove in the Tool options palette and paint out the unwanted bits. As before, as long as you have Smart Edge checked, the bits you paint out of the selection automatically expand up to the boundary between the element and the background. For smaller detail you'll find it helps to reduce the size of the brush and zoom in. You can also switch from add to remove by holding down the Ctrl key.

The Auto Selection tool is even simpler to use than the Smart Selection Brush. Its the last tool on the selection tool fly-out, below the Smart Selection Brush. Once selected, drag a rectangle around the element you want to select and the Auto Selection tool works the same trick as the Smart Selection Brush, locating the edges within the rectangle and creating a selection around them.

One of the nice things about the Auto Selection tool is there's very little for you to do other than draw a box around the thing you want to select. That's it. Of course if it doesn't yield the desired results there's not much you can do other than try something else. But don't be tempted to rely on just one

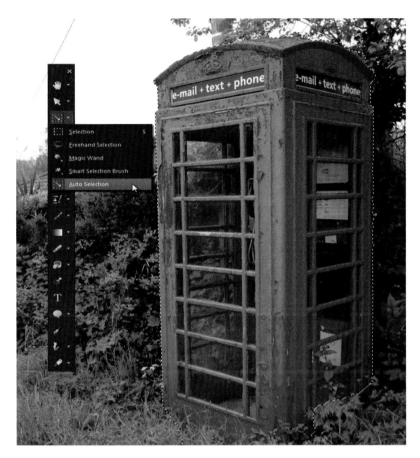

FIG 5.4 To use the Auto Selection tool just select it and drag a rectangle around the thing you want. That's all there is to it.

tool to get the job done. If the Auto Selection tool picks up too much, or not enough of what you were trying to select, switch to the Smart Selection Brush and finish the job by adding to, or removing from the original selection. If that still doesn't work it's time for the next tool in PaintShop Pro's selection armory, the Magic Wand tool.

The Magic Wand Tool

The Smart Selection and Auto Selection tools are quick and easy, but they don't work for every subject. In this case, the Magic Wand tool may be what you need. This is the most versatile selection tool available to you and can capture just about any selection you ask of it. The key to success with the Magic Wand tool lies in correctly setting the options and this often involves some trial and error. With a little experience, however, it will become second nature to you and take very little time. Certainly a lot less time than having to make the same selection manually.

Tip

Feathering is measured in pixels. If you feather a selection by 10 pixels on a low-resolution image, it will have a much bigger effect than on a high-resolution one.

Select the Magic Wand tool from the selection tool fly-out on the toolbar (it's above the Smart Selection Brush and is also a wand, this time with a yellow spark at its tip) and click inside an image on an area of fairly similar color and tone. The resulting selection marquee may cover a little of the image or a lot of it, and it may be one big selection or there could be smaller islands of selected image dotted about – it all depends on the image.

What the Magic Wand does is select pixels of similar values, within a range that you specify, throughout the image. As a starting point the Magic Wand tool uses the pixel that you click on. It then selects all the pixels with an RGB value within the range specified by the value in the Tolerance field of the Tool Options palette; the larger the tolerance, the more pixels will be selected. If what you're trying to select is a very specific color, a red door for example, you can use a low tolerance setting to select all of it. If it contains a wider range of colors, like a sky or the leaves on a tree, you might need to increase the tolerance to capture all of the hues.

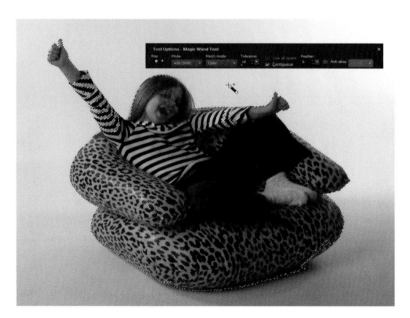

FIG 5.5 Successful use of the Magic Wand tool depends on making good tool options choices and adopting appropriate techniques. In this case it's easier to select the background and invert the selection to capture the subject. Rather than increasing the tolerance in an attempt to get everything in one bite, which will most likely just capture unwanted areas of the image, use a smaller tolerance setting and Shift-click to add to the original selection.

Sometimes, increasing the tolerance means you capture pixels you don't want, which happen to have similar values to those you do. If this happens you need to try a different tack. One method is to Shift-click to add to the existing selection. If you get an unsatisfactory result press Ctrl+Z, rather than trying to subtract from the selection by Ctrl-clicking with the Magic Wand tool. Alternatively, it's often easier to select a background with the Magic Wand tool then invert the selection (Selections>Invert or press Ctrl+Shift+I) to capture the subject.

There are other options that can help you fine-tune a Magic Wand selection. Match modes enable you to make a selection on the basis of color, hue, brightness and opacity as well as RGB values. Using the Brightness Match mode is one way to select shadow or highlight detail if you want to make selective tonal adjustment to an image.

Click the Use all layers checkbox if you want the Magic Wand tool to base its selection on all pixels in the image, rather than just those in the active layer (if you get very unexpected results with the Magic Wand tool, e.g. everything selected wherever you click, it's probably because you're clicking in an empty layer with Use all layers unchecked). 'Contiguous' selects only pixels that are next to each other, so you get one selection marquee. Turn off Contiguous and the Magic Wand tool can jump over non-selected pixels to select in-range pixels anywhere within the image. In non-Contiguous mode you'll get little pools of selection all over the image.

Finally, you can elect to anti-alias a Magic Wand selection's edge pixels. Use the pull-down menu to determine whether pixels outside or inside the selection border will be anti-aliased.

The Tool Options palette isn't the last word on modifying Magic Wand selections. On the Selections>Modify menu you'll find a host of additional fine-tuning adjustments that will allow you to, among other things, expand, contract, select similar, feather, smooth and remove specks and holes from your selections. These can, of course, be used with any selections, not just those created with the Magic Wand tool.

What else can you do with selections?

- All selections can be saved and stored for later use in an alpha channel or to a designated area on your hard drive like any other file.
- Selections can be used like a stencil – to inhibit brush actions along straight.
- All selection tools have an 'Add To' and a 'Subtract From' function. Hold the Shift key when making a second selection and it's added to the first. Keep holding the Shift key to add further selections. In this way you can build, or reduce, extremely accurate selections.
- To further refine the process, selection tools are interchangeable. Make an initial selection using the Magic Wand tool, for example, and add to that using a Marquee tool. Finish off using the Freehand Selection tool. Use the Shift and Control keys to apply additions and subtractions or set the same parameters in the Tool Options palette.
- Use the Options palette to make custom selections using numerical values in the fields provided ('Customize Selection' in the Options palette).

> **Tip**
>
> The results of a Magic Wand tool selection depend on the precise pixel you click on. Even in what looks like an area of flat color pixel values vary, so if your first attempt isn't successful, press Ctrl+Z to undo and click again on a neighboring pixel.

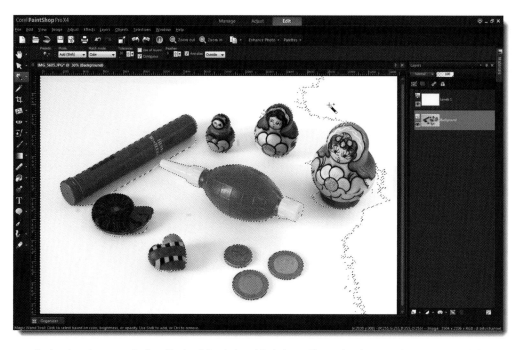

FIG 5.5A To select these objects using the Magic Wand tool I first duplicated the background layer and used a Layers adjustment to make the background as white as possible.

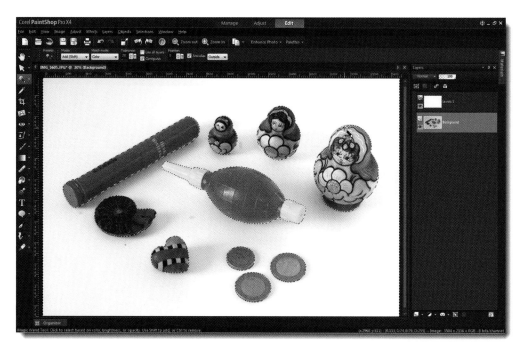

FIG 5.5B Refine the selection using the Magic Wand tool in Add mode (or hold down Shift). You should be able to select all of the background using this method.

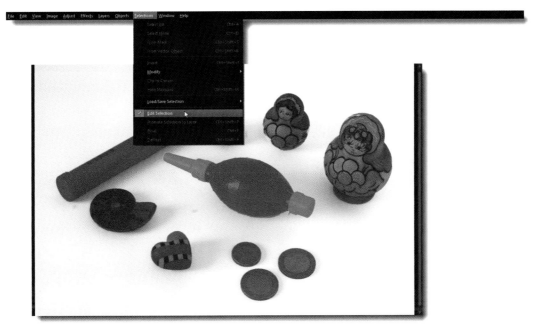

FIG 5.5C Invert the selection (press Ctrl+Shift+I) and choose Edit Selection from the Selections menu to alter the selection using the brush tools.

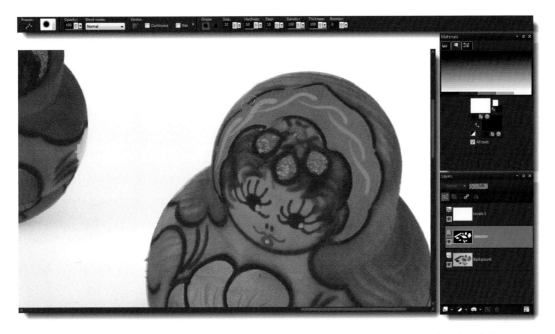

FIG 5.5D Using the brush tools with Edit Selection enables you to make a very accurate, soft-edged selection which won't 'show the join' when you paste.

- PaintShop Pro also has an Edit Selection mode ('Selections>Edit Selection'). In this mode, all the raster painting/drawing tools and many filter effects can be used to modify the selection marquee. In this mode the selection is rendered in a red opaque color so it's easy to see. This is a powerful and fast way to make an average-looking selection into something that has professional accuracy.
- Perfect the selection using the Selection Modify tools. These will allow you to produce surprising accuracy from even the roughest of initial selections.

Using the Geometric Selection Tools

In some ways, PaintShop Pro's Geometric selection tools are the easiest to use because they are 'preset'. They don't rely entirely on the accuracy of the mouse action.

Open a picture and duplicate the Background layer ('Layers>Duplicate') so that you can practice on a copy of the original rather than the original itself. Make sure that the top layer is active (click it in the Layers palette).

Choose the Rectangular Marquee selection tool from the Tools toolbar, left-click and drag the cursor across the picture about 20% from the edge of the image. The moving line that appears where the selection was drawn is called the 'selection marquee'. Any further editing on the picture applies to the area inside this selection only. Because we want to add an effect to the area outside this selection it must be reversed or 'inverted'.

Choose 'Selections>Invert' from the Selections drop-down menu and note how it selects the entire image up to the borders of the original area selected. Use the keyboard shortcut 'Ctrl+Shift+M' to hide the marquee to make it easier to see any tone changes you make. Note that, though it is hidden, the selection is still active.

Open the Levels dialog window ('Adjust>Brightness and Contrast>Levels') and drag the grey diamond slider (the middle one) to the right. This darkens the selected area. Push the slider far enough to make the edges significantly darker, but still keep them semi-transparent.

You can refine all selections using the Feather adjustment. This blurs the selection line across an adjustable pixel width so that you can soften those typical scalpel-sharp selection cut-lines.

Adding to the Selection

To add to a selection, hold the Shift key down and make several more geometric selections, adding one on top of the other to build up a complex irregular but still geometric selection with each new mouse drag.

Change the shape of the selection (circular, square, octagonal, etc.) using the Options palette. Remember at all times to update the save to preserve the selection information in an alpha channel ('Selections>Save to Alpha Channel').

The Object Extractor and Background Eraser

In addition to the selection tools PaintShop Pro X6 has a couple of ways to cut out and remove objects from photos. These aren't strictly speaking selection tools, they go beyond mere selection and actually remove parts of the image for you in one single operation.

The Object Extractor does exactly what it says, it cuts out part of an image – say a person, car flower or whatever your subject happens to be – removing the background. To use the Object Extractor Select Object Extractor from the image menu. The Object Extractor opens in its own window which displays a large image preview below which are some tools and settings. To use it you select the brush tool, set an appropriate brush size and paint an outline around the edge of the object you want to cut out. If you make a mistake you can erase with the eraser. When the outline is complete, click inside it with the fill tool to fill the selected area with a red mask, then click the Process button.

PaintShop Pro X6 now makes a first attempt at extracting the object from the background. If it doesn't get it right the first time, try experimenting with the accuracy slider – each time you move it the image is reprocessed and you'll have to wait a few seconds. Subjects with more detailed edges will require a higher accuracy setting (and better skills with the brush) but as long as the subject that you're attempting to extract is reasonably well isolated from the background you should be able to get a good result. To get a better look check the Hide Mask checkbox and if you want to go back and edit the outline in an attempt to improve the result click the Edit mask button. When you're happy that you've got the best possible result click the OK button to extract the object. What happens now is that the background is deleted leaving your object cut out on its layer.

The Object Extractor like the Background Eraser, which works in a similar fashion, works best on objects that are well isolated from their backgrounds, e.g. those shot against a plain background – like the sky in our example. To cut out objects with more complex backgrounds you'll get a better result using the selection tools already discussed and, even better, masking, which is explained toward the end of this chapter. You could also take a look at the step-by-step project at the end of this chapter that shows exactly how to deal with objects that have fussy edge detail.

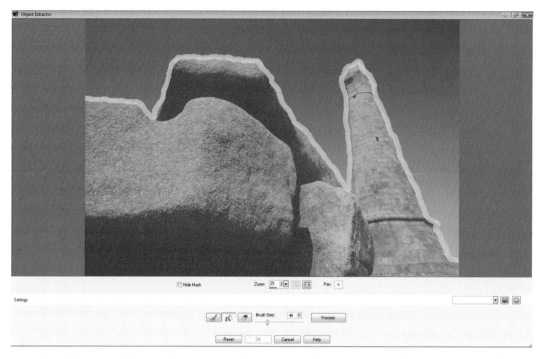

FIG 5.6 The Object Extractor makes light work of removing a subject from its background. It works best on subjects like this, which are clearly defined against a plain background like the sky. It's very simple to use, you just paint an outline around the subject, fill it, then click the process button. PaintShop Pro X6 then deletes the background detail.

The Smart Carver

Tip

Instead of trying to select an object, it's often easier to select the background, then invert the selection (press Ctrl+Shift+I). You can also try using a Levels adjustment to make a light background completely white and much easier to 'grab' using the Magic Wand tool.

One other feature of PaintShop Pro X6 that I want to mention here is the Smart Carver which combines retouching and cropping in one operation, allowing you to resize an image while preserving some details and removing others. Again, though it's not strictly speaking a selection tool, it uses simple selections as a basis for automating what would otherwise be a complex retouching task.

The Smart Carver is on the Image menu just above the Object Extractor and opens in its own window. It has two brushes, one for preserving detail and the other for removing it. You simply paint over what's important with the green brush and daub what you want to lose with the red brush. I use the word daub advisedly. The great thing about the Smart Carver is that you don't need to be too careful about going over the edges. As long as what you want to keep or loose is covered in paint it works just fine.

Having done your painting there are buttons for resizing the image both vertically and horizontally. The most useful of these are the Auto-contract buttons on the right which resize the image sufficiently to remove all unwanted detail.

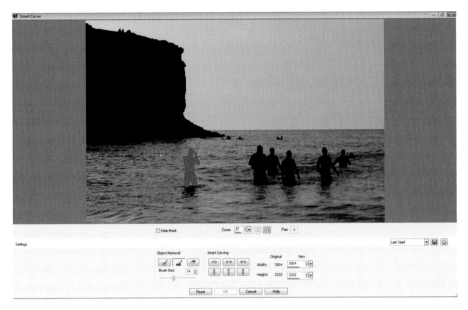

FIG 5.7 Smart Carver resizes photos removing unwanted detail in the process. Unlike cropping, the bits you want to get rid of don't have to be near the edges. You can seamlessly remove detail from anywhere in the frame.

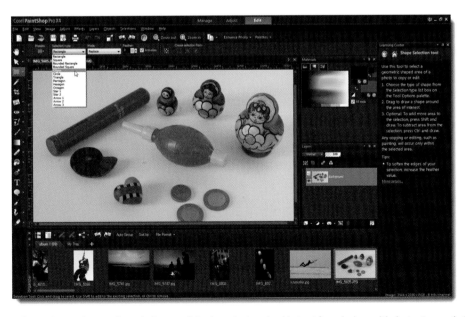

FIG 5.8 PaintShop Pro has a wide range of special selection tools but for cutting irregular objects out from a background the best options are the Smart Selection Brush, Auto Selection tool, Freehand Selection tool or the Magic Wand tool. Few objects are perfect geometric shapes and the geometric selection tools are really intended for producing graphics by making a selection and filling it. If you are taking a photo of objects you intend to cut out, shoot them on a white or plain colored background to make the task of selecting them easier.

Alpha Channels

When you make a selection, PaintShop Pro stores it in an alpha channel. Channels are a bit like layers; an RGB image is composed of three channels, one each for the red, green and blue image data. Alpha channels are greyscale – pixels in them are either black, white or one of 254 shades of grey. In an alpha channel, pixels within a selected area are white, unselected pixels are black and grey pixels are partially selected.

Tip

Using the Brush tools to paint directly onto a mask layer is often a much easier way to obtain a selection than using any of the selection tools.

How can you have a partially selected pixel? Well, pixels in a feathered selection are partially selected. If you looked at the alpha channel for a circular feathered selection, there would be a white hole in the middle with a soft edge gradually fading to black. Any editing applied to image pixels selected using an alpha channel with grey pixels will have a partial effect, which is extremely useful for subtle image editing without 'hard' edges. It means you can apply filters and other effects with a gradually tapering effect.

At their simplest, alpha channels are simply useful methods for permanently storing selections. To do this all you have to do is click Selections > Load/

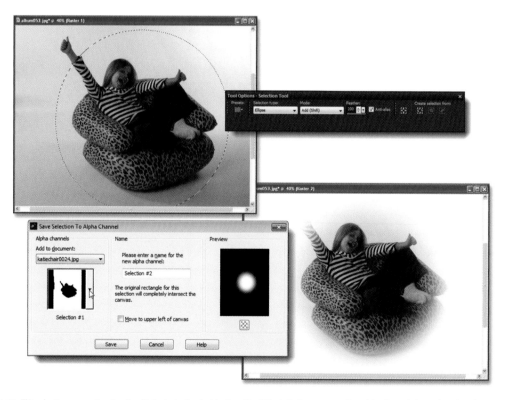

FIG 5.9 This selection was made using the elliptical selection tool feathered by 200 pixels. The corresponding alpha channel shows the selected area in the center, gradually fading to black, and the bottom right image shows the actual selected pixels.

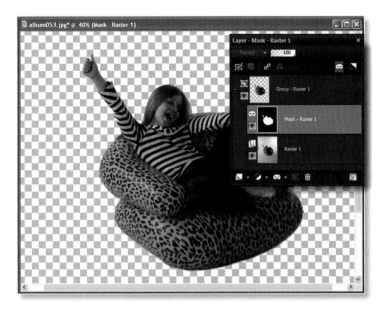

FIG 5.10 A Mask layer hides parts of underlying layers without actually deleting pixels.

Save Selection/Save Selection to Alpha Channel. Usually, you'll want to save a selection to the image you created it from, but you can also save and load selections into other documents.

Masks

Masks are a little like alpha channels in that they use a greyscale image to determine what happens to corresponding image pixels. Masks are in fact a special kind of layer. Greyscale mask pixels determine the opacity of image pixels in underlying layers. Masks provide a useful means of hiding image pixels without actually deleting them. By directly editing masks (and, for that matter, alpha channels) you can perform sophisticated image-editing techniques in a non-destructive way, without altering the pixel values in the affected layer.

To create a mask, first make a selection, then choose Layers>New Mask Layer>Show Selection to show the selected parts of an image layer and hide the rest. To mask (hide) the contents of the selection and show the unselected bits choose Layers>New Mask Layer>Hide Selection.

Selections, alpha channels and masks are interchangeable. You can turn a selection into an alpha channel or a mask, create an alpha channel from a mask, load a mask from an alpha channel and, of course, load selections from masks and alpha channels. You can discover more about masks in the following chapter.

Step-by-Step Projects

Replacing a Lackluster Sky

How often have you taken a shot that you really love, but the weather was a bit dull and the sky just looks grey and boring? Well thanks to PaintShop Pro's great range of selection tools that's a problem you no longer have to live with. The new Smart Selection Brush in PaintShop Pro X6 makes short work of once difficult selections so you can quickly isolate your subject, mask it and drop a new, brighter, more interesting sky into the frame in just a few minutes.

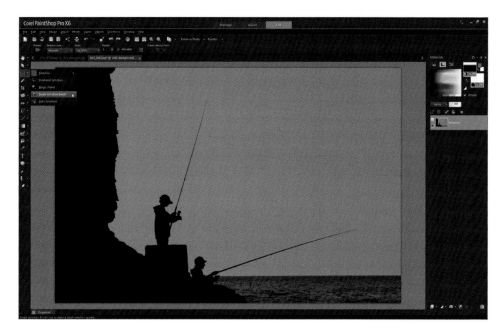

STEP 1 I was quite pleased with this silhouette shot of a couple of lads fishing at one of the local beaches. I deliberately under-exposed the shot so the figures and the rocks would appear black against the evening sky. The trouble is the sky itself, which is a flat, drab grey/blue expanse. I reckon a more interesting sky with a little bit of color could improve the shot hugely. The first step is to get a good accurate selection of the boys and the rocks they're fishing from, plus the cliff behind them and the sea. Everything but the sky in other words. The Smart Selection Brush should make light work of this, Select it from the Selection tools fly-out on the Tools toolbar, it's the fourth one down and looks like a wand with a green star on the tip.

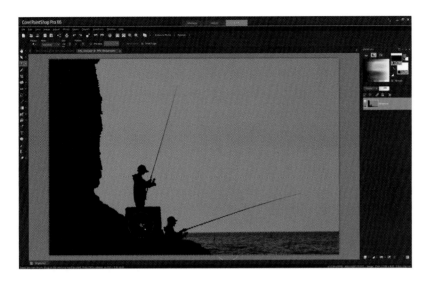

STEP 2 Change the size of the brush in the tool options palette by dragging the size slider to make the brush big enough to paint large sections of the rocks. Then do just that, position the brush over the rocks and click and drag to paint with short strokes. The default mode for the Smart Selection Brush is Add, so each new stroke you paint adds to the selection. In actual fact, just a couple of dabs with the brush have selected most of what I wanted.

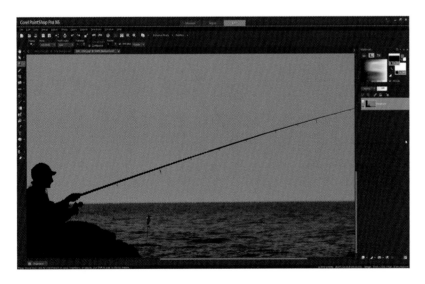

STEP 3 If you zoom in close you'll see that the Smart Selection Brush hasn't picked up the narrow section of the boys' fishing rods. You could try reducing the size of the brush to just a few pixels, but the truth is none of PaintShop Pro's selection tools is great at dealing with very small selections of just a few pixels. Don't worry about it for now, we'll deal with it a little later.

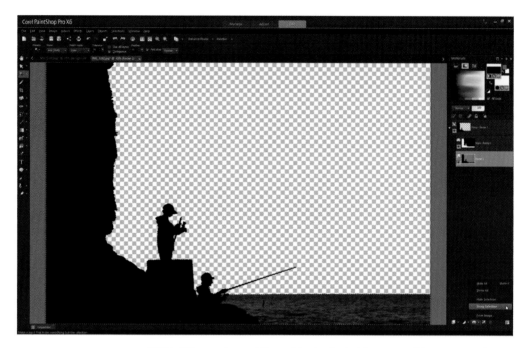

STEP 4 Now we've got the subject selected (or most of it, at any rate) we'll apply a mask layer to it that will hide the parts of the layer that aren't selected. Click the New mask layer button at the bottom of the Layers palette and select Show selection from the pop-up menu. Immediately you'll see the sky disappear and be replaced by a chequer board pattern. That's PaintShop Pro's baseboard, and you can see it through the masked transparent hole we just made in the background layer. Notice also that in the Layers palette the Background layer has been renamed Raster 1 and has been added to a new group called Group – Raster 1 along with its mask layer which is called Mask – Raster 1. Now that the mask is created you can deselect all by pressing Ctrl-d.

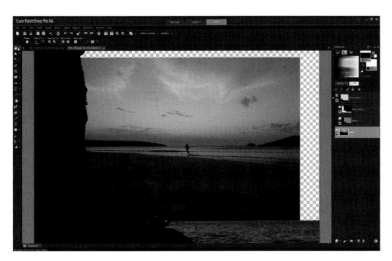

STEP 5 The next step is to paste in the new sky. Open the photo you want to use (it's a good idea to take photos of dramatic skies whenever you see them for just such an occasion as this) press Ctrl-A to select all and copy it. Then go back to your original photo and paste it as a new layer (Edit>Paste as new layer or Ctrl-V). When you paste the sky layer it will appear above the mask layer in the layers palette. Drag it to the bottom of the layers palette so it appears underneath everything else.

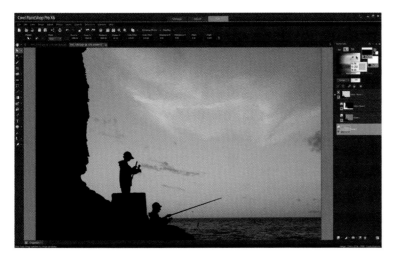

STEP 6 As you can see, my sky photo is smaller than the original so it'll have to be enlarged to fit. Select the pick tool and drag a corner handle to resize the layer, holding down the shift key to maintain the proportions. You can move the sky layer around within the 'hole' created in the upper layer by the mask to position it just where you want it. We're almost there now, except for the truncated fishing rods.

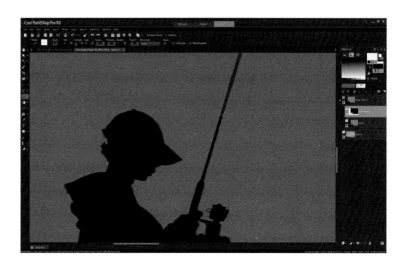

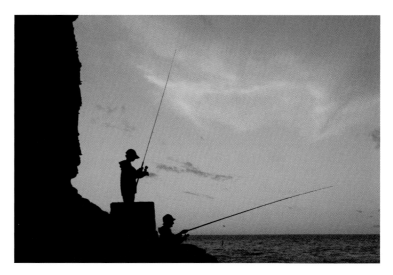

STEP 7 Select the Mask – raster1 layer in the Layers palette and then click the visibility icon (the eye) to turn the mask off. Then click the Highlight mask area button at the top of the layer mask. This displays the mask area as a red overlay so you can see exactly what's masked and what isn't. In the Materials palette click the Set to black and white button (it looks like a square with black and white triangles, hover over it to get a tool tip) then click the swap material button (double headed arrow) and start painting the fishing rod. What you're doing is painting in white on the mask layer, revealing what's on the image beneath (i.e. the fishing rod). Don't worry if doesn't make much sense to you right now, as long as you get the expected result. You'll find out a lot more about masks, how they're related to selections and how to use them in the next chapter.

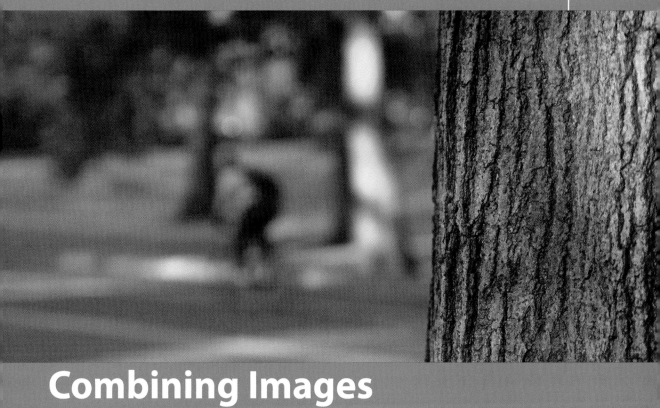

CHAPTER 6

Combining Images
Layers and Masks

What's Covered in this Chapter

- This chapter is all about layers. We've already come across layers in earlier chapters and in some of the step-by-step projects and we've seen how you can use adjustment layers to make editable changes to image tones and color.
- Layers are extremely useful as they allow you to combine different elements – photos, text and graphics – all in the same document. Layers are a little like sheets of tracing paper in a pad – you can see through the topmost layers to those below. PaintShop Pro X6's Layers palette allows you to organize layers into groups, shuffle them around so that some things appear on top of others, change their opacity to make them semi-transparent, even change the way that upper layers interact with what lies beneath.
- As well as learning how to use the Layers palette, this chapter shows you how to combine several photos into one image using layers, how to use PaintShop Pro X6's rulers, grids and guides to position and align layers, what you can do with adjustment layers and how to combine layers.
- We'll also take a detailed look at Mask layers, briefly introduced in the last chapter. In the Step-by-Step Projects section at the end of the chapter,

I'll show you how to use layer deformations to create realistic shadows, how to mask an Adjustment layer to produce a graduated color effect and then finally how to use PaintShop Pro's HDR Exposure Merge feature to create stunning HDR images.

- Layers allow you to combine several images – each stacked one above the other – in a single document. The biggest advantage of layers is that they allow you to put elements on top of one another without destroying what's underneath. But, as we shall see, the advantages of using layers go far beyond that.

Understanding Layers

What is a layer? A layer is simply one picture sitting directly on top of another. Layers can contain whole photos, text, vector drawings, scanned art or anything else that can be digitized. You can add as many layers as you want in one document, depending on your requirements. The reason for building up these layers is to maintain the pictures' editability. While a picture retains its layers, it can always be edited. Flatten those layers, so that it can be e-mailed, for example, and you lose the power to edit it.

PaintShop Pro has quite sophisticated layering capabilities. Not only does it allow you to create montages from multi-layered documents, but also it has a range of features like Adjustment layers that open up further editing possibilities. So much so that every stage in the image-building process can be deconstructed, changed, altered, improved and returned to its place, over and over again, with incredible accuracy and remarkable ease.

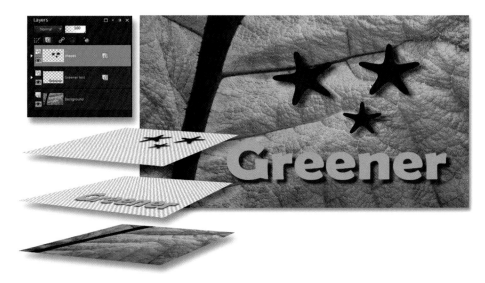

FIG 6.1   The illustration here shows how a layered image works. Viewed from above (i.e. in the work area) the picture looks perfectly normal, but exploring the Layer palette shows that it is in fact composed of three separate layers – all of which can be moved or can have their contents edited independently. Layers files must be saved as either '.pspimage' files or, for cross-computer compatibility, in the '.psd' (Adobe Photoshop) file format. Using either of these file formats preserves the layer integrity.

Who Uses Layers?

Layers are used by anyone who adds text to a document, whether a
single character or a page of copy for a brochure. Layers are used to make
multi-image montages where several pictures blend seamlessly into one.
Layers are used extensively by designers, illustrators, web designers and
anyone, in fact, who uses images that have more than one picture element
in them.

What Can You Do with Layers?

A layer is like a clear sheet of acetate. Layers can be opaque or transparent,
and they can contain pixels (bitmap) or vector data (text and shapes).

You can cut, copy and paste layers from one document to another. Layers can
be flipped, rotated, resized, distorted, rearranged or grouped in any number
of combinations. You can apply color and tonal adjustments to single layers –
and you can add a full range of filter effects, as if one layer were a single
picture. Only while the layered document retains its original layers does it
remain editable. For seasoned image-makers, this layer editability remains
a powerful attraction. How many times have you finished working only to
spot something you missed but now can't change? If you use layers and have
saved the layered version of the image (as mentioned previously), you can
make that change!

Before you get too excited, layers have some disadvantages. Multiple layers
create a spaghetti-like complexity that can be hard to keep track of. And the
more layers you add to a document, the larger the file becomes, occupying
more space on your hard disk and taking longer to process every time you
make a change in PaintShop Pro. If the number of layers in your document
starts to get unweildy, you can merge selected layers into each other. You'd do
this to layers, or groups of layers, that are similar or are finished with (i.e. you
are sure that they'll never need changing).

Layers offer tremendous potential for the creative image-maker. Simply
adjusting the opacity of an individual layer allows you to see everything on
the layer beneath. Each layer also has a range of Blend modes. These can be
adjusted to radically change the way the pixels in the layer react with the
pixels in the layer directly below.

We already know that PaintShop Pro has an almost limitless Undo feature
('Ctrl+Z'). This means that you can reverse the picture-building process by
up to 1000 steps; however, in accepting an Undo command and then saving,
those steps are lost forever. If you are working with layers, you can apply
major editing stages to different layers and retain everything in the one
document, regardless of whether you are using it or not. Each layer has a small
eye icon called the 'Visibility toggle'. Click the Visibility toggle to switch the
layer 'off', click again to switch it back 'on'.

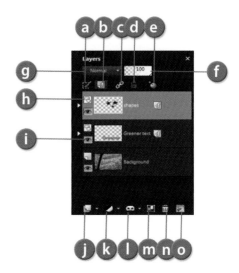

FIG 6.2 The Layers palette is the control center for layers and the things on them. It helps you organize and keep track of all the layers within an image. There are five layer types – Raster, Vector, Art Media, Adjustment and Mask layers. Layers are arranged in order in the Layers palette. The topmost layer in the image appears at the top of the palette; you can rearrange the layers by dragging and dropping. The Layers palette here shows the individual layers and thumbnail images of the content on each . There are several layers, some of which are organized into groups (you can expand and collapse groups by clicking the little triangle button alongside). (a) Edit Selection, (b) Show/hide layer effects, (c) Link/unlink, (d) Lock/unlock, (e) Layer styles, (f) layer opacity, (g) Layer blend mode, (h) layer type, (i) Visibility toggle, (j) New layer, (k) New Adjustment layer, (l) New Mask layer, (m) New layer group, (n) Delete layer, (o) General preferences.

You might also do this to layers that, once merged, can be separated again if necessary using a selection. Though merging or flattening layers frees valuable computer resources, I'd suggest keeping the layers for editing because you never know.

What features can be found in layers?

- Move the picture elements on layers in any direction.
- Change the tone, color, contrast and alignment of any layer.
- Mix Vector and Bitmap layers in one document.
- Create new, blank Vector and Bitmap layers at the press of a button.
- Collect selected layers into Layer Groups.
- Copy single layers, or groups of layers, into the same or a new document.
- Convert selections into layers.
- Paste layers and selections from other documents into a new document.
- Layers can be reordered by dragging them up or down in the Layers palette.
- Layers can be switched 'on' and 'off' by clicking the Visibility toggle (the eye icon) in the Layers palette.

- You can paste the contents of the clipboard into a new layer.
- Duplicate a layer using the Duplicate command (Layers > Duplicate) or by pressing the duplicate tab in the palette.
- Use the 'Edit Selection' button in the Layers palette to edit a selection (Selection Edit mode).

Combining Pictures

PaintShop Pro allows you to create and save every stage of the image-building process as a separate layer. These layers can be switched on or off according to their application. You can also store masks and selections as separate channels in layered documents. These too can be switched on and off. In PaintShop Pro, any document that has layers, masks or selections has to be saved in the native PaintShop Pro file format with a '.pspimage' file ending.

While .pspimage retains layers, this file format is for use only in PaintShop Pro, you cannot use '.pspimage' files on the web or in a word document for example. The file has to be converted first or copied to a more suitable file type, such as JPEG or TIFF. First you must flatten the file

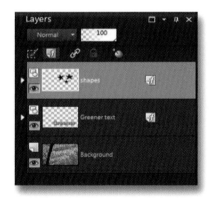
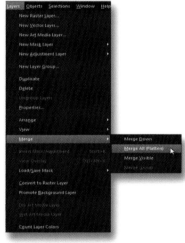
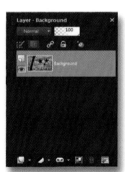

FIG 6.3 A layered (.pspimage) document is more editable than any other format. Because of this it's also too large for many applications, such as e-mailing or storage on a limited size disk. For this reason it is important to make a copy and to Flatten or Merge those layers so that the resulting single-layered document can be resaved in a smaller file format, like JPEG or TIFF.

('Layers > Merge > Merge All (Flatten)'). Doing this turns it into a single-layered document. This loses most of its editability, which is why you should only do this to a copy of the original .pspimage file. Save your layered documents as master files and then make copies from that master for use in other, non-layered file applications.

The simplest way to combine two pictures into one document is to copy one and paste it as a new layer into the other. These layers are totally separate and can be edited at any time as if they were two totally different picture elements. However, because they are in the same document, you also have to contend with their relationship. While copying and pasting one picture into another is by far the easiest way to add another picture to a document, there are a few points to consider first.

The resolution of the pasted image, measured in pixel dimensions or dots per inch, is relevant (see Chapter 9 if you want to know more about resolution). For example, if this is larger than the receiving image it will overspill (bleed off the edges) once pasted. However, even though it looks as if the edges of the pasted image have disappeared, the program does not discard them; they are still there but only become visible if dragged into view using the Move tool ('M').

Another factor to watch out for when combining pictures is their respective color spaces. Providing that the color space of the master document is either 24-bit or greyscale, it will prevail over what is being pasted into it. So, if you copy an 8-bit picture into a 24-bit color picture, the color space of the pasted picture will be increased to match that of the host document. On the other scale, if you try to paste a color picture into a black and white image, it will be converted into the mono color space.

PaintShop Pro offers a number of ways to paste copied images into another document via the Edit menu, by right-clicking in the new document, or using keyboard shortcuts. These are

- *Paste as New Image.* This creates a new picture on its own background.
- *Paste as New Layer.* This adds the contents of the clipboard to the selected document background. PaintShop Pro automatically creates a new layer for the pasted image. If the pasted image matches the physical dimensions of the target image, it will obscure the lower layer or background picture.
- *Paste as New Selection.* This pastes the newly selected picture into the target document, but it remains attached to the cursor, so that it can be positioned somewhere other than directly on top of the background. Left-click to offload the layer and view the selection marquee. The pasted layer then becomes a floating selection until it is deselected. You can save this selection as an alpha channel (in case it is needed again: 'Selections > Save To Alpha Channel'). If you already have a floating selection, it will be defloated and deselected before another picture can be pasted into the document (i.e. you can't have two floating selections in one document).

Tip

The base layer is called the 'Background' and is, in fact, not a layer at all. However, it can be 'promoted' (converted) into a layer if needed (right-click on the Background layer in the Layer palette and choose 'Promote Background Layer' from the contextual menu). If you don't want to promote the background, you can simply duplicate it.

Tip

To maintain the aspect ratio of a layer while resizing it (in other words, to avoid stretching or squeezing it), use the right mouse button to drag a corner handle.

- *Paste as Transparent Selection.* This command does the same as the Paste as New Selection command, but enables you to import transparency from another image. Because of this transparency, the pasted layer is attached to the Move tool for easy repositioning. Click in the image to free it once it is in the right position.

What can you do with layers?

- Change the individual tonal appearance of each layer.
- Make and edit selections on individual layers.
- Add Blend modes to individual layers for special effects.
- Save layer selection and mask information to an alpha channel and to disk.
- Add Adjustment layers.
- Apply any of PaintShop Pro's filter effects to a layer.
- Bend and transform the shape of any object on a layer.
- Convert Vector layers to Bitmap layers.

Advanced Layout Tools

As we have seen, there are many ways to use PaintShop Pro for combining multiple layers into a single document. In the following section we'll take a look at some of the features designed to make laying out and arranging multiple picture documents easier. You'll find these tools useful for positioning and aligning multiple photos as well as for adding annotation labels.

Tip

To remove all of the guides on a photo select Change Grid, Guide and Snap Properties from the view menu (or double-click one of the Rulers) click the Guides tab if it isn't already displayed and check the Delete guides box. You can delete guides from the current image or from all open images.

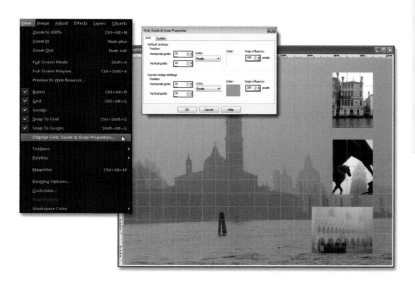

FIG 6.4 PaintShop Pro's rulers, guides and grid enable you to accurately position and align elements. Snap to Grid and Snap to Guides make the grid and guides behave as though magnetized — they attract and hold dragged objects which are in close proximity. Double-click the rulers or select View > Change Grid, Guide & Snap Properties to change grid spacing and other grid and guide properties.

Under PaintShop Pro's View menu, there are a number of highly useful productivity-enhancing features designed to make aligning and arranging multi-layer images faster and easier. These are:

- Rulers. Keyboard shortcut 'Ctrl+Alt+R' adds rulers along the X- and Y-axes of the picture window. You can change the units of measurement (pixels/inches/centimeters) through the program's General Preferences (File > Preferences > General Program Preferences, then click on Units in the Preference Column on the left). Place the cursor anywhere in the image and you can read out the exact location in the corresponding margin. It's a handy tool, especially if you are working with extremely small picture elements on multiple layers.
- View Grid. If you find the grid too heavy, double-click on the rulers in the margin and you'll see the Grid, Guide & Snap Properties dialog. Change the units used and the color to make it appear friendlier. You'll need to make adjustments every now and then for different-sized pictures. This is a useful feature for precise layer or picture element alignment.
- View Guides. This is one of the neatest design assistants in PaintShop Pro. It works only if 'Rulers' are switched 'on'. Guides are colored lines that can be pulled out of the margins (using the cursor regardless of the tool currently selected) and dragged over the picture to form well-design or layout guides. There are no limits to the number of guides that can be used in one document. Guides can be repositioned by grabbing the guide handle (that's the thicker bit of guideline that appears inside the ruler margin as you move the cursor over it). If you want to change the guide properties, double-click the ruler to open its window or just click the guide handle in the margin to open the Grid, Guide & Snap Properties dialog. This allows you to change its color, position or existence!
- Snap to Guides. This function adds tremendous power to the task of aligning multiple layers along a common axis – by selecting this option and making sure that, in the Grid, Guide & Snap Properties dialog, the Snap Influence setting is set to more than one. What this does is if you grab an image layer using the Move tool and drag it toward the guide it appears to be magnetically attracted to the line. In fact, it 'snaps' to the line. Increase this value to increase the magnetic power.

You can change any of these settings for the opened document only, or for the default settings. This feature is a real production enhancer. Under the Layers palette:

- Layer Opacity. All layers have an opacity scale controlled from the Layers palette. Default setting is 100%. Reducing this allows you to see through the layer to whatever lies beneath. Do this to help align specific pictures or graphic elements with stuff that lies beneath.

Under the Layer menu:

- Arrange. This feature allows you to swap the layer order, although you can also do this by using the cursor to grab a layer in the palette and dragging it to another position in the stack.
- View. Controls which layers are visible and which are not. You may also switch a layer on and off by clicking on the eye icon in the palette itself.
- Merge. Merge allows you to do just that: merge or blend selected layers. Merge Visible flattens only the layers with the eye icon switched 'on' (i.e. those that are visible on the desktop).

Using Adjustment Layers

Making tonal adjustments to a digital photo, for example, brightening the midtones and shadows with a Levels adjustment, changing the color balance, or using the Fill Flash filter, changes the value of pixels within the image. Other than by pressing Ctrl+Z to undo, these changes are irreversible. Opening, say, the Levels dialog box and making an adjustment in the opposite direction will not get you back to where you started.

But what if you could apply such changes and, if you later changed your mind, remove them, as if they'd never been applied in the first place? Adjustment layers allow you to do exactly that. Adjustment layers are a safer, more versatile way of applying image adjustments because, as well as turning them on and off just like other layers, you can apply Adjustment layers to one or several layers within the image.

You can also go back to Adjustment layers and edit the settings at any time without causing any degradation in image quality. With Adjustment layers, doing the opposite to a previous adjustment does get you back exactly where you started.

Earlier we spoke of layers as being like acetate sheets stacked on top of the background image. Think of Adjustment layers in the same way – as a clear sheet to which you can apply adjustments and through which you view layers below. The appearance of the pixels in the underlying layers is affected by the Adjustment layer, but the pixels themselves are not altered.

Whereas an adjustment affects only the active layer, an Adjustment layer acts on all the layers beneath it, or all the layers within a Layer Group. By careful positioning of Adjustment layers, you can change only one part of an image. Adjustment layers are frequently used when combining images to make the new image elements match in terms of color and lighting.

Tip

To change the ruler units choose File > Preferences > General Program Preferences and Select Units from the list in the Preferences dialog box. You can choose among Pixels, Inches and Centimeters.

175

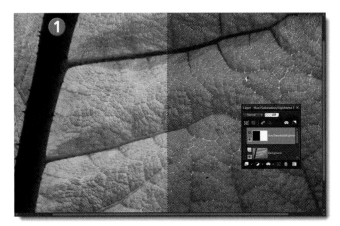
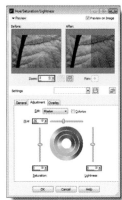

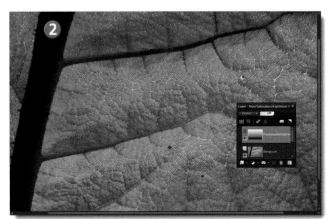

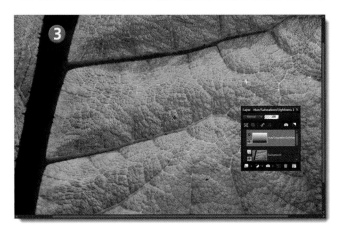
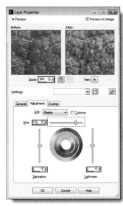

FIG 6.5 (1) Here, I've made a rectangular selection on the right of the image and added a Hue/Saturation/Lightness adjustment layer. The new Layers palette displays a thumbnail of the mask. (2) Filling an Adjustment layer with a linear gradient applies more correction at the top, gradually reducing toward the bottom. (3) An Adjustment layer is infinitely editable with no loss of image quality, to alter the color just double-click the adjustment layer in the Layers palette.

Another way of limiting Adjustment layers is by editing them in the same way as Mask layers. You'll remember from the previous chapter that Mask layers are greyscale and pixel values in the Mask layer affect the opacity of corresponding pixels in underlying layers. Adjustment layers are also greyscale and their effect on underlying layers is likewise dependent on the pixels within the mask. Black pixels apply no correction, white pixels apply the full amount of correction and grey pixels apply varying amounts of correction in between.

You can vary the overall effect of an Adjustment layer using its Opacity slider in the layers palette. Alternatively, you can apply the Adjustment layer to a selection, or paint directly onto it to isolate the parts of the layer you want the adjustment to affect.

Adjustment Layer Types

You can add the following types of Adjustment layer:

- Brightness/Contrast
- Channel mixer
- White Balance
- Curves
- Fill Light/Clarity
- Hue/Saturation/Lightness
- Histogram
- Invert
- Levels
- Local Tone Mapping
- Posterize
- Threshold
- Vibrancy

Advantages of Adjustment Layers

- Add a range of tone and effects changes to a layer or layers without actually changing the original layer.
- Useful for applying overall color or tone changes to multiple layers at a time.
- Can be removed by deleting the Adjustment layer or switching it off.
- Ideal for working with panoramas.

Creating Layer Blend Mode Effects

Blend modes determine how pixels in a layer interact with corresponding pixels in underlying layers. The default Blend mode is 'Normal' – the pixel in the top layer is superimposed on (and therefore hides) the pixel in the underlying layers (subject to transparency settings).

There are 20 other Blend modes in addition to 'Normal' and each provides a slightly different result. 'Darken', for example, displays only pixels in the selected layer that are darker than corresponding pixels in underlying layers; lighter pixels in the selected layer disappear. The Lighten Blend mode does the opposite. 'Color' applies the hue and saturation of pixels in the selected layer to underlying layers without affecting lightness and 'Difference' subtracts the selected layer's color from the color of underlying layers.

Some Blend modes have practical applications. 'Darken' and 'Lighten' are useful for retouching and cloning. You can also use 'Darken' to get rid of a white background on a logo or other artwork. 'Multiply', which combines the colors in the selected layer with underlying layers to produce a darker color, is useful for producing realistic drop shadows.

Because the outcome depends on initial pixel values in the selected and underlying layers, the results of some Blend modes can be hard to predict. If you are working with two layers, simply swapping the layer order can produce very different results. This makes Blend modes an excellent tool for creating special effects with multiple images and works especially well with text, but a certain amount of experimentation is often required to get a good result.

Blend modes can be selected for most of PaintShop Pro's Brush tools as well as layers – the Blend mode pull-down menu in the Tool Options palette provides exactly the same options as are available in the Layers palette.

Using Mask Layers

A Mask layer works a bit like a stencil – holding back some parts of the image and revealing others. We briefly looked at Mask layers in the previous chapter on using selections. Mask layers, alpha channels and selections are a bit difficult to pin down in terms of definitions because they all do pretty much the same thing – control which parts of the image are displayed or affected by an adjustment – in slightly different ways.

Earlier, we saw how Adjustment layers could be used as Mask layers to confine their corrections to one part of the image, but a Mask layer is more often used to hide parts of the image without actually deleting it. The advantage of this should be fairly obvious; you can subsequently edit the mask to reveal hidden parts of the underlying layers or, conversely, to hide more.

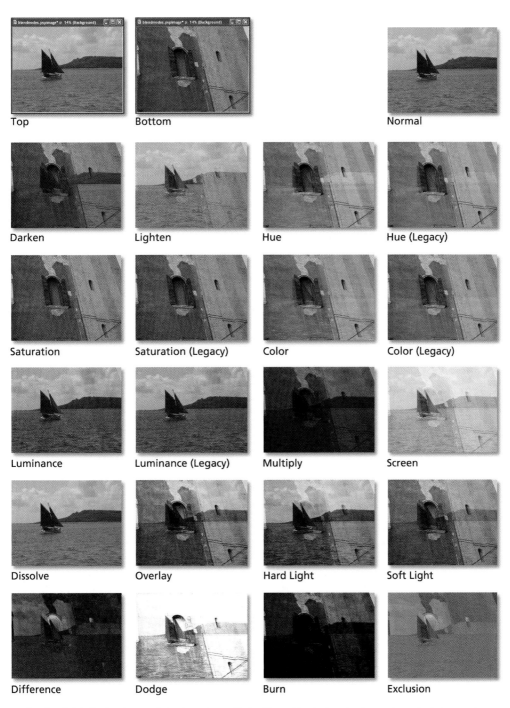

FIG 6.6 PaintShop Pro's 21 Blend modes as applied to the two images 'Top' and 'Bottom'. Results depend on layer content and order. Layer modes can be particularly effective when used with text layers. Legacy modes maintain compatibility with earlier versions, so if you want to replicate an effect you created in an earlier version of the application you shouldn't have any difficulty. Generally though, the newer versions produce better results.

Often, the best starting point for creating a mask is a selection. Make a selection using one or a combination of the selection tools and modifiers and from the Layers menu choose New Mask Layer > Show Selection to create a mask that shows the selected parts of the layer and hides everything else. To create a mask that hides the selected area choose Layers > New Mask Layer > Hide Selection.

PaintShop Pro automatically creates a new Layer Group containing the selected layer and the new mask. This is so that the mask doesn't affect other layers in your image. If you want the mask to apply to all the layers beneath it, drag it in the Layers palette from the Layer Group to the top of the layer stack. With the mask in place, you can press Ctrl+D or Selections > Select None. If you need it, you can recover the selection at any time with Ctrl+Shift+S or Selections > From Mask.

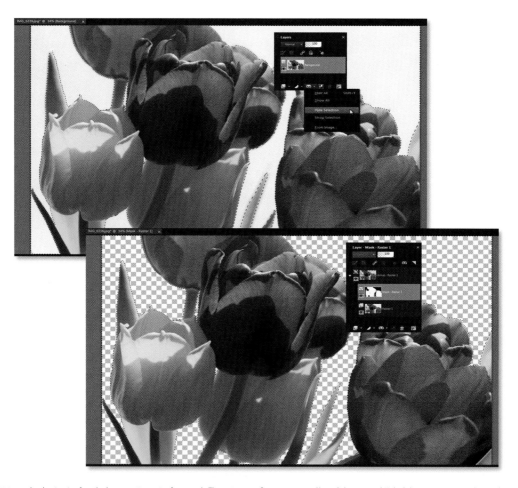

FIG 6.7 A selection is often the best starting point for a mask. The existence of two options – Show Selection and Hide Selection – negates the need to invert the selection if you want to hide the selected area, as here.

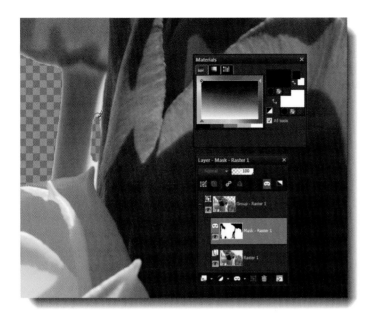

FIG 6.8 Painting on a Mask layer provides a simple, yet effective, method of cleaning up selections. Click the Highlight mask area button to display the mask as a red tint on the underlying layer; turning the Mask layer off allows you to view both masked and unmasked detail.

Modifying Masks

One of the best things about masks is that you can use PaintShop Pro's Brush tools to edit them. Painting masks is often an easier and more accurate way to clean up selections than using the selection modifiers. You can, for example, use a soft-edged brush to clean up the edge-detail of difficult subjects like fur, hair or indeed anything that doesn't have a clearly defined edge.

To use the Brush tools to directly edit a Mask layer, select the Mask layer in the Layers palette and choose the Paint Brush tool. You may have noticed that the foreground and background swatches in the Materials palette change to greyscale when a Mask layer is selected; remember, Mask layers are greyscale, so you can only paint on them using black, white or one of 254 levels of grey. Painting on the mask with black will add to the mask and remove detail from the underlying layer. Painting with white will remove the mask and reveal detail on the underlying layer. If you paint with grey, you'll make parts of the underlying layer semi-transparent. It's usually easiest to use just black and white and change the brush settings in the Tool Options palette to achieve the required effect. As I've said before, this kind of editing is made much easier using a tablet and stylus.

Adding to the mask – painting out detail on the underlying layer – is quite straightforward because you can see what you are doing. Painting detail back in by removing black areas from the mask is trickier because you can see neither the mask nor the detail. To display the mask click the Mask Overlay button on the Layers palette. This overlays the Mask layer with black areas displayed as a 50% red tint over the target layer(s).

Combining Layers

Some digital image-makers work with multiple images and image masks. In this situation it is vital to remember exactly what you are doing and what the final planned result should look like. To this end, try to label all the layers, Layer Groups and masks. Doing this (by double-clicking each layer and entering the details in the dialog) will make the masking and blending process somewhat clearer, especially when there are 20 or more layers to contend with.

As we've seen, images with lots of layers create large file sizes and it's often difficult to discover which bits of the image are on what layer. You can simplify PaintShop Pro images and drastically reduce the file size by flattening them or merging layers together. There are four merge options on the Layers > Merge menu – Merge Down, Merge All (Flatten), Merge Visible and Merge Group. Masks that are associated with underlying layers as part of a Layer Group can easily be merged using Layers > Merge > Merge Group.

When you do this, the mask is applied to the image and masked areas are deleted. Simply deleting the mask has the same effect.

Merging layers means you no longer have the editing flexibility that they provided, so if you're likely to want to carry out further changes later make a back-up copy with all the layers intact using File > Save Copy As before you start merging.

Tip

Displaying the Mask Overlay, but turning off the Mask layer itself, shows the mask on top of the unmasked layer below, making it much easier to see what you're doing when painting onto the mask.

Saving Masks

To save an image with masks use the .pspimage format. You can save a Mask layer to its own file on disk – choose Layers > Load/Save Mask > Save Mask To Disk. The default location for saved masks varies depending on your version, for PaintShop Pro X6 it is in My Documents/Corel PaintShop Pro/16.0/Masks. If you're running an earlier version of PaintShop Pro try My Documents/My PSP files. This folder is where all your custom content (Tubes, Masks, Selections, etc.) is saved. You will also find a selection of ready-made masks in the Masks folder in the PaintShop Pro program folder. These can be used for framing and other effects.

Only two formats support images with masks and other types of layer: they are the .pspimage and .psd (Photoshop) formats. If you want to save your image with all layers intact use one of these two file formats. If you attempt to save your image in a file format that doesn't support layers, PaintShop Pro warns you before flattening the image and saving it.

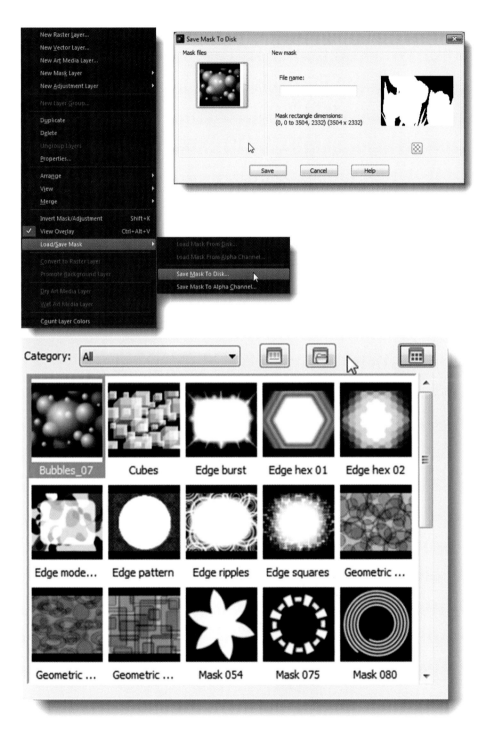

FIG 6.9 As well as saving your own masks to disk, PaintShop Pro provides a selection of existing masks that you can use to frame layers and create special effects.

Step-by-Step Projects

Creating the Perfect Shadow

PaintShop Pro's Drop Shadow Layer Style and filter are great for adding drop shadows to two-dimensional objects like photos and text, but if you want to add a realistic drop shadow to a 3D object you need to create additional layers and use the deformation tools to produce a realistic shadow shape. It's not a difficult technique, and once you've mastered it you'll be able to add realistic shadows to all manner of things from signposts, cars and coffee cups to people, even painters and decorators.

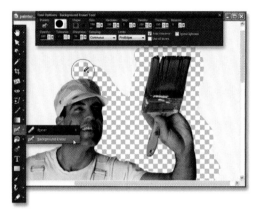

STEP 1 Right-click the background layer in the layers palette and select Promote Background Layer. Unless you're lucky, the object you want to create a shadow for won't be on a transparent background, so you'll have to cut it out. This one has a white background which the Background Eraser makes light work of. While you're using the Background Eraser, hold down the space bar to temporarily access the Pan tool and move around the image.

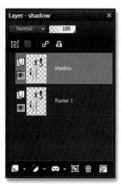

STEP 2 When all of the background is removed, duplicate the layer by right-clicking it and selecting 'Duplicate' from the context menu. Rename the duplicated layer by clicking its name in the Layers palette (or by right-clicking the layer and selecting 'Rename') and overwriting it. Call it 'shadow'. The Layers palette should now look like this.

STEP 3 Open the Brightness and Contrast dialog box (Adjust > Brightness and Contrast > Brightness/Contrast) and drag the Brightness slider all the way to the left until the Brightness field reads –255. You'll see the preview thumbnail turn black and the image window will mirror this change if you check the Preview on Image checkbox. Click OK to apply the adjustment.

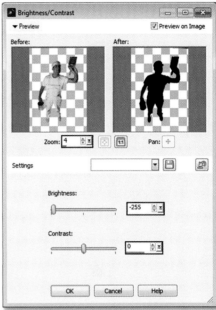

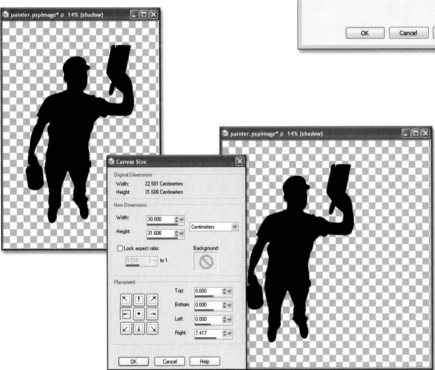

STEP 4 You may need to add more canvas to fit the shadow in. Select Image > Canvas Size and increase the width and height as necessary. To add canvas on the right click the top left placement button, select Centimeters from the pull-down menu and add around 4 cm to the existing width value, e.g. if the original width is 16.5 cm make it 20.5 cm. If you add too much canvas either press Ctrl-Z to undo and try again or remove it using the Crop tool.

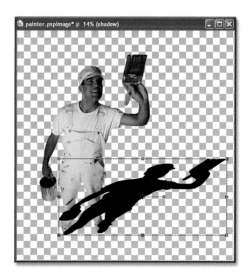

STEP 5 Select the Pick tool and click on the shadow object. Hold down the Shift key and drag the middle handle on the top edge sideways to the right to skew it. Let go, then drag the handle (this time without holding down Shift) downward to shorten it. Make further skew and shortening adjustments until the shadow shape fits with the kind of lighting setup you are trying to create. The higher the light the shorter the shadow will be and the further to the right the more skew you will need.

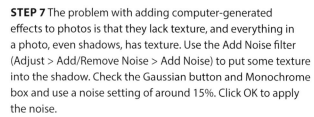

STEP 6 It's beginning to look more like a shadow, but we're not there yet. Select Adjust > Blur > Gaussian Blur and enter a value in the Radius field of around 8, just enough to soften the edges. Click the Preview on image button to preview the effect in the image window. Pixel value settings like Radius are dependent on the size of the image, so if you're working on a smaller photo for the web a lower Radius value of 2 or 3 would be enough.

STEP 7 The problem with adding computer-generated effects to photos is that they lack texture, and everything in a photo, even shadows, has texture. Use the Add Noise filter (Adjust > Add/Remove Noise > Add Noise) to put some texture into the shadow. Check the Gaussian button and Monochrome box and use a noise setting of around 15%. Click OK to apply the noise.

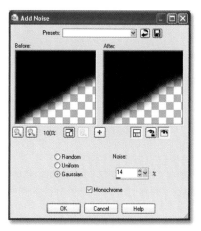

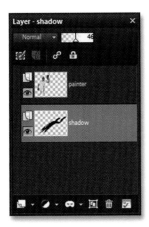

STEP 8 Shadows generally appear behind rather than in front of objects, so drag the shadow layer to the bottom in the Layers palette. You could also rename the other layer 'painter' or something else appropriate to your subject. Naming of layers like this can help you keep track of things. It's not so important when there are only one or two layers, but in more complex images with multiple layers and Mask layers, it helps to keep things organized.

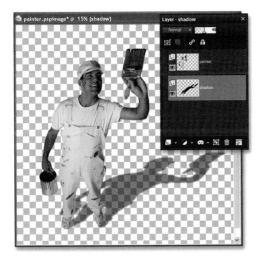

STEP 9 Shadows are rarely solid black. Reduce the shadow layer opacity by dragging the Opacity slider in the Layers palette to around 50%.

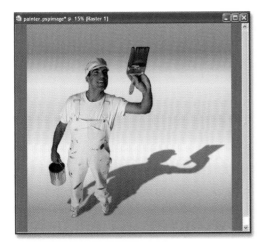

STEP 10 Add a background layer. Select Layer > New Raster Layer and click OK to accept the default settings. Drag the layer to the bottom of the Layers palette, then use the Materials palette to select and apply a solid color, gradient or pattern to the new layer.

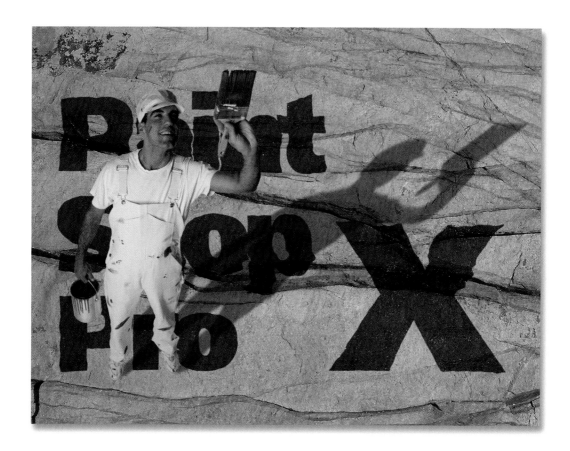

You can, of course, place your transparent object and shadow on any background including other pictures. Here, the painter has been superimposed on the rock image from Chapter 8. His shadow has been deformed, like the type, to follow the contours of the rock face using the displacement map technique described on page 247. The paint on the brush and in the tin has been changed from blue to red using the Hue Map.

Creating Graduated Filter Effects with Masks

As we've seen in this chapter you can use masks to selectively apply adjustments, effects filters and other changes that are usually global to specific parts of the image. We've seen how you can make a selection, save it as a mask and then paint on the mask to restrict the scope of adjustments and effects.

Making selections, creating masks and editing them by painting on them takes time and not a little skill, but by using graduated fills on an Adjustment layer mask you can restrict an adjustment to part of a photo and have it gradually and smoothly taper off.

This technique is perfect for simulating graduated filters used on the lens. One of the most commonly used graduated filters in photography is the graduated neutral density (ND) filter which landscape photographers use to maintain detail in skies. When exposing for the land in landscape shots bright skies are typically over-exposed. A graduated ND filter is grey at the top, gradually tapering off to clear glass, so restricts the amount of light in the sky portion of the scene that reaches the camera sensor. In this step-by-step project, I'll show you how to digitally simulate a graduated ND filter using a masked Adjustment layer.

Before we get started, you're probably wondering why we don't just use PaintShop Pro's Graduated Filter effect (Effects > Photo Effects > Graduated Filter) which was surely designed for this exact purpose? The answer is that this is quite a crude tool that applies a graduated color fill to your image. It's OK for a quick and dirty effect, but it's limited in scope and can't be adjusted or removed later. The technique I'll show you here is a lot more versatile, can be used with any adjustment or effect and is fully editable.

STEP 1 Open the photo you want to work on in the Edit workspace. Click the New Adjustment layer button on the Layers palette and select Levels from the Adjustment layer menu. The new Levels Adjustment layer appears in the Layers palette and the Levels dialog box opens ready for you to make your adjustment.

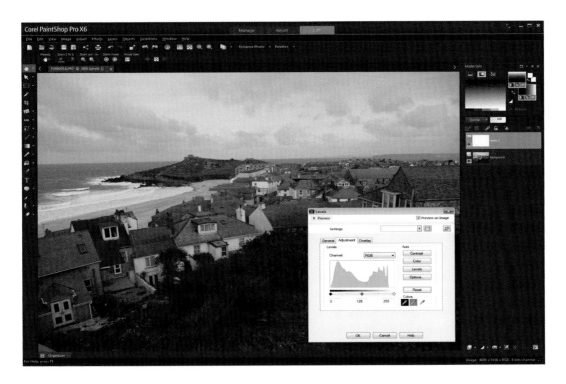

STEP 2 Drag the middle diamond under the levels histogram to the three-quarter tone point on the right to darken the lighter parts of the image. There's now a lot more detail in the sky than previously, but the rest of the image has gone very dark too. Don't worry about that for now, just click OK in the Levels dialog box to apply the adjustment and close it. Now take a look at the Layers palette and you'll see the new Levels Adjustment layer sitting above the Background layer containing your photo. The white thumbnail is the layer mask; it's white because the Levels adjustment is currently applied to the entire image.

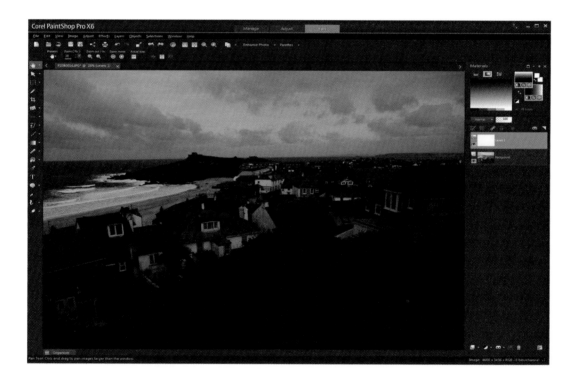

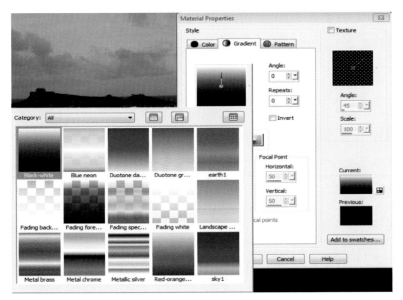

STEP 3 Now to choose a gradient which we'll apply to mask the Levels Adjustment layer. Click the Foreground and stroke properties swatch in the Materials palette and select the Gradient tab in the Material properties dialog box. If it isn't already selected, click the gradient swatch and choose the Black-white gradient preset, then click OK to select the gradient and close the dialog box.

STEP 4 Select the Flood fill tool from the Tools toolbar, make sure the Levels Adjustment layer is selected in the Layers palette and click anywhere in the image to apply the gradient fill to the mask. You'll notice two changes; the Adjustment layer thumbnail now shows the white to black gradient you just applied, it's white at the top and changes gradually to black at the bottom. More importantly, the Layers adjustment is gradually restricted. The white areas of the mask display it at 100% and the solid black completely masks it, with the grey parts of the mask showing it to varying degrees. Click the Adjustment layer visibility icon (the eye) in the Layers palette to toggle the effect on and off.

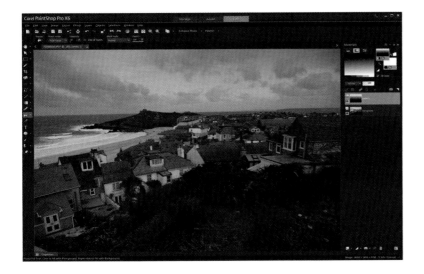

STEP 5 There's one small problem with our mask. It gradually tapers the Levels adjustment, which is great, but the gradient is linear, it changes from solid white at the top to solid black at the bottom gradually throughout the frame. Ideally, we want the adjustment applied full on to all of the sky area, then quickly (but still gradually) tapering to white around the horizon line. We can do that by editing the gradient and re-applying it. Click the foreground color swatch then click the edit button underneath the gradient swatch in the Material properties dialog box. The position sliders under the gradient ramp control the color at that point. There's a grey one about three quarters of the way along, remove it by dragging it of the ramp and dropping it, then drag the white point from the far right end of the ramp until the location field reads around 80% and drag the black point to around 65%. Click the close button, then click yes to save the changes, followed by OK in the Material properties dialog box.

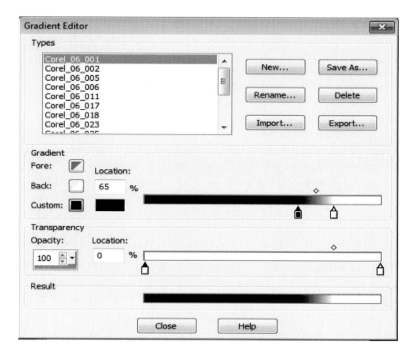

STEP 6 Select Edit > clear to remove the existing gradient fill from the Adjustment layer mask and click the image with the Flood fill tool to apply the new gradient. Now the Adjustment is applied fully to the whole area of the sky and tapers quickly, but smoothly and invisibly at the horizon. Of course, not all horizons are as straight as this one, but the great thing about a mask is that you can paint out any buildings or other obstructions.

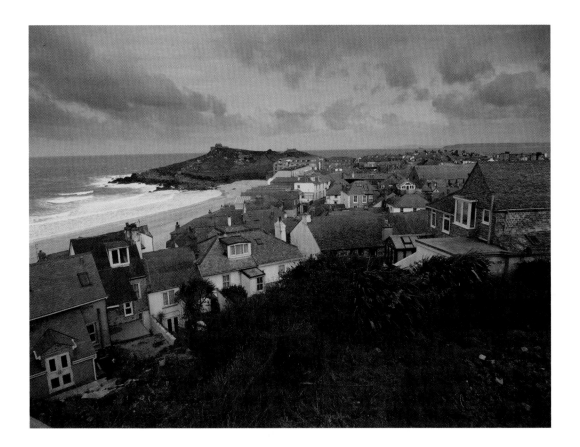

HDR Exposure Merge

In this step by step tutorial, I'll show you how to achieve a natural looking result using PaintShop Pro X6's HDR Exposure Merge feature. Whatever you think of HDR, it looks like it's here to stay. A lot of people are put off by the aggressive tone mapping that's used in many HDR images, rendering the scene more like a painting or illustration than a conventional photo. That's given HDR a bit of a bad name and led a lot of people to assume that it's good for nothing. Not so! HDR, or High Dynamic Range, images are a really useful way to capture the full range of tones in a scene, particularly when that range is beyond what the camera sensor is capable of recording in a single exposure.

STEP 1 The basis of HDR is that you combine several shots taken at different exposure settings, so first a word about that. You'll need to shoot at least two bracketed exposures a stop apart; I'd recommend you shoot at least three and, if you have the patience, five won't do any harm. Some cameras have an auto bracketing mode that will do this for you. If not, choose aperture priority exposure mode and manually bracket with one correctly exposed frame and four at +1, +2, −1 and −2 EV. For example, if the correct exposure is 1/500th at f5.6 shoot four additional frames also at f5.6 but with shutter speeds of 1/250th, 1/125th, 1/1000th and 1/2000th. The reason you change the shutter speed and not the aperture is to maintain the same depth of field in each frame. Finally, it helps a great deal if you put the camera on a tripod, or rest it somewhere steady, and HDR works best with fairly static subjects.

Here's what your five bracketed shots should look like.

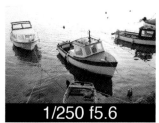
1/2000 f5.6

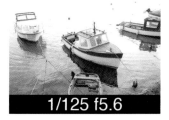
1/1000 f5.6

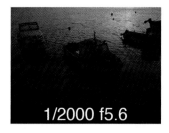
1/500 f5.6

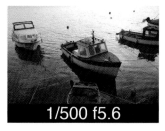
1/250 f5.6

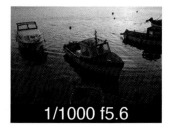
1/125 f5.6

STEP 2 Select your five bracketed frames in the Manage workspace (make a new tray for them if it helps) and choose File > HDR > Exposure merge. The merge window has a number of options, the first of which is the Camera Response Curve Profile. I'm a little skeptical of this as it lists manufacturers, rather than individual models and seems to make little difference to the end result, but you're welcome to give it a try if your camera manufacturer is listed, otherwise just leave it on the default Auto Select.

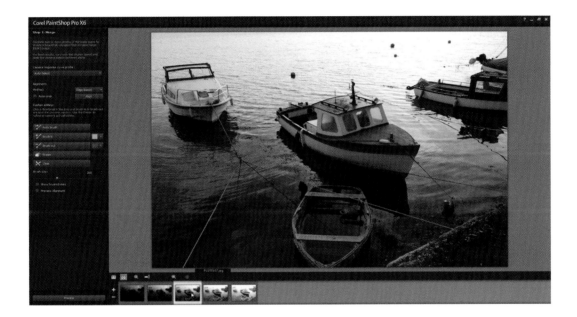

STEP 3 The next section on the Merge Settings window is for alignment; if you shot using a tripod you won't need this, but for hand-held shots you can experiment with edge-based or feature-based alignment to see which produces the best results. Ignore the Custom editing tools for now; I'll come back to those a little later. Just head straight to the bottom and click the Process button.

You'll now see the HDR composited image previewed in the Adjustments window. This is the result using the default settings, you can choose from one of six presets to apply a range of adjustments to alter the white balance, saturation and Tone mapping. It's the last of these that determines how the tones in the original frames are combined and how the vast range of tones in a 32-bit floating point HDR image are mapped to more limited tonal range in a 16-bit per channel integer file.

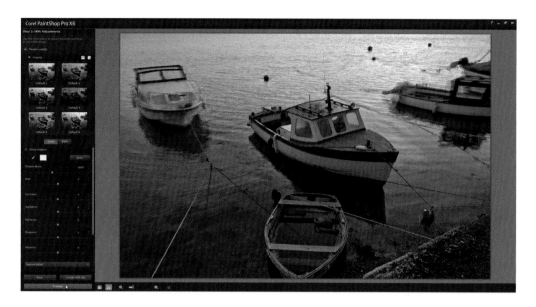

Check out some of these presets. I actually think the default (no preset) result provides a good balance in terms of tonal reproduction, white balance and color saturation. But if you prefer a slightly more stylized look the Default 1 preset is where it's at. If default 1 is a little too much for you, the Default 2 preset is less full-on. Default 3 is like Default 1, but with darker midtones and shadows and less vibrant colors. The remaining presets provide variations with, among other things, varying saturation or vibrancy.

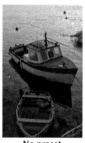
No preset

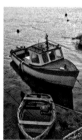
Default 1

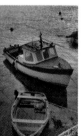
Default 2

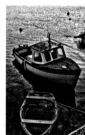
Default 3

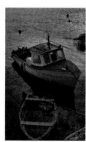
Default 4

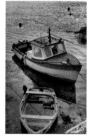
Default 5

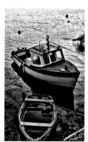
Default 6

STEP 4 The other thing that differs between the presets and that's worth experimenting with is the last pull-down menu which provides two options, Natural detail with three sliders for adjusting local tone mapping in the shadows, midtones and highlights and Creative details with sliders for strength and block size. You can reset things back to the initial processed settings by clicking the reset button at the bottom of the adjustments pane. And, once you've found a combination of settings that works for you, you can save it as a preset of your own by clicking the disk icon at the top of the panel.

Once you've got the HDR image looking the way you want it you can click the 'Create HDR file' button. This doesn't create an image file but saves the HDR settings so that you can reopen and continue editing later. Unless you want to do that, click the Process button to apply your settings.

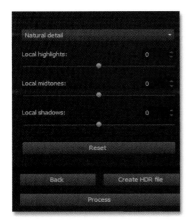
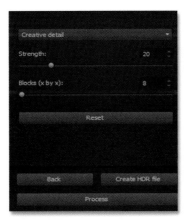

STEP 5 The Fine tune window allows you to do just that, make minor changes to tone and color as well as remove noise from the image and apply sharpening. When you're happy with how everything looks click the save and close button and choose the .pspimage format to save the file as a 16-bit per channel RGB image.

It's looking good, but we're not quite done yet. You don't have to look too hard at the screen grab on the next page to see that there's a problem with this HDR composite image. The boats on the left and right of the frame have moved between exposures and caused 'ghosting' in the final composited result. This is one of the big problems that you'll frequently encounter when shooting HDR, you can avoid camera movement by using a tripod, but people, water, vehicles, and even trees have a habit of moving around and there's not much you can do about it. Or is there?

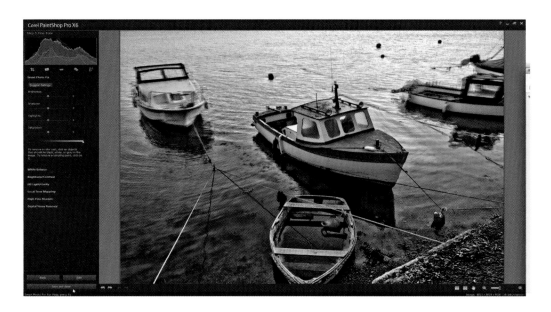

STEP 6 Let's go back to the Merge screen in HDR Exposure Merge (click the Back button twice). Under custom editing, you'll see a selection of tools for holding back and forcing parts of the image in each exposure. The Auto brush tool is worth a try, though I've had limited success with it. It analyses each frame to determine what parts of the subject have moved between exposures then brushes them out. Give it a try and see how it works for you. If nothing else it can guide you to where the problems might be. Click the Auto brush button and after a few seconds, you'll see the problem areas painted in red on each frame. Now click the process button to create the HDR Exposure Merge using those settings.

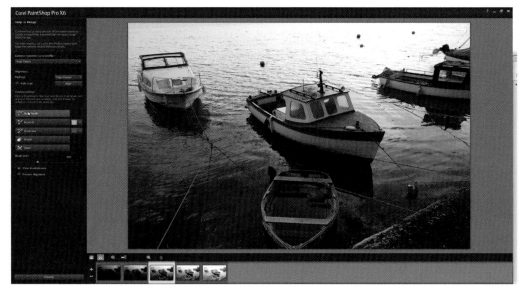

STEP 7 If you don't like what you see click the Back button and this time use the Brush out brush to manually paint out the problem areas. You'll have to decide how many of the frames you need to apply the brush out to, but it's probably best to assume your subject has moved and is in a different place on every one of them, so you'll need to brush out the offending detail on all but the middle exposure. A far quicker and easier way to do this is to use the Brush in tool and paint the same areas on the exposure that you want to use. Here (above), I've brushed in the two boats on the center (correct) exposure and this automatically brushes out those same areas on all the other frames.

The disadvantage is that you won't get any HDR goodness in the brushed in/out areas because only pixel data from a single exposure is used. You can use the Eraser to remove any accidentally applied brush in/out paint.

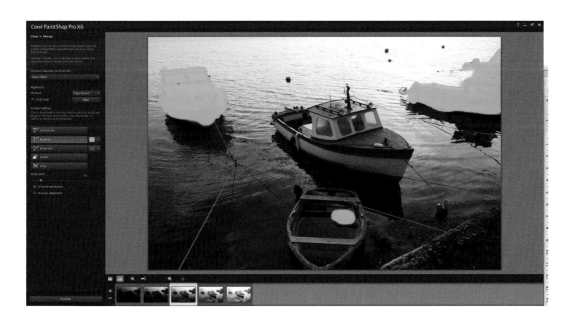

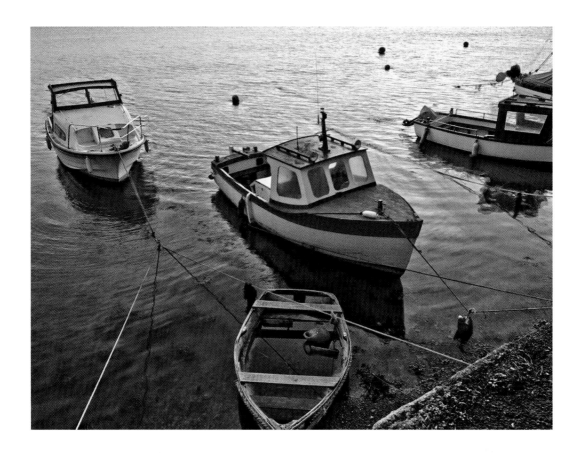

STEP 8 Here's the final result with both of the boats brushed in on the center (correctly exposed) frame.

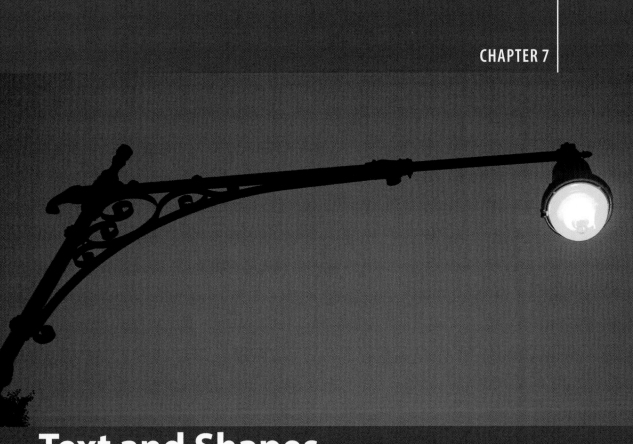

CHAPTER 7

Text and Shapes
Understanding Vector Graphics

What's Covered in this Chapter

- It may seem over the top to devote an entire chapter to text in a book about photography, after all PaintShop Pro X6 isn't a word processor. But the fact is that there are all sorts of occasions when you need to add words to your pictures. Whether it's producing family calendars and Christmas Cards, event posters, advertising or just having a laugh with some speech balloons, PaintShop Pro's text tools will help you get the job done.
- Text works in a fundamentally different way from photos – the shapes are described by mathematical formulae, rather than being just a bunch of pixels. Objects, including text, that are produced like this are called vector graphics, and this chapter starts out with an explanation of the difference between pixel-based things like photos (sometimes called bitmap or raster images) and vectors.
- As well as the Text tool, PaintShop Pro has a range of tools for creating geometric and irregular shapes. You'll learn how to use all of these including the all-powerful Pen tool which can be used to draw any shape that you can imagine.

- As well as creating text, this chapter shows you how you can manipulate it. You can apply any of the filter effects to text providing you first convert it to a raster layer. PaintShop Pro X6's Layer Effects have no such limitations and you'll find out how to use these to good effect to produce striking and impactful typography. You'll also discover how to make text follow any path – around a circle, or along a wavy line, for example, and how to distort letter shapes to create your own type forms.
- At the end of the chapter, you'll find a step-by-step project that shows how to create a text effect using text as a selection.

How Text and Vectors Work

Up to now, nearly everything we've done in PaintShop Pro has involved manipulating pixels. Text and vector objects work in a different way to pixel-based images, and this provides them with some advantages. Whereas a pixel-based bitmap is composed of many individual dots, each described in terms of its red, green and blue component values, vector objects and text are mathematically defined shapes. The object's properties are defined, and from these, the computer constructs them. A circle, for example, might be described in terms of its radius, stroke weight and color, and fill. The user isn't necessarily aware of this and just uses the available Shape tools and the Materials palette to draw the required shape or the Text tool to enter type.

Vectors have two distinct advantages over bitmaps. Because they need minimal data to describe them, they take up very little memory and disk space. And because they are generated by the computer, they are resolution independent, which is another way of saying you can make them as big as you like with no loss in quality.

Vectors also have their limitations. They're a good way of producing regular shapes like letterforms, geometric shapes and even irregular curvy shapes, but they're not great at representing real-world textured, detailed scenes, which is why we need the pixels for photographic images. For this reason, vectors tend to be confined to type and 2D illustration with flat color or mathematically predictable gradations.

Adding Basic Text

PaintShop Pro's Text tool is used to add text to any type of document, whether photo, vector illustration or scan. Choose the Text tool from the Tools toolbar and double-click anywhere in the document. If you're using an earlier version of PaintShop Pro, this will open the Text Entry dialog box. Type what you want in this box, click OK and watch as the text appears somewhere in the document canvas.

When you click on an image with the text tool and begin to type in PaintShop Pro X6, text is added directly in the image workspace (in versions prior to X3, a text box appears and you type text into it, it's then added in its own layer when you click OK).

The program automatically places the text data onto a vector layer in the Layers palette. It remains in a vector format until you need to apply special effects to it. If this is the case, PaintShop Pro asks you to convert the layer from vector to raster (more on this in the next section).

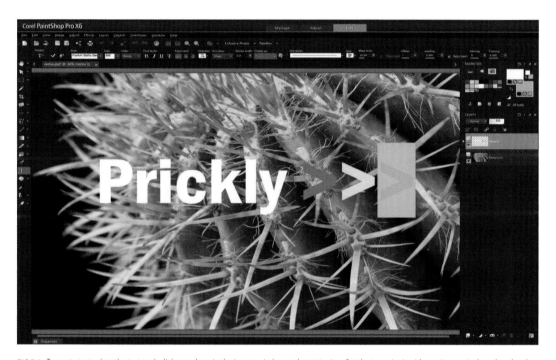

FIG 7.1 To create text select the text tool, click anywhere in the image window and start typing. Set the type size in either points or pixels and apply other text attributes including alignment, direction, antialiasing, stroke width, then click the apply button on the Tool Options palette. Characters within a text block can be individually styled.

You can format text using the tool options palette to select the font, size, style, alignment and other attributes. The text fill and stroke color are determined by the Foreground and stroke properties and Background and fill properties swatches in the Materials palette. To apply the formatting, click the apply changes button (the green tick) on the left of the tool options palette or click the cancel button next to it to exit from text editing mode without saving your text. You won't be able to switch tools, make any menu selections or make any other editing changes until you either apply or cancel your text edits.

Once you click the apply button, the text is added on its own vector layer, but you can click on it with the text tool and change the formatting at any time. And by selecting just a part of the text with the cursor, you can apply individual formatting to sections of the text.

There are a couple of other formatting controls on the tool options palette that are worth a closer look. The Anti-alias menu has three settings – Off, Sharp and Smooth – that determine the amount of smoothing applied to the edges of characters. When set to Off, type is not anti-aliased and you can see the stepped edges that result from the attempt at producing curved edges with square pixels (although text is defined by vectors, it is displayed on screen and when you print using pixels). A smoother look is achieved using semi-transparent pixels to fill some of the gaps. As a general rule anti-aliased text looks much better so, other than for very small type, you'll usually want to set this to either sharp or smooth.

The next control along determines the stroke width of your text and can be used to produce a stoked outline effect if you set different foreground and background colors. For small text, it's best to set the stroke width to zero, though you can use a narrow stroke of the same color as the fill to embolden text slightly. The stroke extends in both directions – inward and outward, so you need to take care not to overdo it and distort the shape of the type characters. Used moderately, however, applying a stroke to text is a great way to quickly produce a very classy-looking text effect.

There's one last thing on the Tool options palette I want to look at before moving on to type effects. The 'Create As' dropdown menu on the Tool options palette is set by default to Vector. This means that when you click the apply button, the text is added as a new vector layer in the layers palette. There are two other options that you might also want to consider using in some circumstances.

Selection creates a marquee selection from your text which you can then use to create text filled with images, text cut-outs and other effect. Floating creates the text as a floating selection – it looks the same as your vector text but is added to the image as a floating selection which you can move and transform. When you defloat raster text (Selections>Defloat or Ctrl-Shift-F), it's merged with the underlying raster layer unless you promote it to a layer with Selections>Promote Selection to Layer or Ctrl-Shift-P.

Creating text as selections is fine for a quick and easy route to text effects, but it's usually better to create the text as a vector layer then make a selection from it. That way you can easily edit the text and reselect without having to start again from scratch. I'll show you the best way to do this a little later in this chapter.

Assuming you've created text as a vector layer, once you click the apply button, the text appears with corner and edge handles and can be moved and transformed in the usual way, by dragging the corner handles to resize rotate

Tip

Use the Presets button on the Tool options palette to save frequently used text font, size alignment and other attributes. You can then apply all the necessary text styling with a single click.

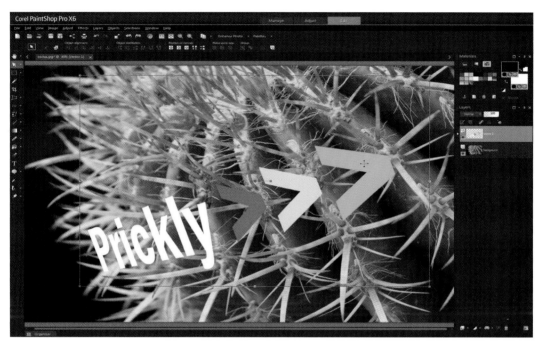

FIG 7.2 Having created the text as a vector layer, it can be transformed – here sheared and rotated, the text remains editable throughout.

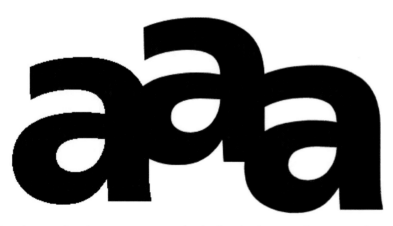

FIG 7.3 Anti-aliasing is the process of introducing semi-transparent pixels at the edges of an object, or text character to smooth out jagged edges, or stepping, caused by square pixels. This is more noticeable at low resolutions, where fewer pixels are used to make up the characters. PaintShop Pro has three anti-aliasing options: off (left), sharp (middle) and smooth (right).

and skew. Transformed text remains editable at all times – just select the text tool and click within the type area.

Now that you have had practice adding text to a picture, you'll want to try adding special effects to jazz up the results. In this section, we run through some techniques for making your text look simply stunning.

205

Layer Styles

Layer styles make it much easier to create, edit and apply certain special effects. You can apply Layer styles to both raster and vector layers and they work particularly well with type. When you apply a filter effect such as the drop shadow from the Effects>3D effects menu, the effect is added as pixels to the layer which makes it difficult to edit. If you decide your drop shadow is too dark or not in the right place, you have to undo it and start over. And if you want to apply effects filters to text you must first rasterize the layer, that is, convert it from a vector to a bitmap or raster layer. This makes it un-editable so, if you later discover a spelling mistake, you're in big trouble.

The great thing about layer styles is that they are 'live' editable effects. If, at any stage in the editing process you decide you want to change the size, opacity, position or color of your drop shadow or any other layer style you can. What's more you don't have to convert type layers to raster layers to apply layer styles to them so you can also edit the text with the Text tool and the layer style will automatically update.

To apply a layer style to some text, double-click the vector layer in the Layers palette to open the Layer Properties dialog box and click the Layer Styles tab, click the Fit Image to Window button if you can't see the text in the preview. To apply a Layer Style and access its controls click the checkbox next to it in the list. The layer itself is also included in the layer styles list, so you apply a layer style but make the layer itself invisible.

FIG 7.4 To access Layer Styles, double-click the layer thumbnail in the Layers palette, and select the Layer Styles tab in the Layer Properties dialog box. You can apply any combination of the six styles available.

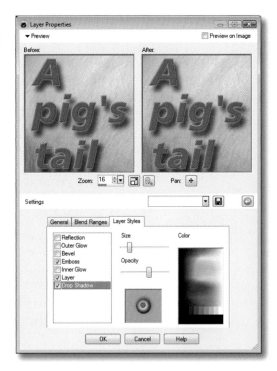

There are six Layer Styles to choose from

- Reflection
- Outer Glow
- Bevel
- Emboss
- Inner Glow
- Drop Shadow

You can apply more than one Layer Style at once – for example, you might want to Emboss your text and add a drop shadow, but be careful not to go overboard. Once you've selected a Layer Style, use the controls to change its size, opacity, position color and any other available attributes. As with most of PaintShop Pro X6's effects, once you've found settings that work well you can save them as presets so you don't have to rediscover them every time you want to apply them in similar situations.

Tip

Preview on image can slow things down to a crawl with Layer Styles. Use the before and after previews to get the job done more quickly.

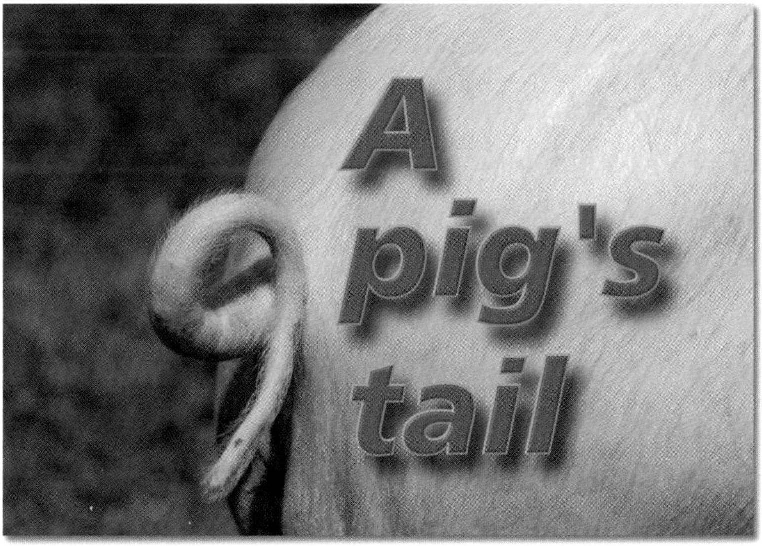

FIG 7.5 Layer styles work well with text layers. Here I've combined the Emboss and Drop Shadow styles to make the type stand out from the pig's, er, rear end.

Special Effects Filters

With PaintShop Pro you can add a wide range of effects to your text layers. For most actions, with the notable exception of Layer Styles, the Vector Text layer must first be converted to a Raster layer – a warning dialog appears and PaintShop Pro asks you if this is OK (if you don't want to be asked every time, click the 'Don't remind me' checkbox from the dialog that pops up on screen).

Select Chisel from the 'Effects>3D Effects' menu. The opening dialog offers a range of control options. The chisel effect extrudes the text shape outward. Use the size slider to determine the extent of the extruded effect and select one of the radio buttons to choose either a solid or transparent color fill. To select a color for the effect you can click the color swatch and use the Color Properties dialog box. Better still, move the cursor over the photo, and it will change to an eye dropper tool which you can use to sample a color from the photo itself.

Other 3D Effects for adding impact to text include: Drop Shadow, Cut-out and Inner Bevel. Most of the 3D Effects are available as Layer Styles and, as a general rule, where you have the option it's better to use a Layer Style than a filter effect. If you need to add something slightly more esoteric, then try some of the filters from the 'Artistic', 'Art Media', 'Distortion' or 'Texture' filter drop-downs. Any of these filters will work on the Text layer as long as it has been converted into a Bitmap (Raster) layer first.

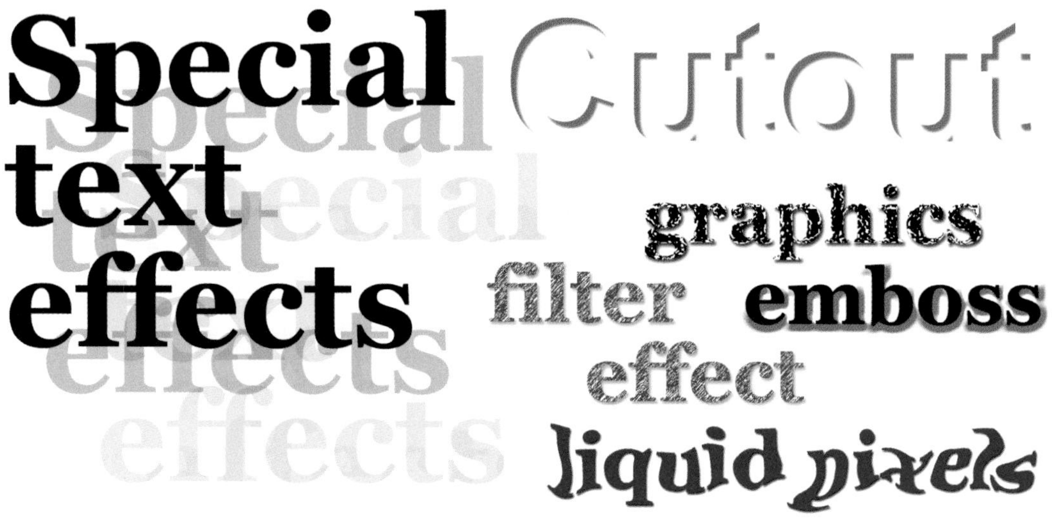

Special text effects

Cutout

graphics

filter emboss

effect

liquid pixels

FIG 7.6 Over and above regular text effects, added via the Materials palette, it's possible to add tremendous three-dimensional power using any of PaintShop Pro's filter effects. To do this, you might have to convert the layer from vector to bitmap but still, the resulting effects, as seen here, are very impressive.

Using Filter Effects: A Warning

Though almost all the filters under the Effects menu will have an effect on Raster Text layers, not all work well and some may not appear to do anything at all. The reason for this is that the filter action works across the entire frame and not just on the text on its own. If the filter has a global effect, then it is more than likely to be seen on the text layer, but if it is of a more random nature, it might or it might not. To make it work correctly, you must first select the text and then apply the filter action. Do this by choosing 'Selections>From Vector Object' or use the keyboard shortcut 'Ctrl+Shift+B' and then apply the filter.

Adding Text to a Path

Adding text to a path can make for a dynamic and interesting design and is especially useful for creating company logos, web buttons, badges, CD and DVD labels and the like. You can add type to shapes created with any of PaintShop Pro's shape tools (see 'Vectors: Learning the Basics on p. 212), but it works best on gently sloping curves. Anything with sharp angles and lots of turns is unlikely to look good or even readable.

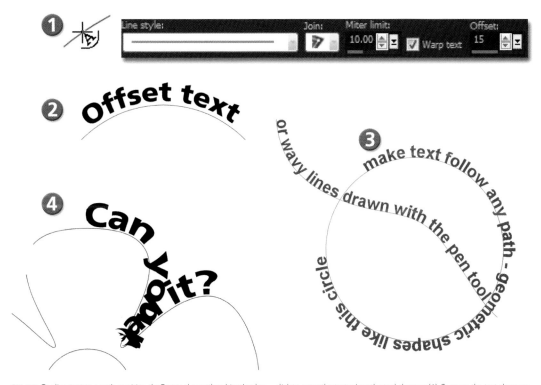

FIG 7.7 To align text to a path, position the Text tool over the object's edge – click to enter the text when the tool changes (1). To move the text above or below the line enter an offset in the Text Tool Options palette (2). You can run text along any vector path (3), but avoid sharp curves and sudden direction changes, which will render it unreadable (4).

To add text to a shape, all you need to do is first draw the shape, then select the Text tool and position the cursor on the edge of the shape. You'll see the cursor change from the normal cross-hairs with a capital A in the bottom right quadrant to cross-hairs with an A at 45 degrees and a curved line below it. When this happens, click on the shape and any text you type will follow the outline of the shape.

- To move the text along the path, choose the Pick tool and click-drag the text. The small circle icon indicates the new start position of the text.

- To raise or lower the text on the path, enter a value in the Offset field of the Text Tool's Options palette. A positive value raises the text above the path, a negative value lowers it.
- If you don't want the path to show, either select a transparent stroke and fill or click the Layer Visibility icon in the Layers palette to turn it off.
- To detach text from the path, select either the text or its path using the Pick tool and choose Detach Object from Path from the Objects menu.
- To attach existing text to an object, select the text with the Pick tool, Shift-select the object and choose Fit Text to Path from the Objects menu.

Editing Text Shapes

By converting text to a vector object you can use PaintShop Pro's Vector Editing tools to alter the shape of individual characters by adjusting individual nodes. To convert text to a vector object, select it with the Pick tool and choose Objects>Convert Text to Curves. There are two options – you can convert the entire text block into one vector object by choosing Objects>Convert Text to Curves>As Single Shape. Alternatively, Objects>Convert Text to Curves>As Character Shapes converts each letter of the text into a separate vector object. Once the text is converted, select the Pen tool and click the Edit mode button in the Tool Options palette to edit the character shapes.

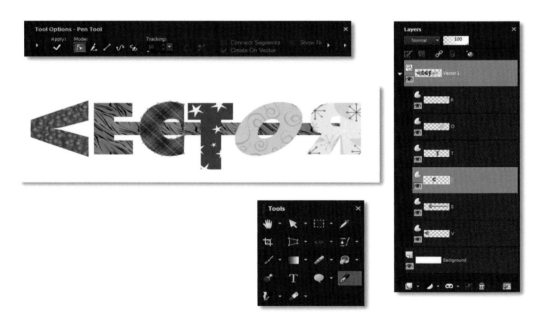

FIG 7.8 Once text is converted to paths, you can edit individual character shapes using the Pen tool.

Bear in mind that once the text has been converted to curves, it can no longer be edited in the usual way, so now is not the time to discover you've made a spelling error! You can cover yourself by duplicating the layer before converting it (make the original text layer invisible by clicking the visibility toggle in the layers palette), so you have the original text to go back to if necessary. Once the text is converted to curves, especially as individual character shapes, you will need to pay special attention to how the individual elements stack up in the Layers palette.

Making Selections from Text

Text selections form the basis for all kinds of effects using photos. You can paste photos inside a text selection, a particularly effective technique when combined with layers. Typically, an image layer is copied, pasted inside a selection and overlaid on top of the original with the opacity reduced, the color desaturated, or some other effect applied.

You can make a text selection directly by selecting the Text tool and choosing Selection from the Create As pull-down menu in the Tool Options palette. This is useful for a quick text selection, but once the selection is made, it can't easily be edited. A better method is to create the text as a vector, then choose

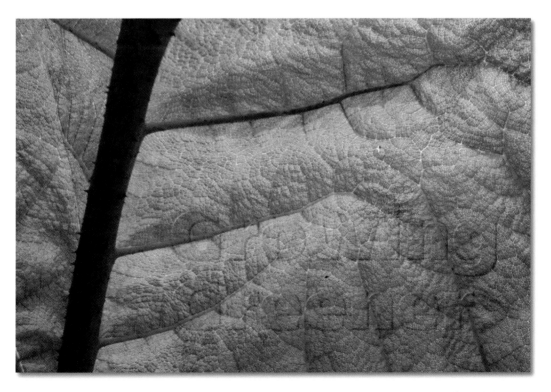

FIG 7.9 To create this text, I made a selection from it using Selections>From vector object, then turned the text layer's visibility off. I pasted the background image into the selection (Edit>Paste Into Selection), then promoted the selection to a layer and applied the Emboss Layer Style. Finally, I made the Background layer black and white using the Black and White Film Effects.

Selections>From Vector Object. That way, if you decide to edit the text, even if it's only to open up the tracking a little, or reduce the leading, you can easily make a new selection.

Vectors: Learning the Basics

Vector images are different to bitmap (raster) images. Whereas a bitmap image is made entirely of pixels, a vector image is made from a set of mathematical instructions or coordinates. Advantages of vectors are

- Vectors are quick to work with.
- Vector file sizes can be small and still display a large dimension.
- Vector graphics are highly editable with absolutely no loss of quality.
- They create perfectly clean, anti-aliased lines and curves.

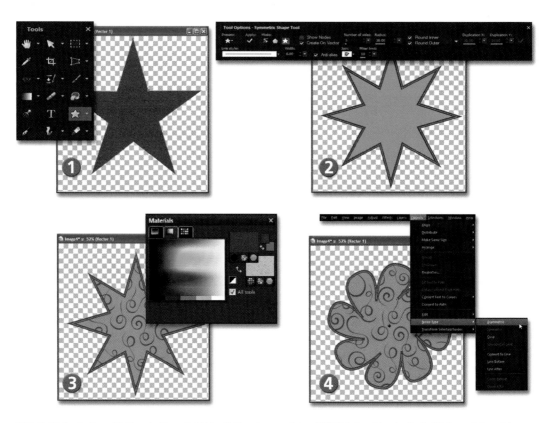

FIG 7.10 (1) Use the Symmetric Shape tool to create highly editable polygons and stars. (2) Edit the line style using the Tool Options palette and choose Stroke and Fill colors from the Materials palette (3). You can edit all of the nodes on a symmetric shape at once (4), so it's easy to quickly create variations on a basic shape theme.

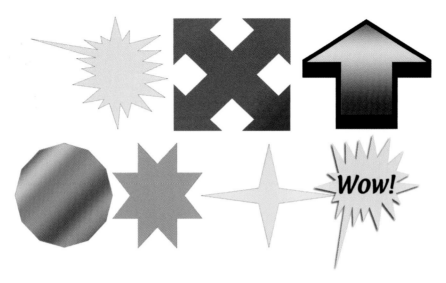

FIG 7.11 The Preset Shape tool is a powerful and quick way to make almost any size or shape of object for illustration.

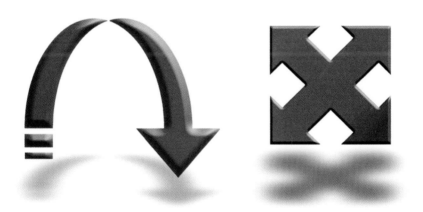

FIG 7.12 Take this one step further, adding drop shadows, bevels and a range of other specialist (filter) effects to make those flat, unexciting shapes something special.

Vectors, therefore, are ideal for illustrations where scalable drawing, text and shapes are required. PaintShop Pro's Preset Vector Shape tool has a myriad range of fully editable subjects in its library. If, for example, you like the shape in one of the presets, but not the color or edge detail, you can edit it using its Edit palette. If you need to create your own vector illustrations from the ground up, use the Pen tool.

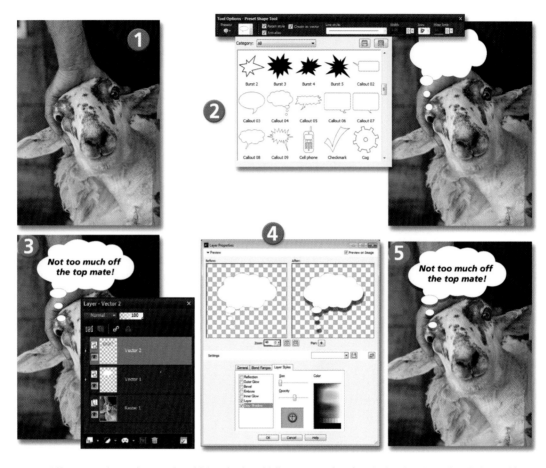

FIG 7.13 Adding a vector shape and text to a photo. (1) Open the photo. (2) Choose a preset shape from the drop-down Preset Shape Tool menu. (3) Use the handles to reposition and rescale the shape if necessary. (4) Reposition, rotate or flip the vector shape using the Pick tool, then choose the Text tool and enter appropriate text in the Text box (do not click directly on the shape with the Text tool, or the text will follow the path as illustrated on page 209) and press 'Apply'. Once happy with the size and positioning of the new text, use PaintShop Pro's Drop Shadow filter to add an effect to the speech bubble and save as a '.pspimage' file.

Working with the Pen Tool

The Pen tool is the ultimate vector shape creation tool. With it, illustrators and graphic designers can create any type of shape, line or layer object they'd care to imagine. The Pen tool gives you scope to design any shape you can imagine; however, because the shapes it creates are formed using vectors, whatever is created remains editable at all times.

Drawing tools rely on manual actions for their accuracy and we all know how tricky it is to try and draw with a mouse. It's like sketching with a house brick, only less accurate. The Pen tool allows you to ignore many of the physical limitations of the mouse and to apply smooth linear accuracy to the most delicate of shapes.

The driving force behind this is the ability to draw using Bezier curves. These are infinitely editable lines that can be used to describe mathematically perfect shapes such as curves and circles. This might not be a tool that you are likely to need but, for anything graphic design based, like producing posters or cards, it can be extremely useful. Check out the stack of controls provided in the Options palette and you'll get an idea of how powerful this tool is. Here are some of its most important features:

- Draw lines and shapes of any size freehand.
- Draw a myriad range of shapes using point-to-point techniques.
- Fill objects with color, texture and transparency using the Materials palette.

The Pen tool works by dropping editable nodes into the picture, whether blank canvas or existing picture. Each mouse-click adds another node that's automatically joined to the previous one with a straight or curved line, depending on the type of drawing implement chosen. Clicking a node back onto the original start point completes the shape. You can add as many, or as few, nodes as needed, though the fewer nodes you use, the smoother your shapes will look.

The Pen tool can be used to create new vector shapes and edit existing pictures in a wide range of styles. You can change any aspect of the Pen tool at any time – for example, thickness of line, color fill, texture, linear aspect, curve aspect and more. Right-clicking displays its principal attributes, which include: Edit, Node Type and Transform Selected Nodes. Using these allows you to perform more than 30 different edit functions.

Uses for the Pen tool:

- Creating accurate masks.
- Creating complex vector shapes and illustrative elements using rectilinear or Bezier-controlled lines.
- Creating perfectly curved lines around irregular objects.

Here's how to make a vector illustration:

Step 1. Create a new document with a white background and a resolution of your choice ('File>New').
Step 2. Click the Pen tool icon on the Tools toolbar and select a line style and width from the Tool Options palette.
Step 3. Select a line application – Lines and Polylines, Point to Point (Bezier Curves) or Freehand, from the Mode section of the Tool Options. You'll need to experiment to discover which suits the task in hand; see the notes below for the differences between these methods.
Step 4. When you've drawn your path, select it with the Pick tool to display its bounding box. The handles on the box allow you to rotate, stretch and deform the vector shape without losing detail. To change the appearance

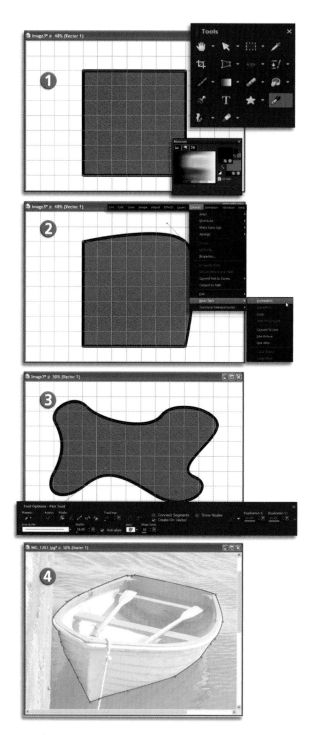

FIG 7.14 (1) Creating geometric shapes with the Pen tool is easy – but you can use the Symmetric Shape tool for that. (2) Change node properties by right-clicking or (3) create curves of any shape by click-dragging. (4) Use the Pen tool to trace shapes from photo layers.

of the line, open the Layers palette, select the vector layer and click the '+' tab. This opens the Vector layer to display the individual elements. Double-click an element to open the Vector Properties box.

Note the following:

- 'Draw Lines and Polylines' draws straight lines between two points.
- 'Draw Point to Point – Bezier Curve' is an infinitely editable freeform line controlled by Bezier technology – grab a controlling handle to bend the line any which way. Bezier curves are ideal for creating seamless freehand shapes.
- 'Draw Freehand' is the same as drawing on a piece of paper.

Step-by-Step Projects

Creating a Type Special Effect with Text Selections

As we saw earlier in this chapter, Effects filters don't work with Vector layers, which must first be rasterized. The same thing goes for text, which by default is rendered as a Vector layer. One of the easiest ways to create stunning type effects, however, is to make a selection from your type and then apply the effect to an image using that selection. Here we're going to produce a beveled glass type effect in four steps.

The success of type effects like this depends very much on choosing the right typeface. The Inner Bevel filter works well on big bold type. So avoid script fonts or anything with fine detail and keep the word count to a minimum – make a bold one-word statement.

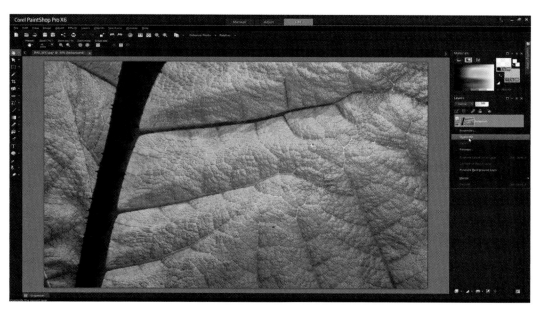

STEP 1 Open your image and create a copy of the background layer by right-clicking it in the Layers palette and selecting Duplicate.

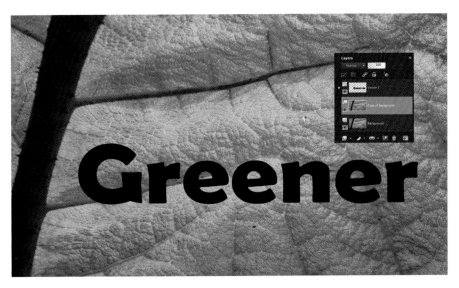

STEP 2 Select the Text tool, click on the image and enter the type. For maximum effect, keep it short – one or two words at most – and use a bold typeface; use capital letters for improved readability and make the type as large as you can. Click the Apply button in the Tool options palette when you are happy with how it looks, then position the type where you want it on the background with the Move tool.

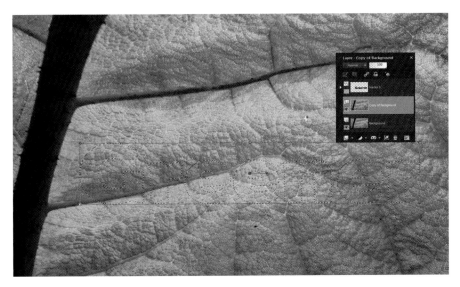

STEP 3 Choose Selections>From Vector Object (keyboard shortcut Ctrl+Shift+B), then turn off the Type layer by clicking its Layer visibility toggle (the eye) in the Layers palette. Click the Copy of Background layer in the Layers palette to make it active.

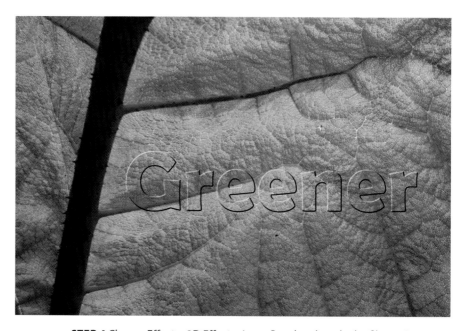

STEP 4 Choose Effects>3D Effects>Inner Bevel and apply the filter using the default settings. Click the Preview icon to see the result in the main image window. You can experiment with angle, smoothness, depth and other settings, or try one of the available presets, but the default setting gives a pretty good result. Click OK to apply the bevel, then press Ctrl-D to deselect all.

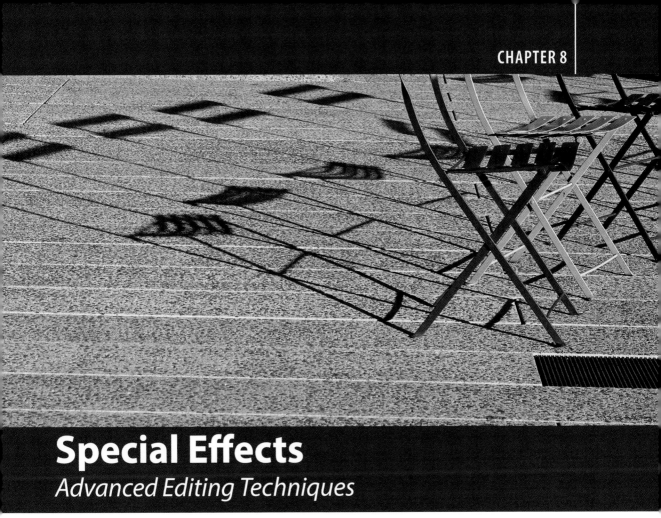

CHAPTER 8

Special Effects
Advanced Editing Techniques

What's Covered in this Chapter

- In this chapter, you'll learn how to add special effects to your digital photos. Applying a special effects filter may be all that's needed to turn a so-so image into something special. But with a little more effort, you can create jaw-dropping effects that defy reality – or what passes for reality in a photo.
- This chapter really covers two things; the first half is all about PaintShop Pro X6's painting and drawing tools, and the remainder explains how to create special effects.
- If you want to create illustrations from scratch, you'll need to familiarize yourself with the workings of the Materials palette and PaintShop Pro's Brush tools. All of this is explained in detail in the next few pages. Creating illustration from a blank canvas can be a demanding task, even if you're a competent illustrator, but by using a photo as a source image and painting over it using layers you can achieve professional looking results. PaintShop Pro's Art Media tools mimic real-world materials like oils and pastels, and you'll learn how to use these to turn photos into paintings.

- Later in the chapter, you'll find a comprehensive run-down of PaintShop Pro's filter effects, where to find them and how to use them. You'll discover how to use the Deformation tools to distort photos as well as how to correct distortion caused by ultra-wide angle lenses using the distortion correction filters.
- Special effect filters and distortion tools are often knocked for not being very 'useful'. That's not a criticism you could apply to PaintShop Pro X6's lighting effects which allow you to add lighting to a photo after you've taken it. Lighting effects are great for adding spotlights or colored lighting to a scene, or simply to shine some illumination and add depth to a picture that suffers from flat featureless light. Turn to page 244 to find out how.
- There are lots of step-by-step projects at the end of this chapter. We kick off with a look at how to make type follow the contours of a surface as if it's been painted on. Following this advanced project.
- We'll tackle something a bit simpler – having a bit of fun with PaintShop Pro's Picture Tube and adding edges and frames to your photos. The final step-by-step project in this chapter shows you how to respray your car using the Color Changer tool.

Using the Materials Palette

One of the most used palettes in PaintShop Pro is the Materials palette. This is where you change the colors used in any of the program's paint or drawing tools. In this section, we look at how the Materials palette can be used in the creation of special effects and how it's used for mixing colors.

Choose the Materials palette from the 'View > Palettes' menu (keyboard shortcut F6). There are three modes in which to work with this tool: Frame, Rainbow and Swatch modes.

The Frame mode provides a quick and fairly intuitive method of picking colors. First left-click to select a foreground hue from the outer hue rectangle (right-click to select a background color), then click in the inner saturation rectangle to alter the saturation and brightness for the selected hue. If you hold down the mouse button and drag within the Saturation rectangle, the value updates and a tool tip window tells you the RGB values at the cursor position. Alternatively, you can fine-tune the saturation and brightness by adjusting the triangular sliders at the bottom and side of the Saturation rectangle.

On the Rainbow tab, position the cursor over the central colors panel; it changes to an eyedropper and a tool tip window displays the RGB values of the color beneath. Left-click to select the foreground color and right-click to select the background color. The Rainbow tab only needs one click to select a color, but provides less accuracy than the Frame tab.

If you're working with a limited palette, you may find Swatch mode simpler to use because you can make your own swatches. In many ways, it's faster and more accurate to work with.

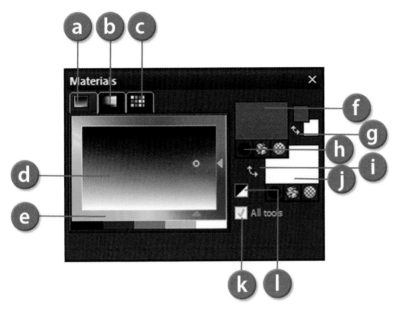

FIG 8.1 (a) Frame tab. (b) Rainbow tab. (c) Swatches tab. (d) Inner saturation rectangle. (e) Outer hue rectangle. (f) Foreground and Stroke Properties. (g) Swap Foreground and Background colors. (h) Click the left button to change the Color/Gradient and pattern selected, click the middle button to change the texture and the right button for transparency. (i) Swap foreground and background materials. (j) Background and Fill color. (k) Apply Materials palette settings to All tools. (l) Select default (black and white) foreground and background colors.

The two large colored boxes on the right of the palette influence the Foreground and Stroke Properties (upper left), and the Background and Fill Properties (lower right). Underneath the Foreground and Background Properties boxes, a Style button provides three options: Color, Gradient and Pattern. To these three modes can be added texture or transparency using the appropriate buttons. Two smaller colored boxes to the upper right are used to set the foreground and background colors.

Double-click either the Foreground or Background Color box to open the Color picker. Use this to choose more colors. To modify the gradient or texture double-click the Foreground and Stroke or Background and Fill Properties box to open the Material Properties dialog box.

- Use the Swap buttons (double-headed arrows) to swap foreground and background colors and materials.
- Click the Style button at the base of the Foreground/Background Properties boxes to choose any of the three styles you wish to work with; Color, Gradient or Pattern.
- Click the Texture button to add texture to the paint strokes.
- Click the Transparent button to add transparency to the brush.
- If you are happy with a particular combination in the palette, click the 'All tools' checkbox to lock it and to apply the settings to all the tools.

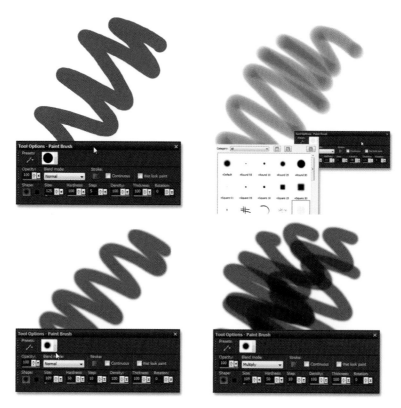

FIG 8.2 Top left: Click once in the Color picker to set the foreground color and paint. Top right: Select from one of the available brush tips to quickly alter the stroke appearance. Bottom left: Even with the default brush tip, you can create a wide range of variation using the tool options palette, here I've created a softer edge by changing the Hardness to 50. Bottom right: Use Blend modes to alter the way new brush strokes interact with existing ones, here multiply mode ovelays strokes to build up color.

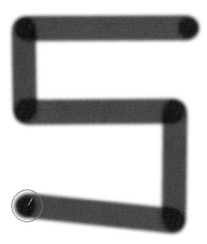

FIG 8.3 To draw a line between two points with the Paint brush, click once, move the cursor to the next point and Shift-click again. I'm still using the Multiply blend mode here which is why each end point appears as a darker spot.

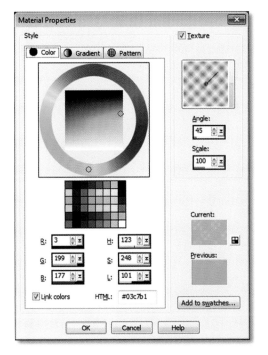

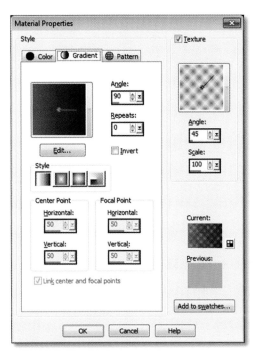

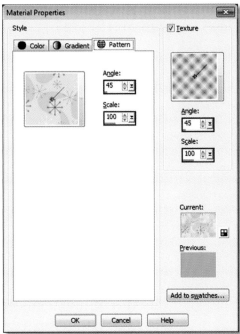

FIG 8.4 The Material Properties dialog box appears when you click the foreground or background color swatch in the Materials palette. It's divided into three tabs (top left) for selecting color, (top right) Gradients and (bottom) Patterns. As well as choosing presets and changing parameters (for example, the start and end colors of a gradient), you can choose and apply a texture.

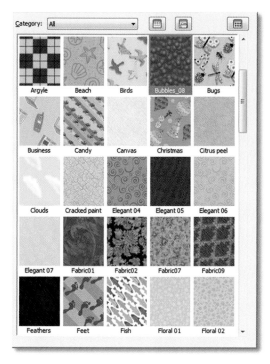

FIG 8.5 Click the Pattern swatch in the Pattern tab of the Material properties dialog to see the list of available patterns.

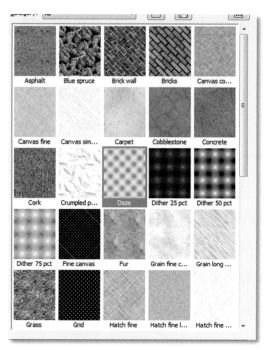

FIG 8.6 You can apply a texture to a color, gradient or pattern, but first make sure to check the Texture checkbox in the Material Properties dialog. Click the Texture swatch to see the range of available textures.

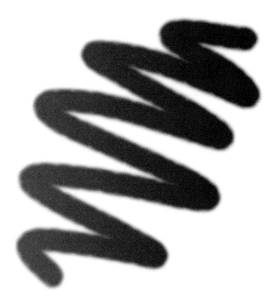

FIG 8.7 Of course, you can paint with a gradient and texture applied.

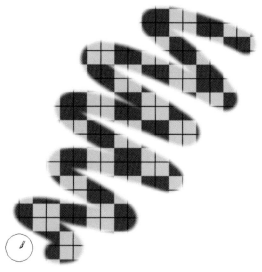

FIG 8.8 And with patterns too.

Working with Brush Tools

PaintShop Pro comes with a staggering array of brushes and brush tips, enabling the user to create a range of simple, or incredibly sophisticated, painting tasks. Brush tools introduce the photographer to the concept of original creativity – you can literally make something from nothing using one of PaintShop Pro's brushes (in the same way that you might with a crayon and a blank sheet of paper).

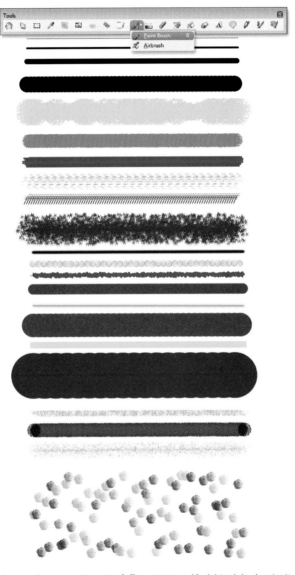

FIG 8.9 PaintShop Pro's Paint Brush can produce a staggering array of effects, textures and 'looks' simply by changing its tool set in the Options and Materials palettes. There are over 20 preset stock tips that vary greatly in each brush.

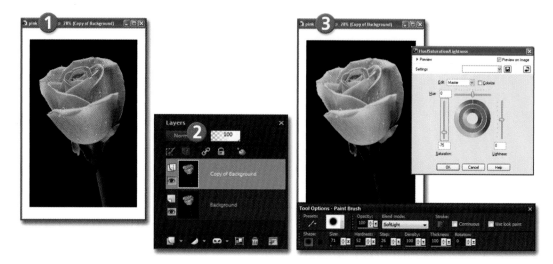

FIG 8.10 This is a very ordinary snap of a very pretty rose. There are a number of preset filter effects that I could apply to the entire photo or even to a selection. However, it is also possible to make quite radical changes merely by using a brush on the canvas. (1) Open the photo and enlarge the canvas to add a white border all round the edges. (2) Duplicate the layer. (3) Desaturate the color. Reduce it almost to black and white.

Use the Tool Options palette to change the physical nature of all brushes. Use the Materials palette to choose different brush colors as well as textures and gradients in the brush action. Simply paint over the image to add texture and additional color.

One way to use this process is to add a non-photographic influence to a picture in order to create the illusion that it's something other than a plain old photo. The most important thing to remember when you're doing this kind of work is to select a blend mode from the Brush Tool options palette that doesn't completely obscure the underlying detail, but allows it to show through your brush strokes.

Brush tools are variable in terms of size, density, opacity and hardness. It's much easier to get good results using a graphics tablet rather than a mouse. A graphics tablet allows you to draw, select, erase and paint with the accuracy and delicacy of a real paintbrush, pencil or crayon. Using the Brush Variance palette (F11), you can assign brush properties like size, opacity and thickness to vary according to how much pressure you apply, or, if your stylus supports it, the degree of tilt or rotation. The bottom line is it's much more natural working with a stylus and you have a lot more control than with a mouse.

Besides the Paint Brush and Airbrush tools, PaintShop Pro has a number of other brush-based tools designed specifically for working on a photographic image for the purposes of adding impact. These are:

- Dodge tool. Lightens pixels under the brush – good for extracting detail in dark areas.
- Burn tool. Darkens the pixels under the brush. Ideal for increasing density in overexposed pictures.

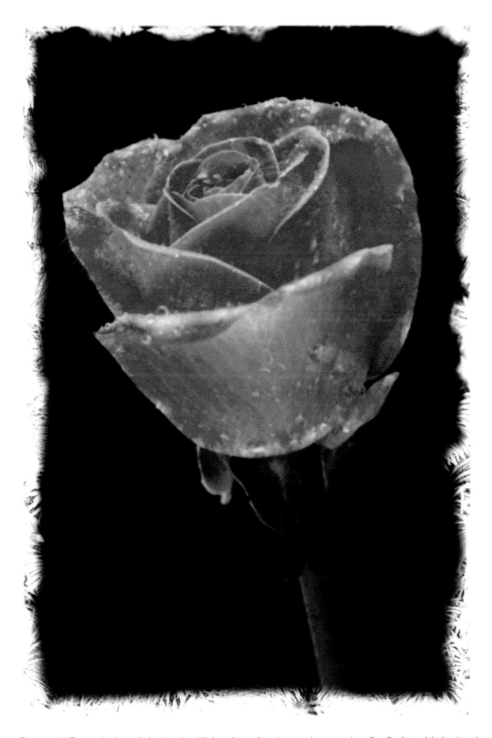

FIG 8.11 The textured effect can also be applied to the edges. Work at a lowered opacity to produce a seamless effect. Too fast and the brush marks become heavy and tell-tale, which is not usually desirable. Original picture: John Shepherd, iStockphoto 1012211.

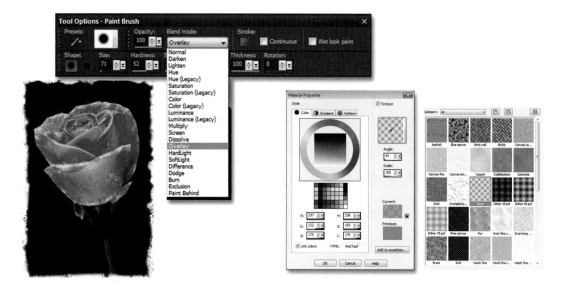

FIG 8.12 Use the Brush Options palette to change the properties of the brush tip. When overpainting choose a blend mode like Overlay, or soft light that will interact with the detail on the image below, rather than completely obscuring it. Use the Materials palette to choose different brush colors as well as textures and gradients in the brush action. Simply paint over the image to add texture and additional color.

- Smudge brush. Blurs and smudges the pixels under the brush action.
- Push. Makes all the pixels behave just like wet oil paint so that they can literally be pushed about the frame
- Soften. Applies a localized soft focus effect.
- Sharpen. Increases the contrast, and therefore the apparent sharpness in the pixels.

Like the Paint Brush, PaintShop Pro's Airbrush also has potential for terrific creativity. Once you hit on one combination, record it as a preset for use on other images.

Using the Art Media Brushes

PaintShop Pro X6 has a range of Brush tools called the Art Media tools. These tools are a radical departure from the usual kind of digital brush tool in that they mimic the behavior of real-world materials like oil paint and pastels.

Altogether there are nine Art Media tools: Oil, Chalk, Pastel, Crayon, Colored Pencil, Marker, Palette Knife, Smear and Art Eraser. These tools can only be used on special Art Media layers; a new Art Media layer is automatically created for you when you start to paint with one of the Art Media tools.

Two of the Art Media brushes – Oil and Marker – are 'wet'; they simulate the wetness of their real-world counterparts. With a 'normal' PaintShop Pro brush, if you paint by holding down the mouse button, or maintain pressure on the stylus tip, the paint just keeps on coming, but with a wet Art Media brush it runs out, just like the real thing. You have to finish the stroke and start a new one with a reloaded brush. Oil and Marker strokes stay wet, so if you paint over them with a new color the paint smears on the canvas.

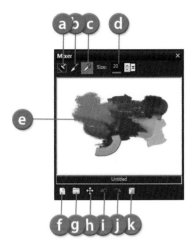

FIG 8.13 PaintShop Pro's Mixer palette works like the real thing, allowing you to partially mix colors and apply a smeared combination with the Oil Brush or Marker tool. (a) Mixer Tube. (b) Mixer Knife. (c) Mixer Dropper. (d) Tool size. (e) Mixer area. (f) New Mixer Page. (g) Load Mixer Page. (h) Navigate button. (i) and (j) Unmix and remix buttons. (k) Mixer Palette Menu button.

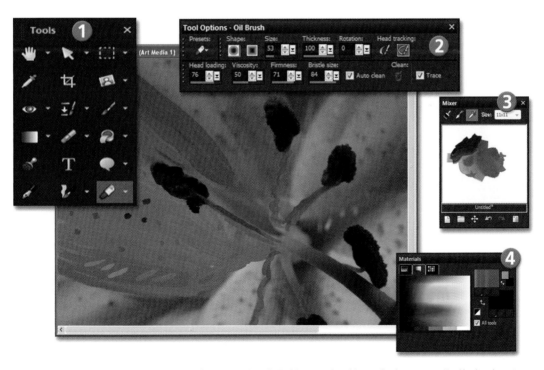

FIG 8.14 Select the Oil brush from the Art Media tools fly-out (1) and use the Tool Options palette (2) to set brush parameters. Head loading determines how much paint is on the brush and how quickly it will run out. Click the Trace checkbox to automatically sample the color from underlying layers. Add color to the Mixer palette (3) using the Mixer Tube and mix the hues together with the Mixer Knife. Sampling an area of the Mixer palette with the Mixer Dropper adds the mix to the Foreground/Stroke swatch in the Materials palette (4) – now you're ready to paint.

Another aspect of real media that these wet brushes emulate is the ability to paint with multiple colors. A real brush might have mostly blue paint on it with a little bit of yellow, producing a smeared blue/green color, and you can simulate this effect with the Oil Brush and Marker tool. There's also a Mixer palette on which you can smear colors around and produce a messy mix of several colors to load onto your brush.

When using the Oil brush or the Palette Knife, the size of the area sampled from the Mixer palette is determined by the brush size setting in the Tool Options palette, so the bigger your brush, the more paint variation you can have. For other Art Media tools, set the sample size using the Mixer palette's Size slider, up and down arrows, or enter in a value with your keyboard.

When using the wet painting tools, painting over existing strokes causes them to smear. You can 'dry' an Art Media layer, or make it wet again at any time by choosing Layers > Dry Art Media Layer or Layers > Wet Art Media Layer.

You can save and load Mixer palette pages and switch between them by choosing Save Page and Load Page from the Mixer Palette menu.

Deformation Tools

Altering the shape or alignment of a layer is easy using PaintShop Pro's Deformation tools. Why use the Deformation tools?

- To change the alignment of a layer.
- To modify the size of the layer.
- To modify the perspective and skew of a layer.
- To significantly change the appearance of a picture.

There are four to choose from:

- Pick tool – used for relatively simple layer changes.
- Straighten tool – especially handy for straightening horizons.
- Perspective Correction tool – for adding exaggerated (or corrective) perspective to objects.
- Mesh Warp – Mesh Warp gives you the freedom to bend, distort, warp and buckle up to 31 sections within a layer.

Transforming layers with the Pick tool is simple enough: open the document and select the layer that needs transforming. Choose the Pick tool from the Tools toolbar. Note the bounding box and 'handles' that appear at the corners of the layer. If you hold the cursor over any of these handles, the normal four-pointed arrow Move symbol changes to a rectangle, indicating that you can scale the layer while maintaining its original proportions. If you don't want to maintain the original proportions, in other words to stretch or squeeze the layer, drag one of the handles located on an edge midway between the corners.

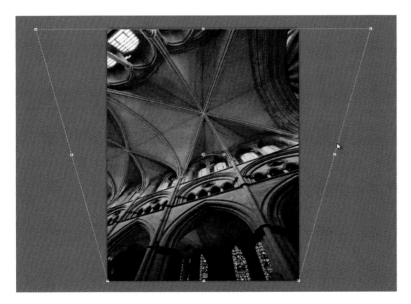

FIG 8.15 Hold down the Ctrl key and drag a corner handle to apply a perspective distortion using the Pick tool.

You can further change the type of the deforming action by holding down the Shift key for a shear action or by holding the Control key to change it to Perspective Deform. The handle in the center which resembles a stroked circle moves all the contents in the bounding box. The Rotation Handle to the right of this (pre-rotation) rotates the layer. Use similar mouse actions to directly change the perspective (Perspective Correction tool) and to align the horizon (Straighten tool). Advanced users can use the Deformation tools to manipulate selected layers to create super-real perspective effects or to add extra realism such as shadows to product photos.

Lens Correction Filters

PaintShop Pro also has a range of filter effects specifically designed for correcting lens distortion found in less expensive and extreme wide angle lenses. They can be used to straighten out the curvature at the edges of the frame that you get with extreme wide angle lenses. You'll find them at the bottom of the Adjust menu. Like all the other PaintShop Pro X6 filters, the lens distortion dialog box provides the option of previewing the result on the image, or displaying before and after thumbnail previews.

The easiest way to find out if your lens suffers from this kind of distortion is to take a photo of something that has a grid pattern – like a brick wall for example. In fact, if you're going to correct for barrel or pin cushion distortion this kind of image will help you judge exactly how much correction to apply using the strength slider. Once you've done that you can save the settings as a preset, so that it can easily be applied in future.

Tip

Many criteria come into play to influence the success or failure of a filter effect. Factors include the quality, focus, color and contrast in the original snap. Don't use a filter to mask the fact that a snap is no good – because the filter effect will invariably be no good either!

Believe it or not, there's also a filter for introducing these kinds of distortions (it works in pretty much the same way as the corrections) which you'll find on Effects > Distortion Effects > Lens Distortions. Use the settings pull-down menu to select the type of lens distortion you want to produce. There are four options: Barrel, Fisheye, Fisheye (spherical) and Pincushion.

Less expensive lenses often suffer from slight barrel or pincushion distortion but, unless straight lines are important to you, it can usually be ignored. Barrel distortion bows straight lines outward toward the edge of the frame, pincushion is the opposite – the lines bow inwards toward the center.

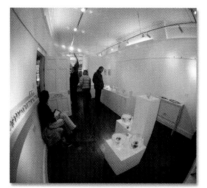
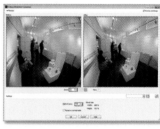
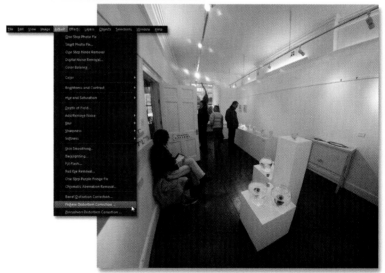

FIG 8.16 PaintShop Pro X6 has three distortion correction filters – Barrel, Cushion and Fisheye – designed to correct for lens distortions. These distortions are often found in less expensive lenses, but they are usually quite minor and difficult to spot. Very wide angle lenses though, and in particular, 'fisheye' lenses with a 180-degree field of view, suffer from severe barrel distortion. The original (top left) was shot with an ultra-wide angle lens – notice how the straight lines, e.g. the lighting rail and skirting board, curve toward the edges of the image. The Fisheye Distortion Correction filter does an excellent job of straightening everything out.

Applying Filter Effects

PaintShop Pro has many filters, designed not only to improve the quality of your work but also to radically change the nature of the picture. For example, you can increase or decrease color, contrast, hue, sharpness and tones in a photo at the press of a button. These filters are regarded as 'standard issue' for most photo-editing products. PaintShop Pro also has a range of creative filter effects that can the nature of a photo from a straight photographic record into something different, like a drawing, painting or even a sketch. In fact, with a bit of patience, you can create almost any type of special effect you care to think of, such is the power of the software filter set.

PaintShop Pro has dozens of filters. The program is also compliant with range of plug-in type filters. These are manufactured by third parties, like Flaming Pear and Auto F/X. These are loaded into the Effects menu just as if they were original integral products.

Tip

Effects filters usually work best when applied to one part of an image, e.g. to text, or a specific area. You can use the selection tools and masks to achieve this and there's a step-by-step project that shows how to apply filter effects using masks at www.gopaintshoppro.co.uk

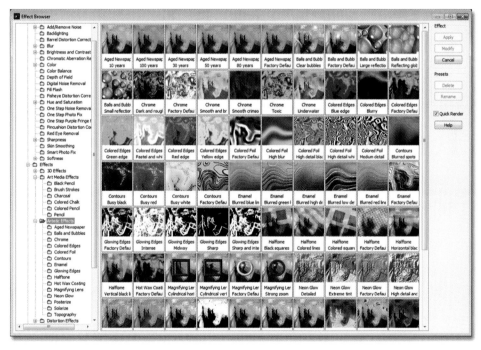

FIG 8.17 This is what the Filter Effect Browser looks like. You can make it display a thumbnail of every filter in PaintShop Pro, or you can be a bit more specific by choosing filters from individual subsets. Double-click the window that you like the look of to apply that filter to an image.

Most of PaintShop Pro's filters are subdivided into types under the Effects menu. These include:

- 3D Effects
- Art Media Effects
- Artistic Effects
- Distortion Effects
- Edge Effects
- Geometric Effects
- Illumination Effects
- Image Effects
- Photo Effects
- Reflection Effects
- Texture Effects
- User Defined.

The User Defined Filter opens a dialog box where you can enter parameters to define your own filter. It's not very easy to work out though and I'm not going to say any more about it here, but feel free to experiment.

You'll also find more filters under the Adjust menu. These include:

- Add/Remove Noise
- Blur
- Sharpness
- Softness
- Red-eye Removal

There's also a filter Effects Browser which previews all the filter effects as thumbnails so that if you've no idea what to use, you can make an educated, illustrated guess.

Tip

If you hit on a filter effect that works really well, save it as a preset that you can later apply to other images with a single click. Click the Save Preset button (the disk icon) at the top of the Filter dialog box.

Each filter sub-folder contains effects that can be applied to any picture globally, to a layer in that document or to a specific selection. For example, Art Media filter effects include: 'Black Pencil', 'Brush Strokes', 'Charcoal', 'Colored Chalk', 'Colored Pencil' and 'Pencil'. Select any of these and the dialog that appears offers further refinements to the filter action. Some are quite basic while others have a range of controls.

The Effects browser is the best way to check out all of the available filters. But PaintShop Pro X5 introduced another feature called the Instant Effects palette, if you're working with PaintShop Pro X5 or X6 you can find out more about the Instant Effects palette below.

The Instant Effects Palette

The Instant Effects palette contains thumbnails showing preset effects available in PaintShop Pro X5 and X6 organized into categories. It appears by default in the Adjust workspace, if you want to display it in either of the other workspaces just select View > Palettes > Instant Effects or press Shift F2.

You won't find the effects shown in the Instant Effects palette in the Effects Browser or the Effects menu. That's because they are presets, applications of those filters using specific settings that have been saved. These effects would ordinarily take you a while to create, experimenting with the settings in the various individual effects until you find something that works. Here, the hard work has been done for you and you can apply the effects 'instantly' with no messing around. To apply one of the effects from the Instant Effects palette, just double-click its thumbnail.

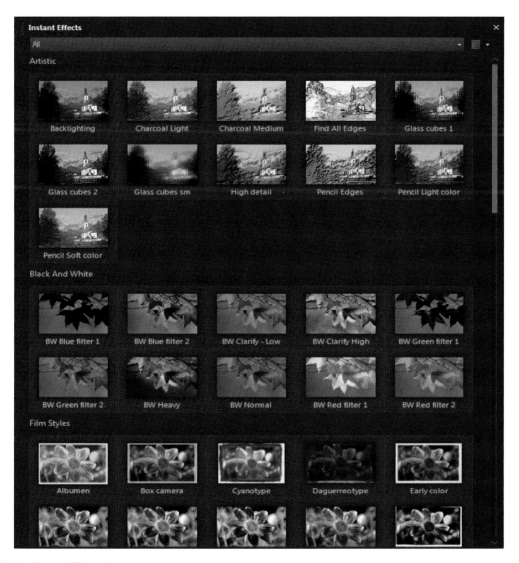

FIG 8.18   The Instant Effects palette.

When you create and save your own presets they are added to the Instant Effects palette in the User Defined category. I'll explain how that works shortly, for now to apply an effect just double-click it. If you don't like the result, just press Ctrl-z to undo it and try another. As I've said, instant effects are arranged in categories, there are Artistic effects, ones for black and white conversions, film styles, those designed for landscapes and portraiture, and so on. If you don't want to scroll through them all you can display a single category by selecting it from the pull-down menu at the top of the palette.

As you make use of the Instant Effects palette, you'll notice that your most recently used instant effects are added to their own category called, strangely enough, 'Recently used', at the top of the palette. There's another group right at the bottom of the Instant Effects palette that's influenced by the filters you use called 'User Defined'. Scroll down to the bottom of the palette, or select it from the Instant Effects palette category pull-down menu and you'll see that, unless you've previously created your own filter presets, it's currently empty.

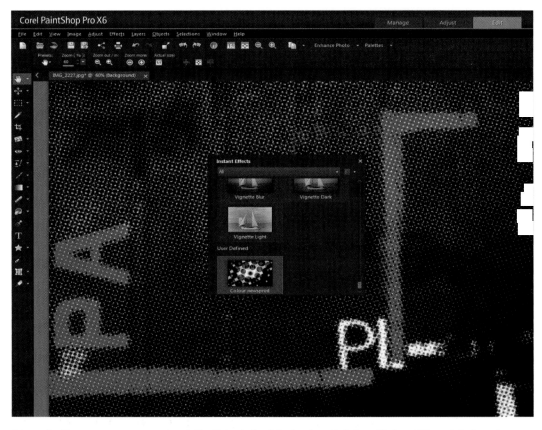

FIG 8.19 Any filters you save as presets are automatically added to the User Defined section at the bottom of the Instant Effects palette. Remember though, you have to exit and restart PaintShop Pro X6 before they appear.

With a photo open in the Edit workspace, choose one of the filters from the Effects menu, for the example in Fig 8.19 I've used the Halftone effect (Effects > Artistic Effects > Halftone) and altered the settings to produce the effect I'm looking for. Next click the disk icon on the effect preview window to save the effect you've just created as a preset and click OK to save it. Now that this effect is saved as a preset you can apply it at any time just by selecting it from the preset pull-down menu in the dialog box for the Halftone effect. But there's an even easier way.

Now that the effect is saved, hit the cancel button to exit the effect dialog box without applying it to the image. If you take a look in the User Defined section of the Instant Effects palette (press shift-F2 to display the Instant Effects palette in the Edit workspace) you'll see it's still empty, or at least it doesn't contain your new preset. To get it to appear you'll first have to shut down PaintShop Pro and restart it. Not an ideal state of affairs, but the Instant Effects palette is populated from the scripts that produce the effects when you start the program, so there's currently no way around it. With the program restarted, you'll see you're new preset thumbnail in the User Defined section of the Instant effects palette. Now all you have to do to apply your new effect preset to any currently open photo is double-click it.

Using Plug-ins

The last item on the Effects menu is Plug-ins and this lists any third-party plug-ins you may have installed. Plug-ins are a great way to add to PaintShop Pro's features and there's a wide range available including lots of special effects. If you register your copy of PaintShop Pro with Corel, you can get a Free copy of the KPT Collection of filter effects. And if you bought PaintShop Pro X6 Ultimate, that includes two plug-in filters, Perfectly Clear by Athentech Imaging and Reallusion FaceFilter 3.

To install any of these plug-ins, you simply run the installer which places the files needed for the plug-in in the appropriate folder. To find out where that is select File > Preferences > File Locations and select Plug-ins from the list on the left. Note that plug-ins and their location are specific to the 32- and 64-bit versions of PaintShop Pro. Some plug-ins are designed to work with the newer 64-bit version of the program, others will only work with the 32-bit version of PaintShop Pro. So it's important to install the right version. Some vendors, Like Athentech, mentioned above provide plug-ins for both versions of PaintShop Pro which are automatically installed. So if you've bought PaintShop Pro Ultimate and installed Perfectly Clear, it'll appear in both the 32- and 64-bit versions of PaintShop Pro X6. The KPT collection on the other hand is 32-bit only.

Why is it worth knowing where your plug-ins are located? Because not all of them have installers, but instead are supplied as .8bf files which you need to drop straight into your plug-ins folder (the right plug-ins folder, remember, there are different ones for 32- and 64-bit plug-ins). Once any plug-in is installed, whatever the method, it'll appear at the bottom of the Effects menu.

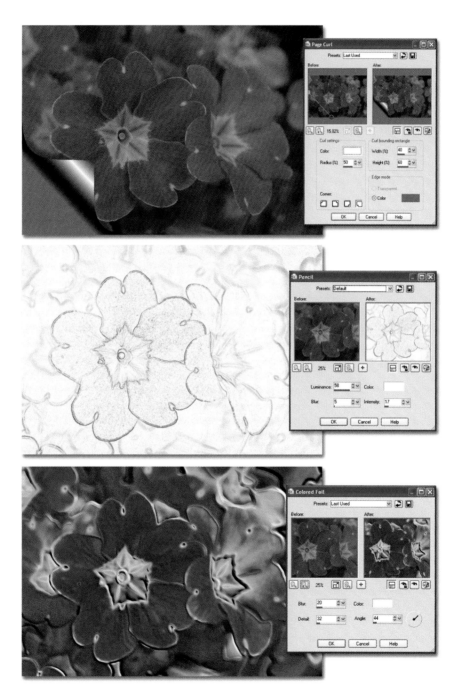

FIG 8.20 Top: Page Curl. Middle: Pencil. Bottom: Colored Foil.

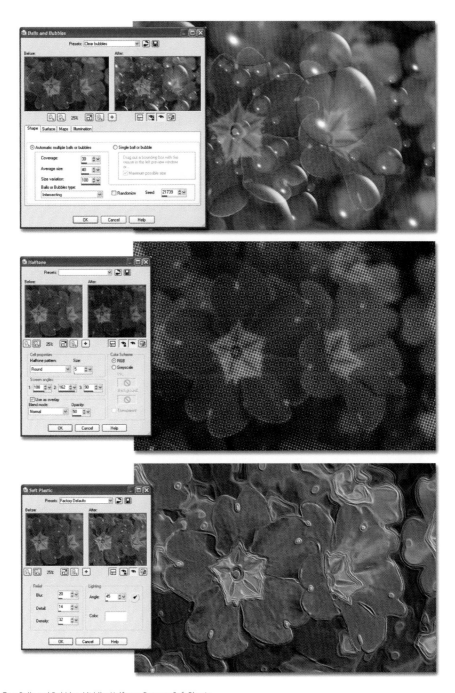

FIG 8.21 Top: Balls and Bubbles. Middle: Halftone. Bottom: Soft Plastic.

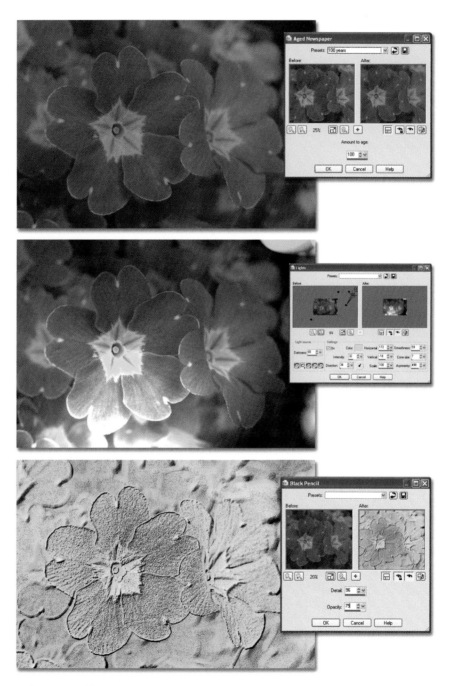

FIG 8.22 Top: Aged Newspaper. Middle: Lights. Bottom: Black Pencil.

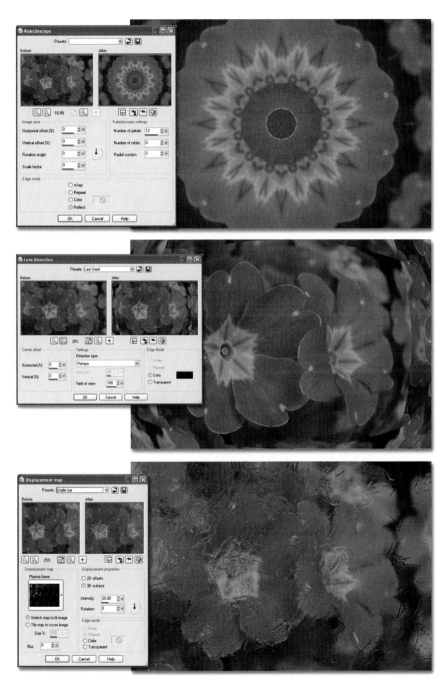

FIG 8.23 Top: Kaleidoscope. Middle: Lens Distortion. Bottom: Displacement.

Adding Lighting Effects

PaintShop Pro has a very powerful feature that allows you to add real studio lighting-type effects after the shot has been taken. It's a pretty cool filter-type effect that, when used with care, can add depth to an otherwise flat or lackluster picture. You'll find it on the Effects menu – Effects > Illumination Effects > Lights.

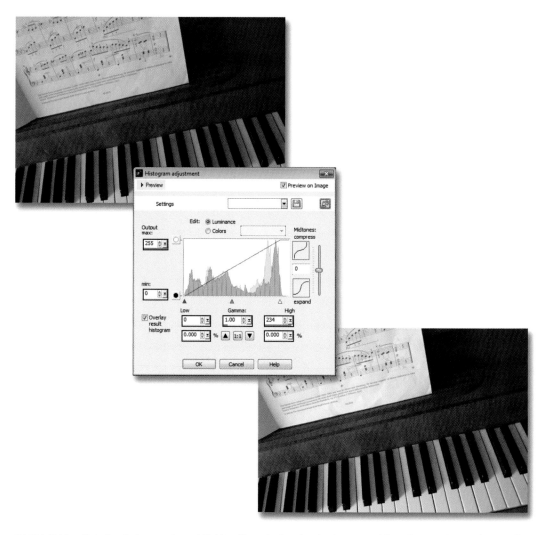

FIG 8.24 Lighting effects allow the image-maker to add lighting effect to the shot after it has been captured. This is done via a clever combination of directional contrast and brightness enhancements, simulating the effect of a floodlight or a spotlight. Though you should never use this as a substitute for shooting a frame properly, the addition of a lighting effect like the ones seen here can make or break a picture that is not as strong as it possibly could be. The first step is to use the Histogram Adjustment dialog to improve the tones and contrast in the photo.

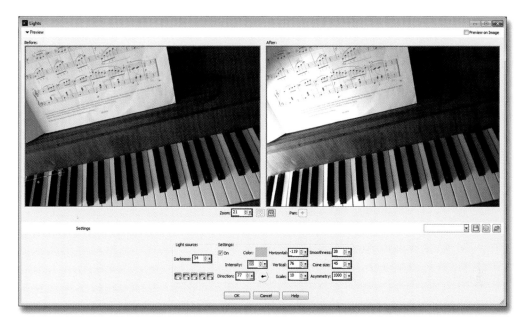

FIG 8.25 The Lights dialog box displays a before and after preview. Drag the lights in the 'before' thumbnail to position them and alter their 'cone size' – narrower angles produce a spotlight effect, broader angles a more diffuse style of light. There are five lights in all, but two, or at most three, will be adequate; uncheck the 'on' box to turn unwanted lights off. Here, I've used a spotlight (cone size 11) to illuminate the keyboard from a low angle and a more diffuse light above for the sheet music. You need to be careful not to overdo the intensity and create 'blown' highlights with no detail. Often, the best way to avoid this and produce creative lighting setups is to position the lights outside the image shining onto it.

PaintShop Pro offers several light sources, exactly as you'd have in a real photo studio. Click on one and you'll be able to edit its behavior – widening or narrowing the spread of light has the effect of increasing or spreading the flood of light onto the picture. A narrow beam intensifies the concentration of added light, so take care not to 'overdo' this; otherwise, you'll end up adding overblown highlights that take away from the subject matter. A little, in this case, will always produce a better result. The great thing about this tool is that its five light sources are infinitely adjustable. If you only need one or two lights, switch the others off by lowering their intensities to a zero value. Take care though, because you might end up spending a lot of time moving the 'lights' around the studio floor (i.e. the canvas). Keeping it simple will produce realistic and genuine improvements to any picture.

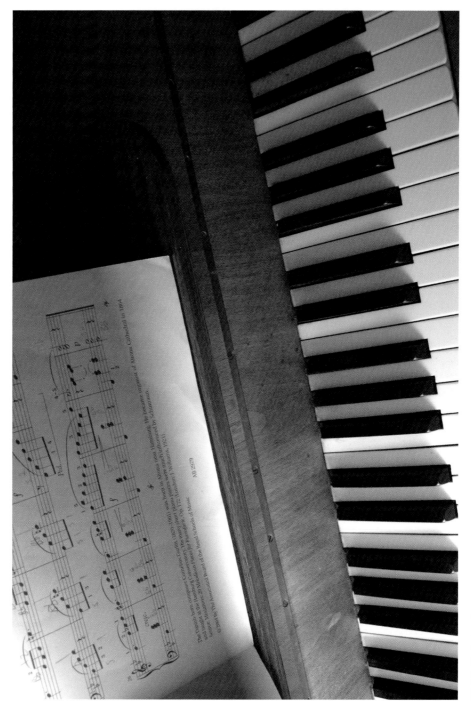

FIG 8.26 The final result.

Step-by-Step Projects

Creating Realistic Depth Effects Using Displacement Maps

The displacement map effect was introduced in PaintShop Pro 9. Displacement maps have been a feature of that other professional image-editing application (OK, Photoshop!) for some time, but even professionals are often at a loss to know what to do with this effect. This is a shame, because you can use displacement maps to create amazingly realistic 3D overlay effects.

Let's say, for example, you want to overlay some type on a heavily textured background – a brick wall, or a rocky cliff face – but you want it to look like it's been painted on, following the contours of the surface below, rather than floating on top the way a normal text layer would. Displacement maps allow you to do just that.

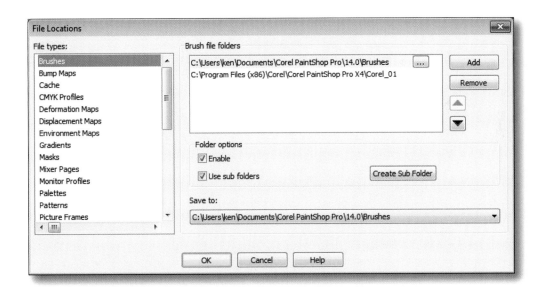

STEP 1 Open the base image (the rock face, or your own textured backdrop) in PaintShop Pro and resave it as a copy (File > Save Copy As) into the folder containing PaintShop Pro's displacement maps. To find out the location of the displacement maps folder choose File > Preferences > File Locations.

STEP 2 Add the type, the bigger and bolder the better. Here, I've added two layers, so that the number 'X' can be sized and positioned independently. Right-click the Type layers in the Layers palette and select Duplicate from the contextual menu.

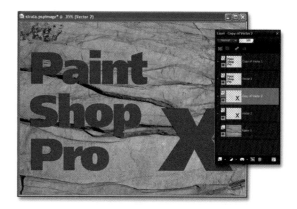

STEP 3 Select the duplicated Type layer in the Layer palette and choose Convert to Raster Layer from the Layers menu. If you used more than one Type layer, turn all the other layers off by clicking their Layer Visibility button (eye icon) in the Layers palette and choose Layers > Merge > Merge Visible to combine them. Double-click the merged layer and rename it 'Type' in the Layer Properties dialog box.

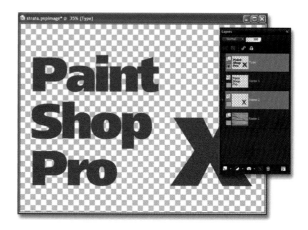

STEP 4 Turn the background layer back on, make sure the Type layer is selected and choose Effects > Distortion Effects > Displacement map. Click the Displacement Map button underneath the 'before' thumbnail, make sure All is selected from the category pull-down menu and locate the copy image you saved in Step 1.

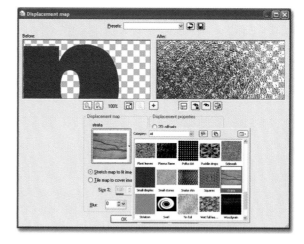

STEP 5 You should now see the type deform in the preview window. The displacement map moves pixels in the target image depending on the value of corresponding pixels in the map. There are two buttons in the Displacement Map pane that allow you to stretch or tile the map, but our map is the same image, and therefore, the same size as the target, so we don't need to bother with these.

Tip

You can use the background from the current image as a displacement map if you turn off visibility for all the other layers. But make sure you have the (invisible) Type layer selected before you apply the displacement effect.

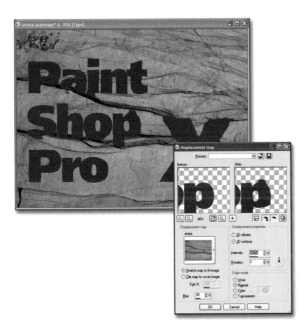

Tip

Sometimes you can get a more realistic overlay effect by switching the layers around and placing the Background layer on top of the Type layer and choosing an appropriate Blend mode. You'll need to promote the background layer to a full layer to do this.

STEP 6 In all likelihood, the default settings won't produce a satisfactory distortion; there will either be too little or too much. There are two ways to control this. First, click the 3D Surface radio button in the Displacement Properties pane and change the intensity. The Displacement Map dialog box only shows the Type layer. If you want to see the effect overlaid on your background image click the Proof button (the eye icon). Clicking the Auto Proof button will update the proof each time you make a change, but this can be quite time-consuming, especially with larger images.

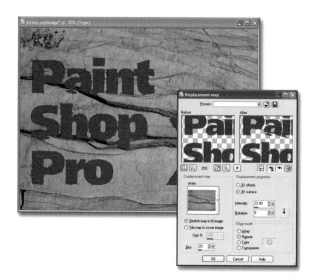

STEP 7 Generally, it's sufficient for the type to deform along the larger cracks and fissures in our background image, but ordinarily every little detail would produce unwanted distortions. The effect of the finer detail can be reduced by blurring the image. Drag the Blur slider until only the edges of the type are deformed and appear to be following the contours of the background image. Using trial-and-error, find the best combination of Blur and Intensity and, when you're happy with the result, click OK.

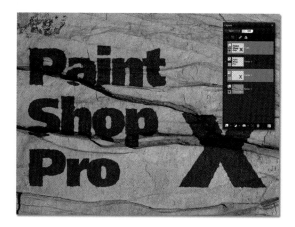

STEP 8 The type is now following the contours of the rock, but it doesn't look painted on and has an unnaturally flat look. Real paint would show through some of the rock texture and detail. You can create this effect using a Layer Blend mode; here I've set the Blend mode for the Type layer to Burn. Hard Light, Color and Multiply are also worth trying – different images require different approaches. Sometimes, reducing the layer opacity helps heighten the realism of the effect.

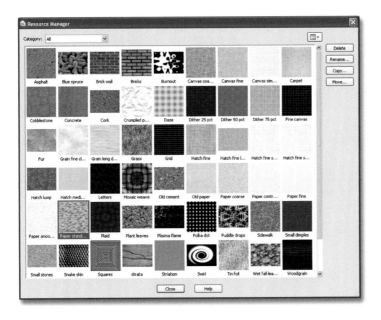

STEP 9 PaintShop Pro X6 has an assortment of ready-made displacement maps, including geometric patterns and texture photos which you can use to distort images. You can also make your own – save them in the Displacement Map folder or use the File Locations button on the Displacement Map dialog box to add a folder of displacement maps. Greyscale images work best. Mid-grey pixels produce least distortion; black and white pixels distort pixels in the target image the most.

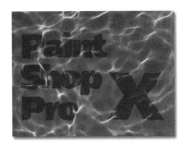

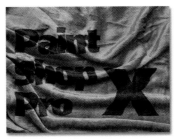

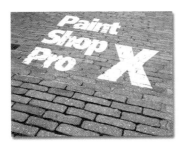

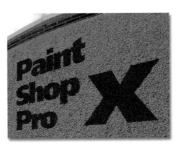

STEP 10 This technique can be used to apply all kinds of images to all kinds of surfaces. You can use it for lighting effects – to make a laser beam deform as it passes over objects; to produce realistic shadow effects; and to superimpose designs onto all kinds of backgrounds from crumpled material to water.

How to Create a Picture Tube File

PaintShop Pro's Picture Tube tool is one of the weirdest around. What does it do? The Picture Tube literally 'pours' pictures out of a tube onto the canvas.

Using graphics and photos as 'liquid paint' rather than flat color is an interesting concept, but it's one of those esoteric type tools that's almost impossible to find a proper use for. Unless, of course, you create your own specific Picture Tube files.

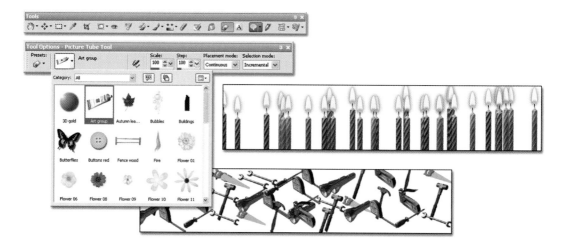

Use the Picture Tube to have fun, create borders and even to decorate artwork destined for the inkjet printer.

Picture Tube applications:

- Creating fun effects.
- Cool edges and borders for pictures.
- Making unusual picture frame effects.
- Entertaining your kids (and yourself).
- Creating textured backgrounds.
- Adding specific, custom views to a picture (such as image grain, noise and even textures).

STEP 1 Open the pictures chosen to be in the set, ensuring that they are dust-free and clear from JPEG artifacts (use PaintShop Pro's JPEG Artifact Removal filter to do this). Ensure that all pictures are a similar resolution and physical dimension.

STEP 2 Create a new document ('File > New') with a transparent background to accommodate the picture elements. For example, if you are making a four-image Picture Tube, set the fields to 800 pixels wide and 200 high. Choose 'Transparent' as the background color and then click 'OK'.

STEP 3 Open PaintShop Pro's Rulers palette ('View > Rulers') and drag the guideline to the 200 pixel mark. Drag another to the 400 pixel mark and a third to the 600 pixel mark.

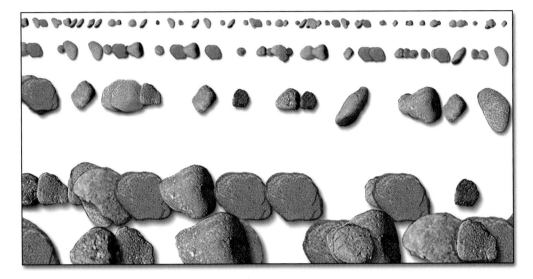

The Picture Tube icons can be of different sizes and randomness. Shift-clicking creates a point-to-point straight line.

STEP 4 You should now have a document with a transparent background (a checkbox pattern indicates transparency) with colored grid lines dividing a long, wide frame into four sections. Copy and paste (Edit > Paste as New Layer) the four pictures into this document. At this stage, it's a good idea to save a copy of the file in case the resulting tube is no good. Give it a unique name and save it as a '.pspimage' (layered) file for later use.

STEP 5 Merge all the layers ('Layers > Merge Visible') that PaintShop Pro has created (don't flatten this as it will produce a default background color which is not required at this stage). Once merged, the four pictures should be sitting on a single layer that has a transparent background.

STEP 6 Select 'File > Export > Picture Tube' and another dialog opens. Enter the amount of cells that you have made for the tube (in this case, four). Make a unique name for the tube and click 'OK'. To test the tube, create a new document with a white background (any size and resolution will suffice) and select the Picture Tube tool. Open its Options palette and, after pressing the Image Selection tab, scroll through the preset tube files to find your alphabetically placed file. Select this and paint away to test the tube.

> **Tip**
>
> In the Picture Tube Tool Options palette, you can control the scale of the Picture Tube elements, the frequency of their placement and selection modes (how they are placed from the file).

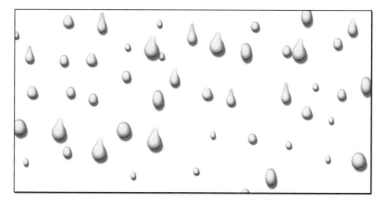

By setting the randomness to a high value and reducing the frequency, you can use the tube to paint individual objects one at a time over the canvas.

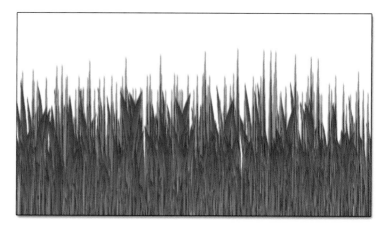

You can use the tube to create cartoon-like effects. Download new tubes from the Corel website's community page.

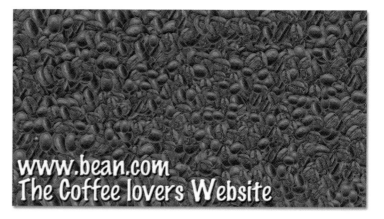

Another use for the tube is to create backgrounds If necessary, lower the opacity on the layer, so that text can be read more clearly over the top.

You'll soon discover whether the selections you made, the scale of the images and their colors are attractive or not. If you are not happy with the result it's simple enough to open the '.pspimage' version again, make changes, save it over the previous tube file and try again.

While a few photo-purists might swear at the Picture Tube, there are still a heap of devotees that swear by it. So many that there are entire websites dedicated to its use, offering loads of free tubes. Start by visiting Corel's site for further resources and downloads at www.corel.com.

Adding Edge and Framing Effects

PaintShop Pro gives you the power to not only add frames to any picture you import into the program, but also to add a great range of frame edges using the Picture Frame tool.

PaintShop Pro's Picture Frame tool is fantastic, providing a great range of paint style edges (among others) that normally would take hours to create. Why use edges? Photographers live in a rectangular world, so it is great that we can now change that to recreate the look of a painted or sketched edge, film, crayon, and heaps more edges. If you habitually work with the program's specialist filter effects, you'll find this extremely useful.

STEP 1 Open the picture in the Edit workspace, choose 'Image > Picture Frame', and choose a frame or a picture edge from the dialog's many options.

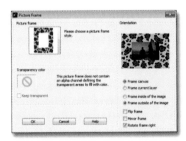

STEP 2 Once the frame dialog is open, choose a frame or edge that you like the look of and click OK to add it to the full-resolution picture. If you don't want the frame to obscure detail at the edges of your photo, check the 'Frame outside of the image' radio button.

> **Tip**
>
> If you don't want the frame to cover part of your picture, select 'Frame outside of the image' in the Picture Frame dialog box. PaintShop Pro will automatically increase the canvas to make space for the frame. This option is particularly useful with the larger frames.

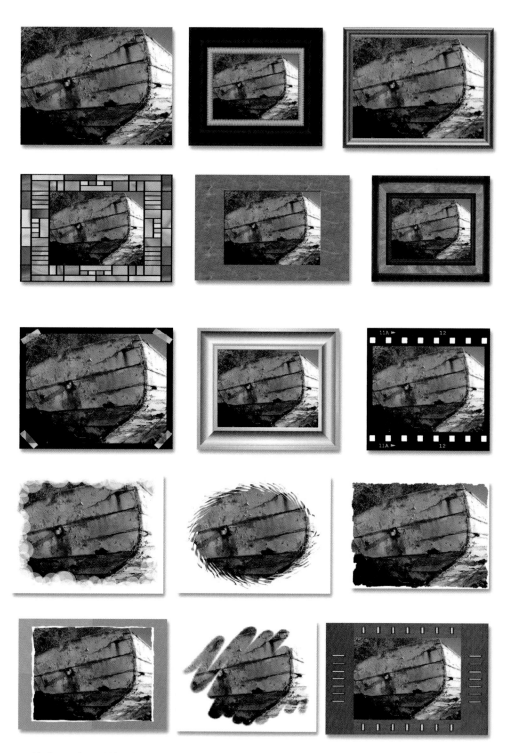

Just some of the frame styles available with PaintShop Pro's Picture Frame feature.

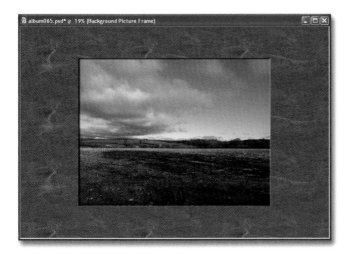
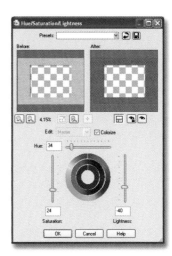

STEP 3 PaintShop Pro puts the frame on its own layer, so you can apply adjustments to the frame, leaving the photo untouched. Here, I've used the Hue/Saturation/Lightness tool to change the frame color. You could just as easily change the Layer Blend mode, transparency or apply any of the Effects filters.

Using the Color Changer Tool

Changing colors in a photo is something you'll find yourself wanting to do all the time. Whether it's someone's shirt, a front door, or a car, PaintShop Pro has the tools you need to make a neat job of it. In a previous edition of this book, I showed how you can use the Color Replacer tool to change a front door from red to green. The Color Replacer tool remains a good choice for some color-change jobs, but PaintShop Pro X6 has a tool which is much easier to use called the Color Changer tool.

One of the advantages of the Color Changer tool is that it works on the entire image. The Color Replacer tool is a brush tool – you paint over the parts of the image you want to recolor and, depending on the color of the original pixels and the tolerance setting, the pixels the brush touches are changed to the new color. The Color Replacer tool remains the best option for fiddly detail, but to change large areas of similar color in a photo the Color Changer tool is the way to go. Here's how to use it to respray your car or change the color of any other large object.

STEP 1 Right-click the Background layer in the Layers palette and select Duplicate from the context menu. You can make your changes to the duplicate layer and still have the original to fall back on if anything goes wrong. Select the color you want to change to on the Foreground color swatch in the Materials palette.

STEP 2 Select the Color Changer tool from the Flood Fill fly-out on the toolbar. There are only two settings on the Tool Options bar for the Color Changer tool – Tolerance and Edge Softness – and you'll need to experiment with both to get the results you want.

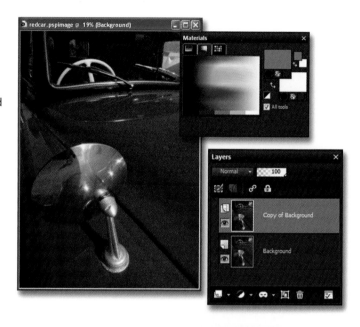

STEP 3 The Tolerance setting determines the extent of the color change. If you set a low value only pixels which closely match the color of the pixel you click on will be changed. Here I've set a Tolerance of 10 and, although there's a lot of red, only the red pixels that are very close in terms of color to the red pixel I clicked on have been changed. One great feature of the Color Changer tool is that you can adjust the tolerance after you've clicked to change pixels and the preview updates to color new pixels using the new Tolerance settings.

STEP 4 Rather than trying to get all of the red paintwork in one hit you can use the Color Changer repeatedly, clicking on different parts of the car to add to the original selection. Continue clicking with the Color Changer tool until most of the paintwork is the new color.

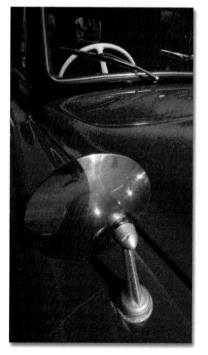

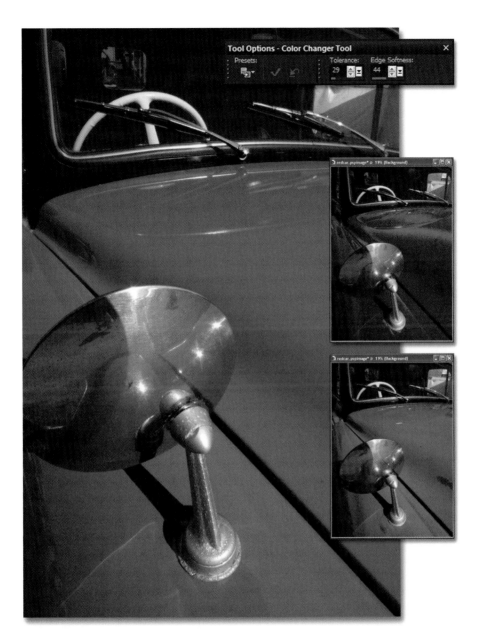

STEP 5 Incrementally increase the Tolerance setting until all of the red goes green. Incrementally increase the Edge Softness setting to produce a soft, more natural-looking edge to areas of changed color. When you're happy with the new paint job, press the Apply button to apply the color change.

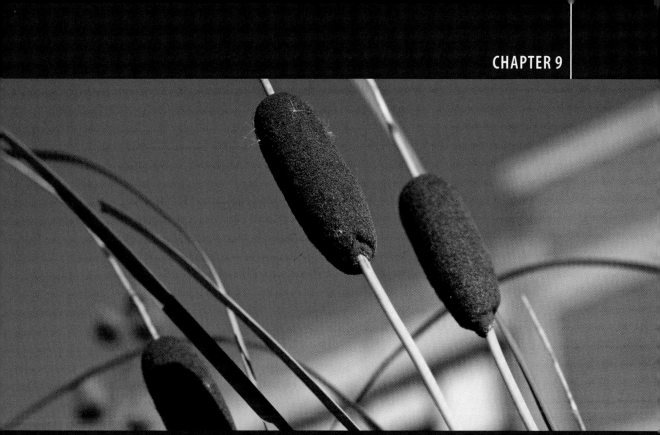

CHAPTER 9

Printing

What's Covered in this Chapter

- This chapter is short, but it contains a lot of things worth knowing if you ever want to turn your photos into real physical things that you can hold in your hand and put on your wall, rather than something you only ever see on a screen. What with web photo sharing sites, e-mail and Wi-Fi enabled electronic photo frames, most of your photos may never find their way onto paper. Believe it or not though, not everyone owns a PC and, even among those who do, there are people who will always prefer a physical printed photograph over an electronic one. Some photo competitions still insist on you sending hard copy prints and if you want to exhibit your photos or just hang them on the wall you'll need to know how to print them.
- This chapter kicks off with a discussion about resolution and how it affects print quality and if you read nothing else you should at least try and get your head around this concept as it's one of the most important factors affecting print quality.
- If you're having problems getting what comes out of your printer to match what you see on the screen you're not alone, it's one of the most common problems digital photographers face. Read the section on monitor calibration and color management to find out how to overcome the problem and stop wasting precious ink and paper.

- Another way to save on expensive consumables is to print several photos on one sheet of paper. PaintShop Pro's Print Layout application is designed to help you do just that. The step-by-step project at the end of this chapter shows you how.
- Printing can be a frustrating business because there are many factors which affect final print quality – the quality and resolution of the digital image, the type of printer, the inks and paper used, color management and printer settings. By following the advice provided here you'll be able to consistently produce the best results possible from your printer.

Image Resolution

In order to get good results when printing it's important to understand a little about image resolution. If you've bought an inkjet printer recently, one of the things that may have influenced your decision is the printer resolution. Your inkjet printer may boast a resolution of 1440 dpi or even more. Similarly if you've recently bought a digital camera, somewhere on the box, it will say 12 or 16 or maybe even 32 megapixels.

Like printer and digital camera manufacturers, makers of flatbed scanners use resolution as a selling feature – the higher the better. But what do all these numbers mean and how are they related? Perhaps more importantly, how does the number of pixels produced by a camera's sensor affect how your photos will look when they are printed?

When it comes to digital images, cameras, scanners, printers and PaintShop Pro, all deal in the same currency – pixels. The starting point with any digital image, therefore, is its size in pixels. The image in Fig 9.1 has a size of 3888 × 2592 pixels, giving a total pixel count of 10,077,696. If you view this image in PaintShop Pro at 100% magnification you would only be able to see a small part of it. As well as the number of pixels in an image, we also need to take account of the resolution, measured in pixels per inch (ppi). The resolution of most screens in use today is around 100 ppi. If you divide the pixel dimensions by the resolution, you get the physical size of the image. 3888/100=38.8 and 2592/100=25.9, so a ten megapixel photo would measure approximately 39 × 26 inches on screen at 100% magnification.

Shuffling Pixels

Open an image in PaintShop Photo Pro and select Image > Resize. The Pixel Dimensions pane in the Resize dialog box tells you the pixel dimensions of the photo, in this case 3888 × 2592 pixels. The Print Size pane shows the physical dimensions of the image at the specified resolution; at 72 ppi, this image measures 54 × 36 inches.

Click the Advanced Settings box and make sure the 'Resample using' box is unchecked and enter 144 in the resolution field; notice how the width and

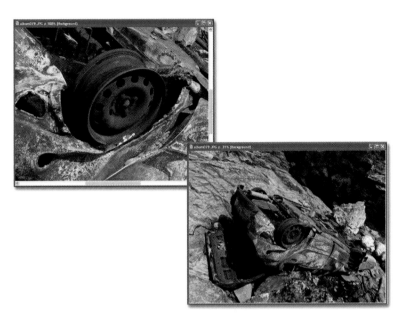

FIG 9.1 At 100% magnification, only a small part of this 2592 × 3888 pixel image is visible on screen; to see the whole thing it's necessary to reduce the magnification using Window > Fit to Window.

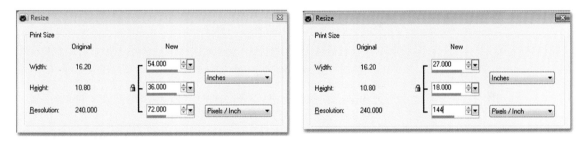

FIG 9.2 There's an inverse relationship between resolution and print output size – doubling the resolution halves the output size.

height print dimensions half when you double the resolution. If you enter 288 in the resolution field, the print size decreases again by a factor of 2. All you are doing here is rearranging the same information – the 10,077,696 image pixels – into a progressively smaller space.

There's an inverse relationship between resolution and print output size – doubling the resolution halves the output size.

On the screen at 72 ppi, the pixels are packed so closely together that you can't see them individually. But inkjet printing technology requires images of higher resolution to produce good quality results. Generally, your photos should have a minimum resolution of 200 ppi to print well.

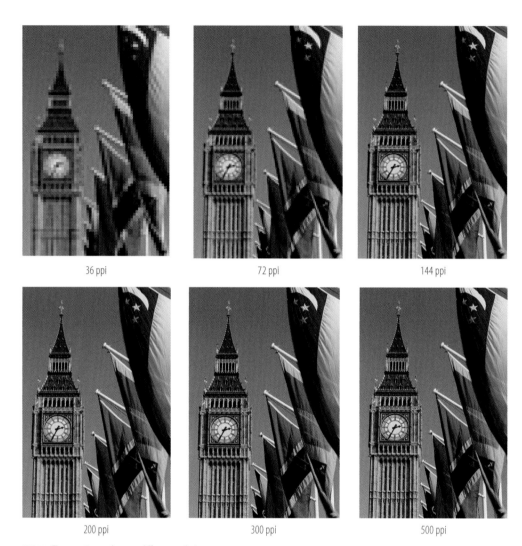

36 ppi   72 ppi   144 ppi

200 ppi   300 ppi   500 ppi

FIG 9.3 The same image shown at different resolutions.

Although the commercial printing process used for this book is technologically dissimilar to inkjet printing, these images nonetheless provide a good example of what you could expect to see if you output images at these resolutions to a desktop inkjet. At low resolutions, pixelation is clearly visible. A good quality image is produced at 200 ppi, but at higher resolutions, no improvement in picture quality is discernible. The minimum recommended resolution for the offset litho process used to print this book is 300 ppi, so you may see some improvement from the 200 ppi to the 300 ppi image above (look at the detail in the clock face), but this is unlikely to be the case with an inkjet printer. Try carrying out your own resolution tests to determine the point at which increasing the resolution produces no apparent quality improvement on your printer.

Resampling

Go back to the Resize dialog box and enter a value of 200 in the Resolution field. This gives a print size of roughly 10 × 15 inches. What if you don't want to make a print almost A3 in size? That's easy, just enter the size you want in the Width or Height box – changing one automatically changes the other to maintain the aspect ratio. Say you want to fit the photo on a 6 × 4 inch piece of photo paper, enter 4 in the Width field (for a portrait-shaped photo), and the Height field automatically changes to 6. Wait a minute, though, now our image resolution is 648 ppi, far higher than the 200 ppi required for inkjet printing. This doesn't really matter too much, and it certainly won't affect the print quality, which will be no better and no worse than at 200 ppi. It will take longer, though, for your computer to send all that data to the printer and for the printer to process it. You can speed things up by downsampling the image – removing the extra pixels that aren't required for printing at this size.

Downsampling

Check the 'Resample using' box and select either Smart Size or Bicubic from the interpolation pull-down menu. Now enter a value of 200 in the Resolution field. This time, rather than changing the physical dimensions to accommodate all the image pixels at the new resolution, PaintShop Photo Pro has done something different. It has removed pixels to produce the requested resolution at the existing size (it hasn't done it yet, but it will when you press OK). Take a look at the Pixel Dimensions pane and you'll see the new pixel dimensions are 800 × 1200. If you do the maths yourself you'll discover that this does indeed produce a 6 × 4 inch image at 200 ppi.

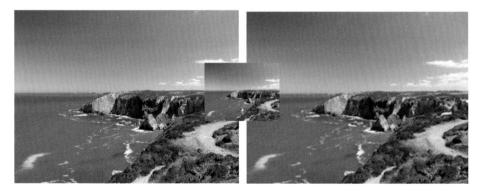

FIG 9.4a–c The photo on the left has been downsampled from an original 2560 × 1920 image to 6 × 4.5 at a resolution of 300 ppi – suitable for printing. Its pixel dimensions are now 717 × 538. The smaller middle photo was downsampled to 2 × 1.5 at 300 ppi, giving new pixel dimensions of 237 × 178. The middle photo was then upsampled to the original 6 × 4.5 size at 300 ppi. You can clearly see the loss of detail and sharpness caused by the interpolation, hardly surprising as only one-third of the pixels in this image are original. You can improve things marginally by unsharp masking, but there's no substitute for the original pixel data, so always make sure you keep originals backed up before resizing!

Removing pixels in this fashion will not affect the picture quality. This 4 × 6 inch print will be indistinguishable from one printed at 512 ppi, but you'll have it in your hand much sooner. But what if you change your mind and decide that an A3-sized print would look pretty cool after all (assuming you're lucky enough to own an A3 color inkjet printer)?

Upsampling

Open the Resize dialog box once more. (In PaintShop Pro Photo XI and earlier, when you open the Resize dialog, it applies the last-used settings to the current image. To get back to the current image size, select 'Percent' in the Pixel Dimensions units pull-down menu and enter 100 in the Width field.) Make sure the 'Resample using' box is still checked and enter the original pixel width of 2592 in the Width field (the Height box will automatically increase to 3888). Click OK and PaintShop Pro will upsample the image, taking us back where we started, right? Wrong!

Take a look at the new image and you'll notice it's not quite as sharp as it was to begin with. PaintShop Pro has added new pixels in between the existing ones to bring the image up to size. The values of these new pixels are based on those of neighboring ones using a process called 'interpolation'. Interpolated pixels are OK if you're in a fix, like you need to make a large print from a small digital file, but they are no substitute for the real thing.

So, you can take pixels out of a digital photo with no loss of quality, and this can help speed up printing, but you can't put them back without things starting to look mushy. What are the implications of this for storing and printing your digital pictures? If you follow one simple rule, you won't go wrong. Always keep a full-sized original copy of your digital photos backed up on removable media (i.e. CD or DVD). Then you can downsample your images for printing, e-mailing, uploading to the web or whatever, but if you need to make a full-sized print that requires the maximum image resolution you'll always have the original to fall back on.

Printing with Corel PaintShop Pro

Having opened the picture, make sure that the quality is the best possible and choose Print Layout from the File menu. The Print Layout dialog shows the files selected for printing in the left margin. Click 'Open Template' to view your options. The default template group is Avery. This group has over 50 templates which cover most everyday options, but you can also make your own and save them in the template library ('File > Save Template').

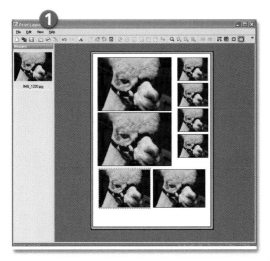

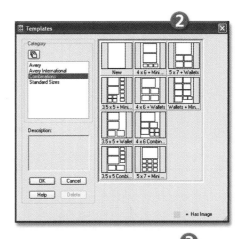

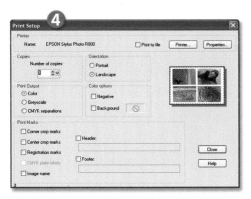

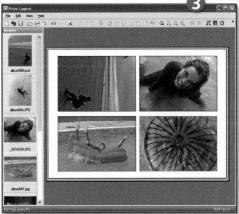

FIG 9.5 Clockwise from top left: (1) Print Layout provides an easy way to print multiple copies of the same photo, or a selection of photos on a single sheet of paper, saving you time and money. (2) A range of templates is available, including Avery standard sizes so you can, for example, produce one large print for your album, or framing, and several smaller versions to send to friends. (3) You can print multiple photos by selecting thumbnails in the Manage workspace and choosing File > Print Layout. The selected images appear in a strip on the left and are dropped in position on the template layout. (4) Click the Print Setup button to change the paper orientation and add captions (though this is better done in the Print Layout dialog box). Most of the settings here are for producing film separations for commercial printing.

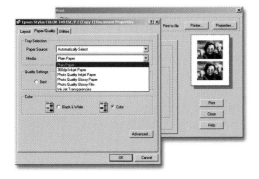

FIG 9.6 Don't forget to select the appropriate inkjet paper type. If you don't, the color may not come out as you'd hoped.

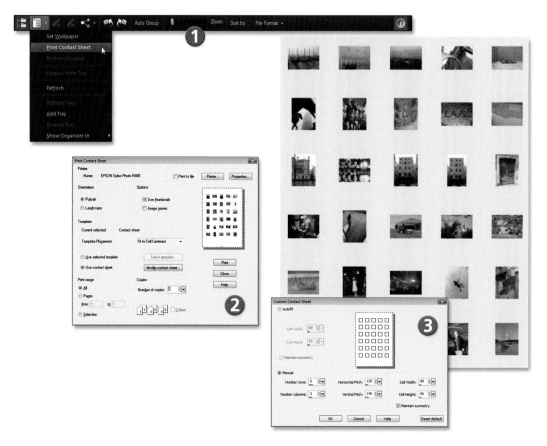

FIG 9.7 Select Print Contact Sheet from the More options menu in the Manage workspace (1) to quickly print a sheet of thumbnails for the current folder. This opens the Print Contact Sheet dialog box (2), where you can use the default template or choose another. Click the Modify Contact Sheet button to open the Custom Contact Sheet dialog box (3) and produce your own layout. Doing this with a folder containing a large number of images may take a while.

What can you use templates for?
- Creating unique contact sheets.
- Customizing for specific jobs such as cards, receipts, invitations, business cards, etc.
- For making mini-stickers.
- For creating your own business and address labels.

Color Management

If you've ever asked the question, 'why don't my prints match what I see on the computer display?', then you need to know about color management. A color management system (CMS) ensures that individual devices – digital cameras, scanners, computer monitors and printers – treat color in the same way, so that you get consistent color from one to the other.

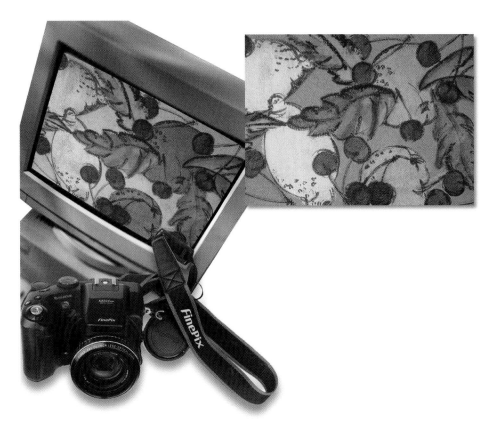

FIG 9.8 A color management system can help you avoid problems like unexpected variations in color from monitor to printer by ensuring consistent color from your digital camera to your monitor and finally to printed output.

To return to the original question, it is in fact impossible for your printer to reproduce exactly what's on your monitor as the two devices use different physical systems to produce color. The monitor transmits light using red, green and blue phosphor dots (or, in the case of an LCD panel, a fluorescent backlight passing through a colored filter) and a color print uses pigment or dye-based inks to reflect light. Color printers can use up to seven inks; even so, it is not possible for them to reproduce all the colors on your computer display. In color reproduction terms, the two devices are said to have different gamuts.

It's not just different kinds of devices that vary in the way they handle color. As anyone who has visited the TV department of a high street electrical store can verify, no two TVs look the same. A picture viewed on your PC at home will quite probably look different on your work PC, and if you e-mail it to your friends, each one of them is likely to see a slightly different version, due to the individual color characteristics of their display.

Color Profiles

To try and sort out this mess, an organization called the 'International Color Consortium' (ICC), which has as its members companies like Adobe, Apple, Agfa and Kodak, developed a system of profiling for color imaging devices. Each device has a profile which describes its color characteristics and which can be read and understood by imaging software. Windows has built-in support for ICC-compliant color management.

Using ICC profiles, a color management system can accurately convert color information from one device to another. In short, this means more accurate color from your camera to your monitor and finally out to your printer. It also means that, providing they use a CMS, what everyone else sees on their monitor is the same as what you see.

Calibration

In order for color management to work successfully, it's important that your monitor is correctly calibrated. To do this, select File > Color Management > Monitor Calibration and complete the Monitor Calibration wizard. Once your monitor is calibrated, the next step is to ensure you have profiles installed for all of your devices or at least for your monitor and printer. These should have been installed automatically when you installed the devices but it doesn't hurt to check. To find out what profile your monitor is using in Windows XP, right-click on the desktop and select Properties from the contextual menu. Click the Advanced button on the Settings tab and then the Color Management tab. In Windows Vista right-click on the desktop, select Personalize and select Display Settings. Click the Advanced Settings button, select the Color Management Tab, then click the Color Management button. For Windows 7, right-click on the desktop, select Screen resolution, click Advanced settings, select the Color Management tab, then click the Color Management button.

If your monitor profile isn't listed, click the Add button and try to find it. All Windows color profiles are stored in the folder C:\Windows\system32\spool\drivers\color. If you can't find it here, check any disks that were supplied with the monitor, or the manufacturer's website.

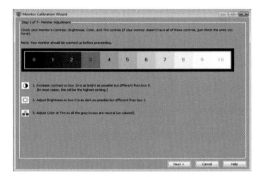

FIG 9.9 A color management system can help you avoid problems like unexpected variations in color from monitor to printer by ensuring consistent color from your digital camera to your monitor and finally to printed output. Monitor calibration is important for accurate color management. Let your monitor warm up for half an hour before running the wizard.

For your printer, select Printers and Faxes from the Start menu, right-click the printer icon, select Properties from the contextual menu and click the Color Management tab. It's not always easy to identify the correct color profile from its name. Windows should automatically assign the right profile, if it's available, though you can add it manually if necessary. As with monitor profiles, if one wasn't supplied with your printer, the best option is the manufacturer's website.

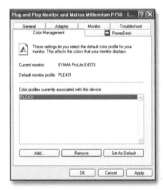 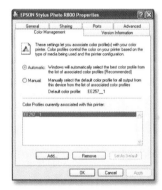

FIG 9.10 You can check the currently installed default profiles for your monitor and printer by opening the Display and Printer Properties dialog boxes.

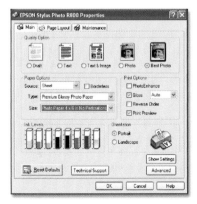 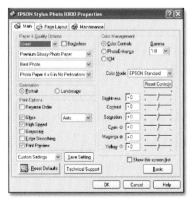

FIG 9.11 In Basic mode (left), the printer driver for the Epson Stylus Photo R800 helpfully indicates ink quantities remaining. Advanced mode (right) provides a range of color controls, but these should be avoided, if you are using color management.

Printer profiles are less straightforward than monitor profiles because they are designed to work with a specific combination of inks and paper. A profile generated for photo-quality glossy paper is unlikely to produce satisfactory results with matt paper. Furthermore, there is a wide variation in different manufacturers' paper characteristics, so a profile designed, for example, for Epson Premium Glossy Photo Paper will not provide good results with another manufacturer's glossy photo paper.

Color Management in Corel PaintShop Pro X6

PaintShop Pro X introduced support for ICC color profiles which makes getting consistent color from your monitor to your printer that much easier. To turn on color management, select File > Color Management > Color Management and check 'Enable Color Management' in the Color Management dialog box.

FIG 9.12 Use the Color Management dialog box to turn on color management and configure your display and printer profiles.

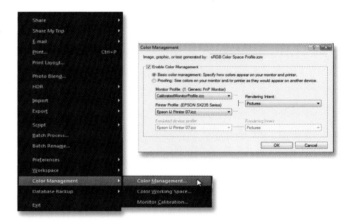

Select your monitor and printer profiles from the pull-down menus – unless you have several profiles installed there will be only one, the default profile for the device that you installed previously. That's nearly all you need to do.

If you have an image open, the color profile, if it has one, will be displayed at the top, after the message 'Image, graphic, or text generated by:'. Not all images are tagged with a profile, but if it's a photo from a digital camera, it will most likely have an embedded sRGB profile.

Don't worry if the image has no embedded profile, you will still be able to see how it is going to look when printed. All of the elements for a color-managed workflow are in place, and the color management system can correctly interpret the numbers in the profiled image and translate them for display on your monitor or printer using the profiles for those devices.

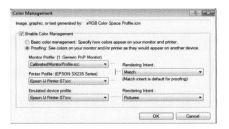

FIG 9.13 To produce a 'soft proof' – an on-screen view that accurately simulates output from your printer – check the Proofing radio button and select your printer profile from the 'Emulated device profile' pull-down menu.

Despite all of this, for the reasons explained earlier, it's still not possible for the image displayed on your monitor to match your printer. But, PaintShop Photo Pro can show you on screen what an image will look like when printed on your desktop color inkjet, or any other printer for which you have a profile. This is called 'soft proofing' as opposed to 'hard proofing' which involves making a hard copy print.

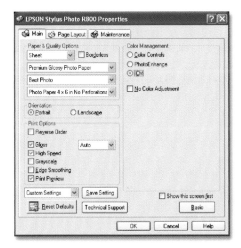

FIG 9.14 Click the ICM checkbox to enable color management using the currently installed default printer profile.

To display a soft proof on your monitor, open the Color Management dialog box and check the radio button labeled 'Proofing'. To see colors on your monitor and/or printer as they would appear on another device, select your printer in the 'Emulated device profile' pull-down menu and click OK to view the proof.

Printing Using Color Management

How your Print dialog box looks will depend on the printer you are using and the driver software. The examples shown here use the Epson Stylus Photo R800 printer, but other printer drivers will provide similar options. First, make sure your image is the correct size and resolution for printing on your chosen paper as described earlier in this chapter. Select File > Print and click the Properties button on the Print dialog box.

The Stylus Photo R800 driver provides Basic and Advanced options. It also provides an extremely useful graphical representation of the ink levels. Click the Advanced button and select the paper type, size, orientation and other print options.

On the right-hand side of the dialog box, you'll find the Color Management settings. In Color Controls mode, you can alter the brightness, contrast, saturation and color balance of the print output using the slider controls. Only use these controls if you don't want to use color management. PhotoEnhance mode allows you to apply a number of effects to the printed output, including monochrome and sepia toning and soft focus, canvas and parchment texture effects.

The button we are interested in is the one marked 'ICM'. Click this and the driver will use the color management system to correctly interpret and print the colors in the image. Once you click the ICM button in the Epson R800 printer driver dialog box, the other color controls disappear as you won't be needing them. Don't check the No Color Adjustment box, as this is intended for use where the conversion to the printer color space has already been made in the image-editing software. There's a save button that lets you save this configuration. I'd recommend you use it as it's easy to miss just one thing if you have to do all this manually each time you print.

No Profile?

If you can't get a color profile for your printer and ink/paper combination, there are three options available to you. You can pay a company to produce a profile for your individual setup. The way this works is that the company supplies you with a set of images composed of color swatches which you print out and return to them. They then analyze these using sophisticated spectrophotometry equipment and produce a profile based on the results. This kind of profiling is very accurate, because it is tailor-made for your specific printer, paper and inks, as opposed to a generic profile. One company that produces printer profiles is Chromix (www.chromix.com). These services aren't cheap, but if accurate color is important to you, and certainly if you are producing images for commercial use, they are well worth the cost.

The second option is to produce your own color profiles using a device such as the Datacolor Spyder 4 or the X-rite ColorMunki Smile. These are spectrophotometer devices that you connect to the front of your monitor, so that they can take readings and compile a profile. These monitor profiling devices used to be the expensive preserve of imaging professionals but are now very affordable.

If you are making prints for personal use and can't justify the cost of a profiling service or dedicated hardware, you can make your own printer adjustments. As I said at the beginning of this chapter, you will never get your printer to emulate exactly what you see on your monitor (even professional setups have to content themselves with soft-proofing – getting the monitor to show what the print will look like), but you should be able to improve an existing unsatisfactory setup.

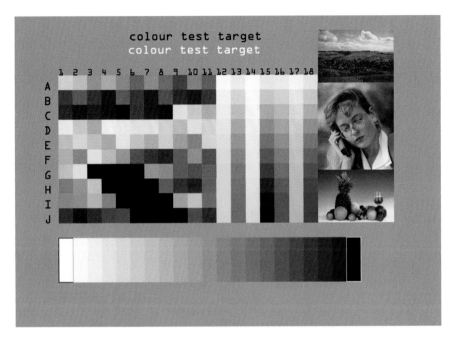

FIG 9.15 Use a target such as this one to compare printed output with what's on your screen.

You can do this in one of two ways. Either use the printer driver's color adjustment controls to alter the color balance or use PaintShop Photo Pro's Adjustment layers to make temporary adjustments prior to printing. In either case, you will need to compare printed output to what is on your screen and for this you should use a test calibration image that displays a wide range of colors, including naturally occurring hues like sky, foliage and skin tones. Professionals use specially designed color targets for this, but you can easily create your own, like the one pictured here. If you haven't got time to make your own, you can download this target image from www.gopaintshoppro.co.uk/test-target.html

Step-by-Step Projects

Printing Multiple Photos with Print Layout

Print Layout is a straightforward layout application that you can use to make multiple prints on an inkjet printer, saving time and money. Using Print Layout, you can print several copies of one photo on a single A4 sheet of paper, cut them up and send them to friends and family. You can print out multiple photos for passport or driving license applications, or you can use Print Layout to arrange different images on the same page for quick and convenient printing. There is a range of templates which you can adapt to fit your own needs and save for future use.

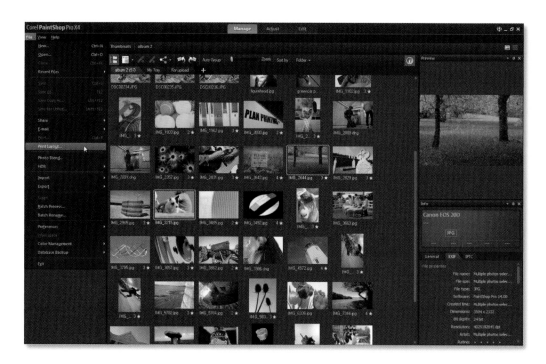

STEP 1 We're going to use Print Layout to print a selection of photos onto template pages. Select the images you want to print in the Manage workspace and select File > Print Layout. The photos you selected appear in the Images window on the left. The default Template is 21.59 × 27.94 cm. Drag the images to the layout window and size and position them.

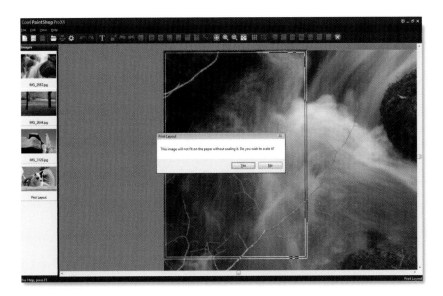

STEP 2 If the images exceed the size of the template, you will get an alert box telling you they won't fit and asking if you want to resize them. This can happen if you have not resized your image. Click OK and they will be scaled to fit the width of the default template. Drag a corner handle to make them smaller – the proportions are automatically retained so you don't need to worry about stretching or squeezing them.

STEP 3 Don't worry too much about neatly laying everything out at this stage, just get the pictures in the layout window at roughly the size you want them. If you want to get four pictures on a template, make them slightly smaller than a quarter of the page size to allow a border around them.

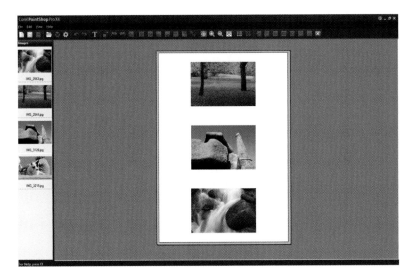

Tip

If you're printing multiple images on a page for cutting out, it helps to minimize wastage if you sort your photos into landscape and portrait format and print only one kind at a time. Don't mix landscape and portrait format photos on the same layout.

STEP 4 You can position the images manually, but Print Layout has a few auto positioning features to help out. The four buttons in the center of the toolbar will position an image in any of the four corners of the page or dead center. To the left of these, you'll find the Auto Positioning button. Roughly arrange your images on the page, click the Auto Arrange button and they will be automatically sized and positioned for the best fit.

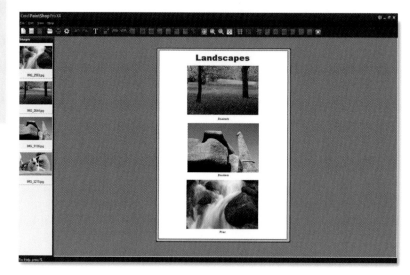

STEP 5 Manually arranging images like this is the best way to create poster layouts. Use the Text tool to add a headline at the top of the page and to put a caption under each image.

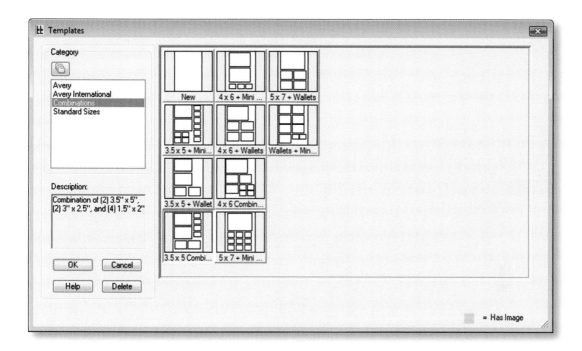

STEP 6 To choose a template layout, click the Open Template button on the toolbar or select File > Open Template. Select a category, click on one of the template thumbnails and click OK. This will replace your previous layout so, if you want to keep it, save it first using File > Save Template.

STEP 7 To add photos to the template, just drag and drop them from the Images window onto the 'cells' in the template. If the image isn't an exact fit, you can drag a corner handle to resize it and drag it around within the rectangle to change the crop, or click the Fill Cell with Image button; there are buttons to help with this on the right of the toolbar.

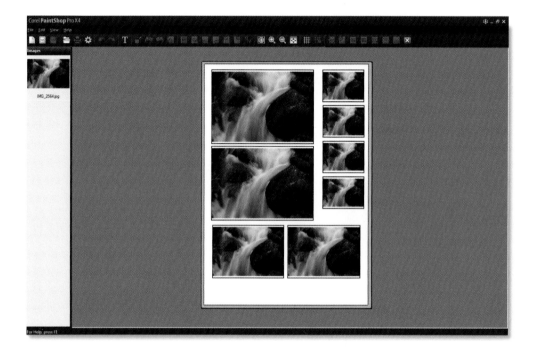

STEP 8 If you are making a page that contains only one image, click the Fill Template with Image button to copy the image to every cell on the template. Otherwise, drag the remaining images into position and resize them. Right-click on any of the images and select 'Apply placement to all cells' to have the positional changes you make to one image automatically applied to all of the others.

STEP 9 Add captions using the Text tool and click the Print button on the toolbar, or select File > Print to print the page.

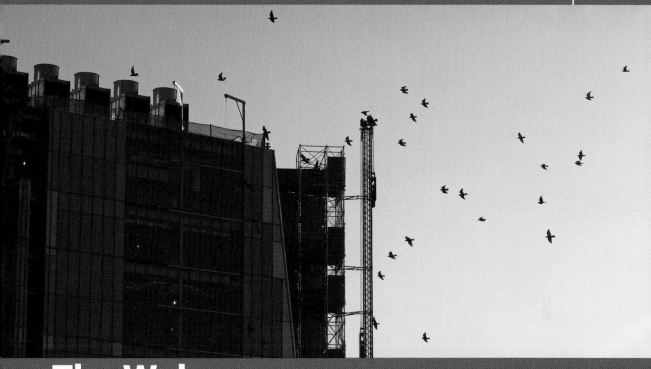

CHAPTER 10

The Web
Sharing Images

What's Covered in this Chapter

- In this chapter, you'll discover how to produce pictures for the web. Whether you want to share images on social networking sites like Facebook and Flickr, to produce a decent photo of your old camera to put on eBay, to e-mail a few snaps to friends, or if you have something more ambitious in mind like an entire website, the following pages will tell you everything you need to know.
- If you're not sure of the difference between GIFs and JPEGs and PNGs and when and how to make use of the different web image file formats then read through the opening pages. Experiment with Paint Shop Pro's GIF and JPEG Optimizers, try to reproduce some of the examples shown here and you'll soon understand what optimization is all about.
- In these days of fast broadband connections, it's tempting to think that file size doesn't matter, but even a broadband link can sometimes slow to a crawl. If your site downloads in a flash, regardless of connection speeds, you'll get and keep your visitors' interest.

- In the step-by-step projects at the end of this chapter you'll learn how to add a visible watermark to your photos and how to use PaintShop Pro's enhanced sharing features to upload photos to Facebook, Flickr, and Google Plus.

Sharing Photos on the Web

PaintShop Pro X6 allows you to upload and share your photos on Facebook, Flickr and Google Plus. Obviously, you'll need an account on those networks, but if you're part of the dwindling minority yet to have discovered social networking, here's the opportunity you've been waiting for.

These new upload features are pretty basic – they'll allow you to upload a bunch of photos, but that's about it, and they have some shortcomings which I'll discuss as well as looking at ways to overcome them.

Uploading Photos to Flickr

If you want to upload your photos directly to Flickr, you first need to authorize PaintShop Pro X6 for access to your Flickr account. This happens automatically the first time you attempt an upload. First though, you'll need to select the photos you want to upload and the easiest way to do this is in Thumbnail mode in the Manage workspace. One way to do it is to organize all the photos you want to upload into a tray. Click the New tray + button at the top of the Organizer (if it isn't visible, click the down chevron on the right end of the Organizer toolbar and check Tray) and give the tray a name. Select the folder containing the images you want to upload in the Navigation palette (ctrl-click to add to your selections), then drag them to the tab of your new tray and drop them in.

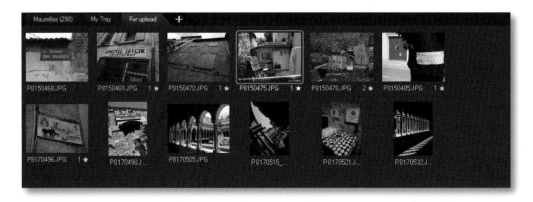

FIG 10.1 Organize all the photos you want to upload into a tray, Click on one thumbnail then press Ctrl-A to select all. Create a new tray and drag the images to its tab.

With the contents of the New tray visible in the Organizer, press Ctrl-A to select all, then click the Share button on the Organizer toolbar and choose Flickr from the menu. A window like the one in figure 10.2 will appear, enter your Yahoo login details and click the Sign In button. Next, you'll be asked by Flickr to authorize PaintShop Pro to access your Flickr account and upload, edit and delete photos, click OK to agree to this and the Social Sharing window, shown in figure 10.3, will appear with your selected photos ready to upload. In future, you'll come straight to this without having to go through the login and authorization screens.

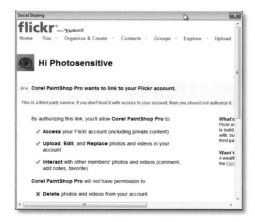

FIG 10.2   The first time you upload photos to Flickr, you'll be asked to authorize PaintShop Pro to access your Flickr account. You can later withdraw the authorization if you decide you no longer want to use PaintShop Pro to upload photos to Flickr.

The save to Album pull-down should list all of your Flickr sets (for some reason Corel likes to call Flickr sets albums, instead of giving them their proper name) but only your public sets are shown here. If you have sets containing photos that are private (viewable only by yourself, friends and family), they won't appear in this list.

That leads us to a more serious privacy issue with the PaintShop Pro X6 Flickr uploader – you can't set privacy preferences. Any and all photos you upload to Flickr from PaintShop Pro X6 will, at least initially, be public. Once your photos are uploaded, you can visit your photostream in your web browser and edit the privacy settings (fortunately Flickr makes this easy and I'll show you how to do it in a moment). This applies to Facebook and Google plus as well.

In the meantime, the best you can do is upload your photos, then immediately change the permissions on the Flickr website using your browser. Your photos will only be publicly visibly for the time it takes between uploading and changing the permissions, but if absolute privacy is important to you, I'd recommend you use the Flickr uploader.

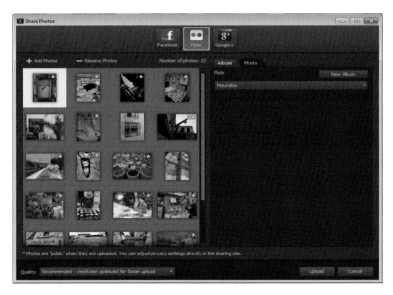

FIG 10.3 The Social Sharing dialog with photos ready to upload.

Even though you can't see sets with private photos, you can create a new set by clicking the New Album button. The only thing that remains to be done is to select the maximum size of your uploaded photos from the Quality (why not size?) menu at the bottom of the share photos window. If you leave this on the default 'Original Pixels' then the largest size will be the same as the original. If you'd rather restrict your Flickr uploads to smaller images choose Recommended – resolution optimized for faster upload. In Paintshop Pro X6, this reduces your images to a maximum size of 1600 × 1200 pixels before uploading them, which is probably plenty big enough and will reduce the upload time – considerably if you're uploading a big batch of photos. But if you want to keep your originals on Flickr at their original size as backups, stick with the 'Original Pixels' option. Older versions of PaintShop Pro offer several different sizes for reduced resolution uploads on this menu. Now all you have to do is press the upload button and wait for the process to complete. When the upload is finished, an alert box will appear to tell you so.

If you do decide to upload your photos to Flickr from PaintShop Pro X6, here's how to change the permissions for the whole batch. Launch your browser and sign in to your Flickr account. Select Organize from the You menu then, from the pop-up menu at the bottom of the content area, select the date on which you uploaded the photos, select them and drag them to the content area. Select 'Who can see, comment, tag?' from the Permissions menu and make the appropriate selection from the popup box, e.g. check the Only You(private) radio button plus the 'Your friends' and 'Your Family' checkboxes, then click the Change Permissions button.

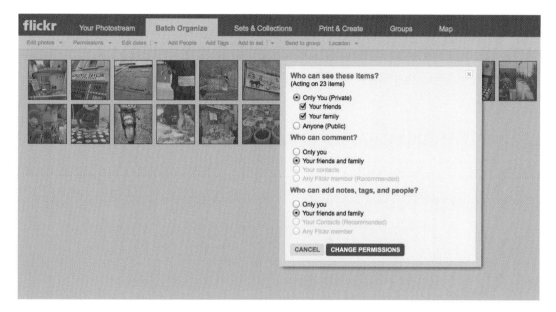

FIG 10.4 Though you can't assign privacy settings to your pictures when uploading from PaintShop Pro to Flickr, you can easily do so subsequently using Flickr's batch organize feature.

If at some point, you no longer want to use PaintShop Pro X6 to upload photos to Flickr, you should de-authorize the permission you granted for the application to access your Flickr account. To do this, you need to access your Yahoo account information page. To find out how to do that, click the Need help? Start here! Link at the bottom of your profile page.

Uploading Photos to Facebook

Paintshop Pro X6 also provides a convenient way to upload photos to Facebook. As with Flickr, the best way to organize this is to create a new tray containing all the photos you want to upload (see above). Then, click one of the thumbnails, press Ctrl-A to select all and choose Facebook from the Share button on the Organizer toolbar.

Now you'll need to sign in to your Facebook account. Enter your details and click the Login button, then click the Allow button to let PaintShop Pro access your Facebook account. Once you've done this, you'll be presented with the Facebook upload screen. You only need to do the authorization stuff once then you'll come directly to this window when you select Facebook from the Share menu.

All the pictures you selected are shown in this window, you can add more by clicking the Add file button, but then you need to locate the image files on your hard drive which isn't very clever. If you don't have all the photos you want, the easiest way to get them is to hit the cancel button and redo your selection in the Manage workspace.

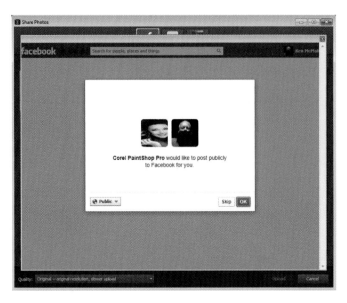

FIG 10.5 The first time you upload photos to Facebook, you'll be asked to authorize PaintShop Pro to access your Facebook account. You can later withdraw the authorization if you decide you no longer want to use PaintShop Pro to upload photos to Facebook.

You can select an existing Facebook album to upload your images to or create a new one, and, as with the Flickr uploader. Click the Photo tab to add a description to each picture by selecting it and filling in the description field. You'll only have to do this, if you haven't already captioned your photos. In the Photo tab, you'll also notice there's a people field. This shows the name of anyone you've tagged in the selected image (using the People feature) who you've linked with your Facebook friends and saves you having to tag the images all over again once you've uploaded them.

For this work, you've got to first link your PaintShop Pro people tags with the corresponding Facebook friends. To do that (you'll need to click the cancel button in the Share photos dialog box for now and come back to it later) select anyone listed in the People category of the Tags section of the Collections tab in the Navigation palette. Next, look in the Organizer palette toolbar at the top of the Organizer and on the left you'll see link tags for Facebook and Flickr. Click the Facebook icon and Paintshop Pro will connect to your Facebook account and download your Friend list. Now you just click the Friend that corresponds with the selected person and the two are linked.

If you now return to your upload, you'll notice that the people field in the photo tab contains the Facebook names of anyone you've linked in this way. When the photos are uploaded they'll be automatically tagged and your friends will be notified. It works in the same way for Flickr contacts.

When all is ready, click the upload button. The photos will be uploaded to the album you selected or created, and an alert box appears to tell you when

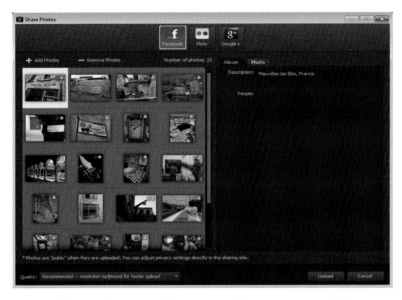

FIG 10.6 Uploading to Facebook. You can add photos to existing albums, create new ones and add a description for each photo.

the upload is complete, if you're uploading a lot of photos or have a slow connection this could take several minutes.

Once your photos are uploaded to Facebook, you'll need to login to your Facebook account using your browser if you want to view them, change the privacy settings, edit, or delete them.

Uploading Photos to Google Plus

If you have a Google Plus account, you can upload photos in pretty much exactly the same way as for Facebook and Flickr. As with Facebook and Flickr, PaintShop Pro will ask you to sign in to your G+ account and provide authorization to manage your photos and videos as well as your contacts. Once you've done that, the upload process is very similar, choose the album you want to upload to or create a new one, decide whether you want to upload full-sized images or smaller ones and click the upload button. As with Flickr, you'll need to make any adjustments to privacy settings on Google Plus.

One final thing that's worth pointing out, as it's easily overlooked, is that you can upload the same batch of images to all three sites at the same time. So long as the icon at the top of the Share photos window is highlighted, your photos will be uploaded there. So it's possible to simultaneously upload an album of photos to Facebook, Flickr and Google Plus simultaneously. A real time saver.

> **Tip**
>
> Though in some circumstances, i.e. uploading to an existing Facebook album, PaintShop Pro will respect your existing privacy settings, always assume that photos uploaded using the Share photos feature will be published publicly on social network and photo sharing sites. Once the upload has completed, log in using a web browser to check and change privacy settings if necessary.

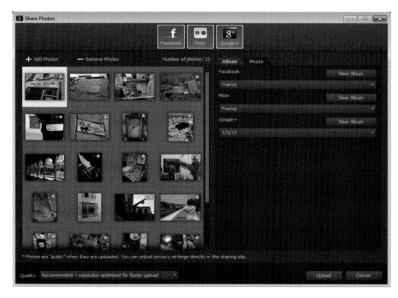

FIG 10.7 To upload to Facebook, Flickr and Google plus simultaneously, just click all three buttons at the top of the Share photos window. Remember to Assign an 'album' for each site and to add a description and tags where appropriate.

Creating Your Own Images for the Web

Social networking sites have made it easy to upload and share photos, but PaintShop Pro X6 has a range of tools which you can use to prepare photos for your own websites. If you have your own business website, or a blog, or you want to upload photos to an online forum, auction site or enter them for a competition, you'll want to produce the best possibly quality image without creating an enormous file. The rest of this chapter is devoted to the tools PaintShop Pro X6 provides to help you do just that. Even if you're content to use the Share button to upload and e-mail photos, you might find the explanation of web files formats and image compression useful.

How the Web Displays Images

You're probably aware that web pages are written in HTML, Hyper Text Markup Language, and that your web browser interprets that code to display formatted text and pictures on your screen. To see what HTML looks like, in Internet Explorer select View Source from the Page menu. You don't need to be able to write or even understand HTML in order to produce web pages as there are plenty of applications that will help you do this while keeping the code at arm's length.

Picture files are loaded into a browser page by HTML code which looks something like this:

```
<img src="images/pelican_02.GIF" width=234 height=53>
```

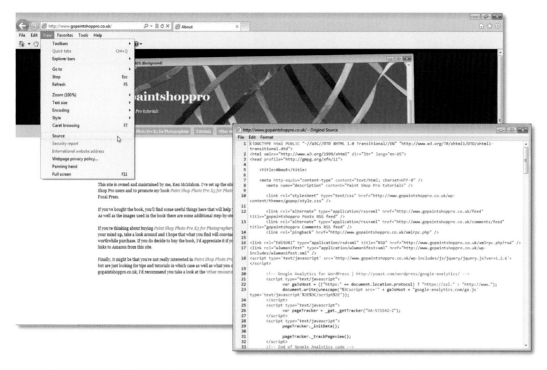

FIG 10.8 You can display the HTML code for the currently displayed browser page by selecting View Source from the Page menu in Internet Explorer. The source code is opened as a text file in Notepad, where you can edit and save it.

The HTML code tells the browser what the image is called, where to find it on the server and what size it is. Once the browser interprets this line of code, it will download the image and display it.

If it's a large image, or if the PC on which the browser is running accesses the Internet via a slow connection, it could take a while for the image to download and display, and trying to keep this delay as short as possible while maintaining good image quality is the main aim of web image-editing.

The first, and most often overlooked, method of reducing image file size is to reduce the size of the image itself. The resolution of most display monitors is around 100ppi, so the first thing to do is open the Image, Resize dialog and change the resolution to 100ppi. If you work at a higher resolution than this, your images will simply appear bigger on the web page. Because of this, most web designers prefer to work in pixels rather than other units, and if you are doing a lot of web work, you should try to get into this habit. If you make an image 100 × 100 pixels, it will be roughly an inch square on screen.

If you want to include big images, link them to a smaller thumbnail and give your viewers the option to sit through a lengthy download if they wish. Another effective but little-used file-shrinking strategy is to aggressively crop images. Get rid of extraneous background detail and crop right in on the subject.

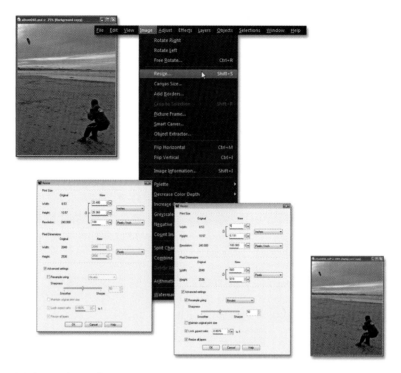

FIG 10.9 The Resize dialog box provides lots of options and it's important to pick the right ones. First, check the 'Advanced settings' box, uncheck the 'Resample using' box and enter 100 pixels per inch in the Resolution field. This 5 megapixel image would be approximately 20 × 25 inches on a web page if we didn't downsample it. Check the 'Resample using', 'Lock aspect ratio' and 'Resize all layers' boxes and enter the 100ppi size in the width box of the Print Size pane. Click OK and view at 100% to see how it will look on the web.

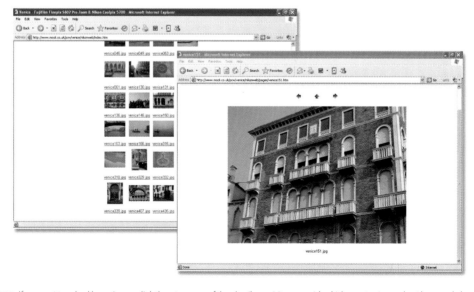

FIG 10.10 If you want to upload larger images, link them to a page of thumbnails, so visitors can pick which ones to view and not be overwhelmed with lengthy downloads.

Web File Formats

Nearly all images on the web are saved in one of two file formats – JPEG and GIF. If you own a digital camera, you'll know about JPEG even if you don't know much about the Web. GIF has been around even longer than JPEG and is used pretty much exclusively for web graphics. There's a rule of thumb that says you should use JPEG for photographic images and GIF for graphics with flat color, and like most rules of thumb, it's a good one 99% of the time, but there are situations when it's best ignored. As always with web images, the objective is to produce the smallest possible file size, while maintaining the best possible image quality. By experimenting with both JPEG and GIF compressions, you'll soon learn what works best for particular images.

If you look hard enough, you'll find some web images that are saved in the PNG format. This relative newcomer was introduced in an effort to combine the strengths of JPEG and GIF and eliminate some of their shortcomings. Despite some advanced features, like drop shadows and support for layers, PNG has never really taken off, though you can easily create PNG files using the PNG Optimizer from Paint Shop Photo Pro's Web toolbar.

JPEG in depth

JPEG is actually a compression algorithm, a process which reduces the size of digital picture files, but it's come to be used to describe the file format which uses it. JPEG is a lossy compression method, which in plain English means that when you use it some loss in quality occurs and the compressed file won't look the same or as good as the original. Compression algorithms that maintain the exact same data and image quality are called 'lossless'. Although JPEG doesn't offer lossless compression, at low compression settings it comes pretty close. A newer version of JPEG, called JPEG 2000, provides a lossless option as well as other advantages, but, like png, hasn't gained widespread support.

JPEG is pretty good at removing quite of lot of picture detail, and thereby considerably reducing file size without anyone noticing, because the algorithm is designed to remove the kind of color information that the human eye doesn't perceive that well. You can compress image files by a factor of about three and you would have to look very hard to spot any degradation in image quality.

Using the JPEG Optimizer

Most image editors, and Paint Shop Pro is no exception, leave it to you to make the decision about how much compression to use. It's up to you to decide just how much image quality you are prepared to sacrifice in return for smaller file sizes.

Tip

The most effective way to reduce the size of images is to crop them. A good quality, closely cropped photo is always better than a highly compressed one with lots of extraneous detail, so get into the habit of making the Crop tool your first step in web image preparation.

To make this decision you need to know two things. What will the image look like if you compress it using a given JPEG setting? And how long will it take to download? The answers can be found in Paint Shop Photo Pro's JPEG Optimizer, which you launch by clicking the JPEG Optimizer button on the web toolbar or selecting File > Export > JPEG Optimizer.

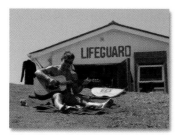
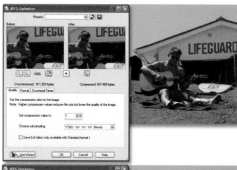

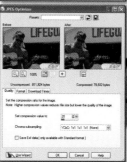
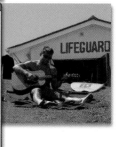

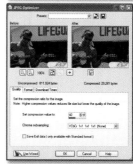
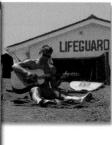

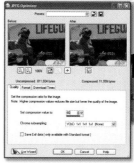
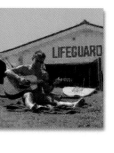

FIG 10.11 The more JPEG compression you apply to an image the smaller it gets, and the worse it looks. At a setting of 1, the compressed image (top) is indistinguishable from the original, but the file size is nearly halved. At a setting of 20, (2nd from top), you can begin to see JPEG artifacts creeping in — look closely at the lettering on the hut.

Increase the compression setting to 40 (3rd from top) and the file size drops to a mere 25 Kb — down from an original 784 Kb. On a cable or DSL Internet connection this would take a fraction of a second to download, but the image quality has suffered badly, with JPEG blocking visible just about everywhere you look.

If 40 is a step too far, 80 (bottom) is just ridiculous. It's interesting to note that, beyond a certain point, not only does the image quality suffer horrendously, but file size savings get correspondingly smaller. A setting of 20 slices 670 Kb from this file; increasing it to 80 gains you only another 53 Kb.

The JPEG optimizer has three tabs – Quality, Format and Download Times – and Before and After preview windows. Make sure the preview is set to 100% view, so you can see the image exactly as it will appear on the web page; enlarge or maximize the dialog if necessary. Enter a number between 1 and 100 in the 'Set compression value to' box or use the slider. The higher the value entered here, the more compression is applied, resulting in a smaller, lower-quality image. 1 is virtually no compression; you'll start to see the preview deteriorate at around the 20 mark, and beyond 60 things will start to look very bad indeed.

Bear in mind that these figures are not percentages, and if you enter the same values in a different Web Optimizer, you're unlikely to get similar results. These values just represent Paint Shop Photo Pro's maximum and minimum JPEG compression settings.

Judging Picture Quality

Just below the Before and After preview windows, you'll see two figures. The left-hand one under the Before window says 'Uncompressed' followed by the file size in bytes and, on the right, the compressed size is given, again in bytes. Notice that even at the lowest compression setting of 1, the size of the compressed file is only about a half to one-third that of the uncompressed one. If you want the approximate file size in kilobytes, just divide by a thousand. Generally speaking, compression settings in the range of 10 to 30 will give acceptable quality images with high compression ratios, but let your eyes be your guide and as soon as the image becomes unacceptably grubby, drag the slider back toward the low side.

Feel free to experiment with the various Chroma subsampling presets on the pull-down menu, though it's unlikely you'll achieve any improvement by changing this. Even the Paint Shop Photo Pro Help file recommends leaving it on the default setting.

Use the Format tab to select either Standard or Progressive format, the latter preloads a low quality preview into the browser, so that the viewer has something to look at while waiting for the real thing. With standard format, nothing is displayed until the entire image is downloaded.

Estimating Download Time

The Download Times tab provides the answer to our second question. In actual fact, it provides several answers, any one of which might be true, depending on the kind of link visitors to your website are using to access the Internet. Four download times are displayed. These provide a guide to the time, it will take to download the optimized file on links operating at 56, 128, 380 and 720 Kbps (kilobits per second).

Tip

You can increase the JPEG compressibility of images by blurring them slightly before compressing them. A small degree of blur softens the contrast in edge detail, which is where JPEG artifacts are most noticeable. Use the Gaussian Blur filter with a radius of between 0.5 and 1 before JPEG optimizing.

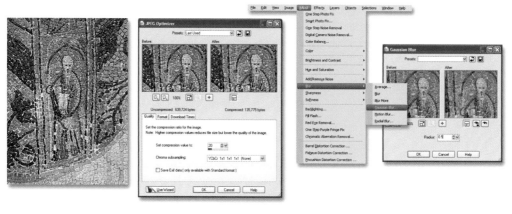

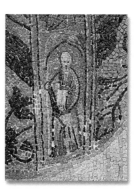

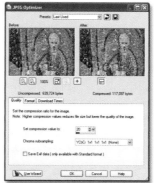

FIG 10.12 Compressing the original (top left) with a compression value of 20 produces a 135 Kb JPEG. By first applying the Gaussian Blur filter with a radius of 0.5, compressing with the same settings produces a file 20 Kb smaller. The resulting image is slightly softer, but perfectly acceptable.

It's a little disappointing that Corel has passed up the opportunity to update the jpeg optimizer for several years now, with the result that the download speeds in the jpeg optimizer are looking pretty archaic. 56 Kbps is the speed at which someone using a modem connects to the Internet. 720k would be the speed of a very slow broadband connection. These days, most web connections are broadband ones operating at speeds measured in Megabits per second (Mbps) rather than Kilobits and, depending where in the world you live average broadband speeds are in the 5–80 Mbps range and getting faster all the time.

Of course, a 10 Mbps line doesn't guarantee 10 Mbps transfer rates. Speeds could be affected if the line is shared via a network router, or if there's Internet congestion, or if the server can't cope with the level of traffic so, regardless of the increase in the speed of Internet connections, it still makes sense to optimize your images.

It's good practice to ensure that most people can access your site without having to wait all night for the images to download, so if the JPEG Optimizer is telling you that just one of the many images that may end up on your home page will take several seconds to download on a 720 Kbps link, you need to think about how you are going to speed things up. As a general rule, you can use the 720 Kbps readout to provide an estimate of the worst performance someone on a broadband connection is likely to experience.

Once you're happy with the quality and size of the Optimized file, press the OK button to save the file.

GIF in Depth

Whereas JPEG images are full color 24-bit files, GIFs make use of an indexed color palette to help keep file size down. Each pixel in a JPEG file needs 24 bits (or 3 bytes) of data to describe it. But the same pixel in a GIF needs only 8 bits and in some circumstances even fewer. GIF does this by referencing each pixel to a color lookup table or palette. The palette has 256 colors. The first color is numbered 0, the next 1 and so on, all the way up to 255; to describe the color of a pixel all you need is its number, and as there are only 256 possibilities, 1 byte is sufficient to describe them all.

One shortcoming of this approach is that, compared with the 16 million or so colors that a 24-bit format like JPEG can display, 256 seems a bit meager. This is one of the reasons GIF is recommended for graphics images that often contain very few colors. Indeed, some graphics contain far fewer than 256 colors, and in such cases, it's possible to make further file size economies by reducing the color palette to as few as four, or even two, colors. A four-color palette can be defined with 2 bits. That's 2 bits for every pixel in the image compared with 24 for JPEG – a massive saving.

Although 256 colors may not sound like a lot, it's surprising how little image quality suffers when you convert even complex photos containing lots of colors into GIF format. GIF can also expand the palette of perceived colors using a process called 'dithering' in which colors are combined to produce intermediate hues.

Once the palette has been defined, GIF further reduces the file by applying a lossless compression algorithm called 'LZW'. So GIF has two methods of reducing image file size: color palette reduction and LZW compression. Typically, LZW compression reduces the file size by a factor of two, in other words halves it, so most of the work involved in reducing GIF size involves making careful choices about how the color palette is created, so you can represent all the colors in your image with the smallest possible palette.

Using the GIF Optimizer

To open the GIF Optimizer, click the GIF Optimizer button on the Web toolbar or select File > Export > GIF Optimizer. Expand the window, so you can see the previews at 100% and click the Colors tab. The first input field, 'How many colors do you want?', lets you specify, well, just that. The maximum and minimum values

> **Tip**
> Avoid using drop shadows on images that you intend to convert to GIF. It's impossible to render subtle gradations of tint with a limited color palette.

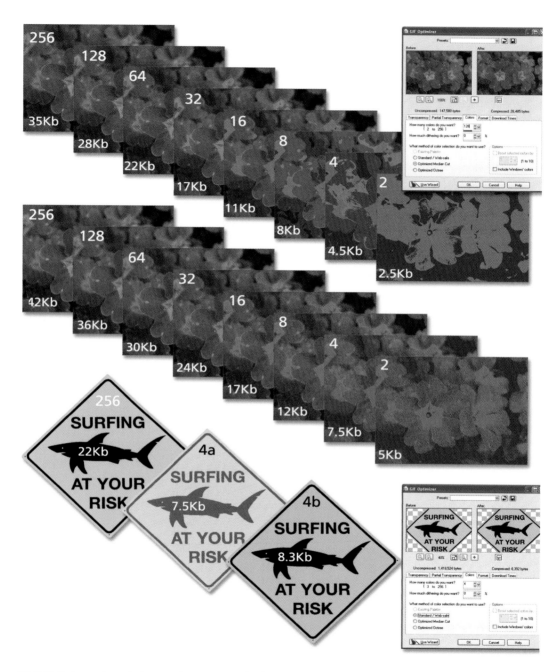

FIG 10.13 The top row shows what happens when you progressively reduce the GIF color palette from 256 to two colors. The second row shows the same process with 100% dither selected. GIF is best suited to graphic images like the bottom one. Reducing the palette to four colors produces little noticeable quality loss because there were few colors to begin with. The GIF Optimizer doesn't always select the best color palette (4a). In this case, choose Image > Decrease Color Depth > X Colors, then optimize using the existing palette (4b).

depend on the method of color selection and there are four choices here, Existing Palette, Standard/Web-safe, Optimized Median Cut and Optimized Octree.

The Existing Palette option will be greyed out unless the image was an 8-bit indexed image to begin with, or you converted it prior to opening the GIF Optimizer. The Standard/Web-safe option uses a palette of standard colors devised to provide the best viewing experience for those using Internet Explorer on an 8-bit display, but now that 24-bit color displays are commonplace; this isn't such an important consideration and you can safely ignore this setting, unless of course it provides better results than the others.

Optimized Median Cut and Optimized Octree are two different algorithms designed to derive the most representative palette of 256 colors from all of those in the unoptimized 24-bit image. If your existing image contains only a few colors use Optimized Octree and if you want to reduce the image to fewer than 16 colors use Optimized Median Cut.

For now, select Optimized Median Cut and drag the slider under the 'How many colors do you want?' box as far as it will go to the left until the box contains the value 2. This is what your image will look like if it's displayed with 1 bit per pixel, allowing two colors. Unless there were only two colors to begin with, the odds are it will look terrible. Highlight the 'How many colors do you want?' box with the mouse and enter the value 4. Things will look a little better, but not much. Double the number of colors to 8, then 16, 32, 64, 128 and finally 256, taking a look at the compressed preview each time.

Dare to Dither

Assuming your original image was a color photo, it probably will have begun to look something like normal when you got to 16 or 32 colors. Even so, some of the colors may not look right and you may get 'banding' – discrete bands of color where the original showed subtle gradations – in skies, for example. What's happening is that the original colors in the image are being mapped to the closest one available in the palette and it's one of the reasons GIF is a poor choice if your original contains lots of colors (but a good one if it only contains a few).

There is something you can do about banding. Enter 100 in the box marked 'How much dithering do you want?' This will considerably reduce and perhaps even eliminate the banding and posterization, but it also introduces a speckly graininess into the image which you may find no more acceptable than the banding. Another drawback is that dithered files are slightly larger than undithered ones. By dragging the dithering slider, you should be able to reduce the graininess to an acceptable degree without reintroducing the banding.

Try Transparency

One very useful feature of the GIF format is that it supports transparency. You can tell the Optimizer to use the existing image or layer transparency or define a color from within the image as transparent. The advantage of including transparent areas in the GIF is that you can place irregular graphics – logos or text, for example – over different backgrounds on your web page and the background will show through. The Partial Transparency tab of the GIF Optimizer provides sophisticated controls to deal with semi-transparent pixels (for example, those around the edges of anti-aliased text), which can cause problems.

Whatever file format you choose, Optimization is a trial and error process. Every image is different, and while you can Batch Process similar images using the same settings, if you want to get the best possible quality at the smallest file size you will need to give each one individual attention, selecting the settings, you think will provide the right balance between quality and download times, and then fine-tuning depending on what you can see in the Optimizer preview window.

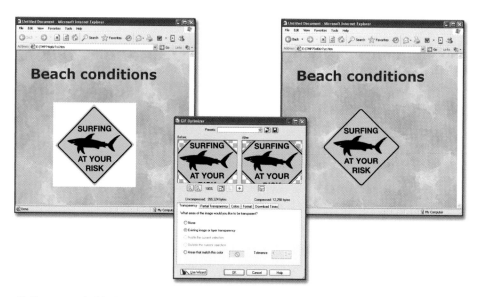

FIG 10.14 The Transparency tab of the GIF Optimizer allows you to use existing layer transparency, or specify a color from the image (usually the background). Use the Partial Transparency tab to specify a blend color for the edge pixels which is similar to the background on your web page.

Step-by-Step Projects

Protecting Your Photos

Adding a Copyright Message and Watermark

If you're going to put your photos on the Web, you need to be prepared for the risk that they may be used without your permission. Horror stories abound of how people's snaps have ended up on advertising hoardings on worse and though you can't entirely avoid it (apart from not uploading your photos), there are some steps you can take to make it less likely. In this step-by-step project, you'll learn how to add a copyright message to your photo file metadata which tells people they can't use it without your permission. We'll also look at how to add a discrete, but visible watermark.

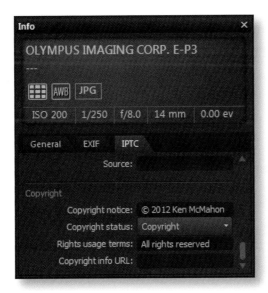

STEP 1 First, add a copyright statement to your image metadata, you should add this to all your photos as a matter of course. Select the IPTC tab in the Info palette and scroll down to the copyright pane. In the Copyright notice field type ©2012 Ken McMahon (substituting your own name and the correct year). To add the © copyright symbol, hold down the ALT key and type 0169. Select Copyright from the Copyright status pull-down menu and type All rights reserved in the Rights usage terms field.

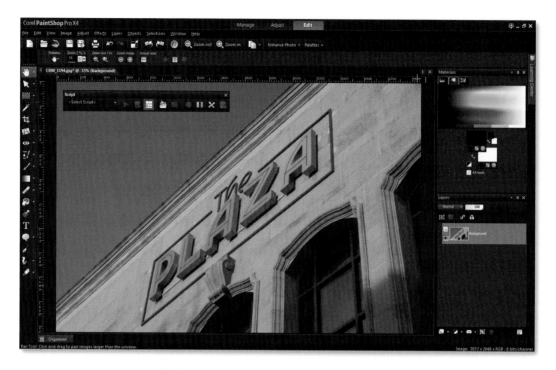

STEP 2 Now we're going to create a semi-transparent watermark which will appear across the bottom (or wherever you want) of your photos using the same type effect described in Chapter 7. This time though, we're going to save the process as a script, so you can add it to other images. First you need to display the Scripts toolbar, from the View menu Select Toolbars > Script. Then click the red record button on the Script toolbar to begin recording. From here on in everything, you do is recorded, so don't mess up! If you do, you'll have to press the cancel script recording button (the X button two to the right of the record button) and start again. If you're not sure about a step, you can click the pause script recording button, try it out, then undo back to where you were before unpausing and continuing.

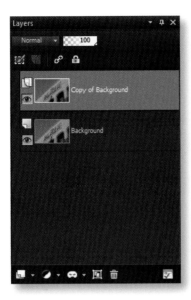

STEP 3 Duplicate the background layer, this is just a precautionary step in case anything goes awry. Eventually you'll Save as to create a new watermarked file. Right-click the background layer in the Layers palette and select Duplicate.

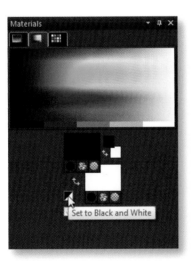

STEP 4 Now click the set default colors button in the materials palette. It's important not to skip this step even if the colors are already set to the black and white defaults as this may not be the case, when you run the script in future. As we'll be making a selection from the text, the color doesn't actually matter, but it doesn't hurt to get into the habit of being thorough when recording scripts.

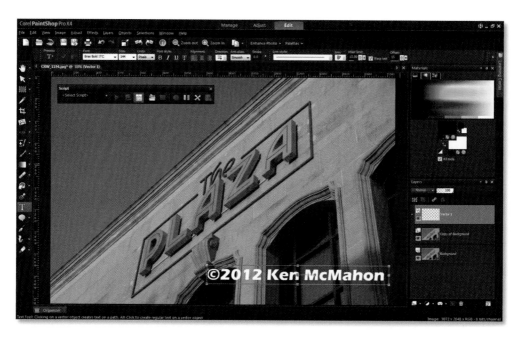

STEP 5 Select the text tool and type your watermark message, for mine I've used the copyright statement ©2012 Ken McMahon. Choose a bold typeface and make the type big enough to be clearly visible but not so large as to overwhelm the image. Click the apply button on the Tool Option palette to OK the text, then select the pick tool and position it.

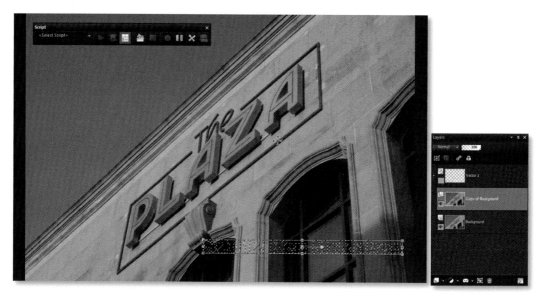

STEP 6 Go to the Selections menu and choose 'From Vector Object' to turn the text into a selection (or press Ctrl-Shift-B). You should now see the selection marquee surrounding the text. Select the Copy of Background layer in the Layers palette, and turn off the text layer by clicking its visibility (eye) icon.

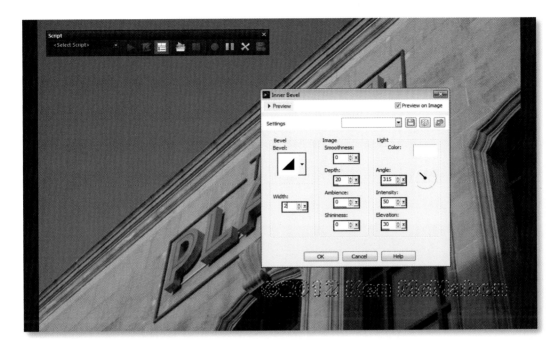

STEP 7 Select Effects > 3D Effects > Inner Bevel to apply a bevel effect to the Copy of Background layer using the text selection. The default bevel is a bit clunky, so I've reduced the width to 2. Click OK to apply the bevel, then press Ctrl-D to deselect all and get a proper look at your handiwork. For the sake of tidiness, you can now delete the 'Vector 1' type layer.

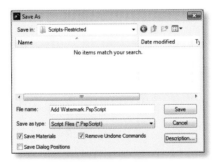

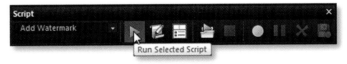

STEP 8 Press the Save script button at the end of the Script toolbar and when prompted for a name call it 'Add Watermark'. Now you can add the watermark to any image with a single click by selecting it from the pull-down menu in the Scripts toolbar and clicking the Run Selected Script (play) button.

Sharing to Facebook, Flickr and Google Plus

PaintShop Pro X6 provides a range of really useful features to help you get your photos uploaded to social networking and photo sharing sites with the minimum of effort. Whether you just want to post a couple of quick snaps or get the results of several weeks worth of shooting online, the share button is the first step. In this step-by-step project, I'll show you how to upload a folder of photos simultaneously to Facebook, Flickr and Google Plus. If you don't have an account with all three of those platforms don't worry, it's easy to share with just one, two or all three, pretty much by just pressing a button, or three.

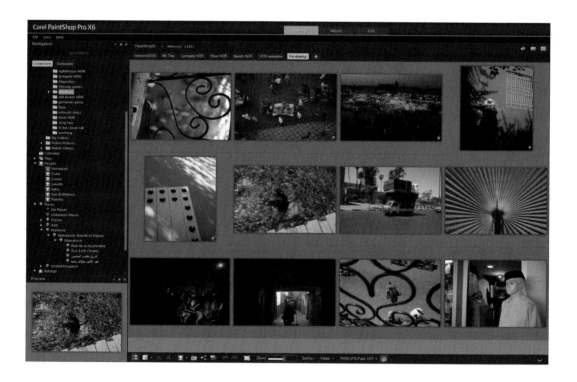

STEP 1 The first thing to do is decide on what photos you want to upload. Though you might want to upload an entire folder, it's more likely that you'll choose a selection of photos for sharing and the easiest way to do that is to create a new tray and add the photos to it. In the Manage workspace, click the downward pointing chevron on the right of the Organizer toolbar and check the Tray box to display tray tabs at the top of the Organizer. Click the + sign to add a new tab and call it 'For sharing'. Select and drag the thumbnails of the photos you want to share to the new tab.

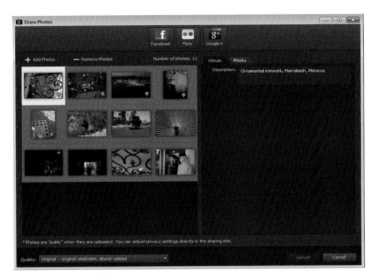

STEP 2 Press Ctrl-A to select all of the thumbnails and then click the Sharing button on the Organizer toolbar, it looks like three nodes or dots connected with two lines. Click the Photo tab and check the description. This is taken from the IPTC caption field, so if you've captioned all your photos (see page 40 or the step-by-step project on page 51), it'll be fine, but if you haven't, it will either be blank or say something like 'Olympus camera'. As this is what will appear beside your photo when it's uploaded you'll want to make sure it says something relevant and informative.

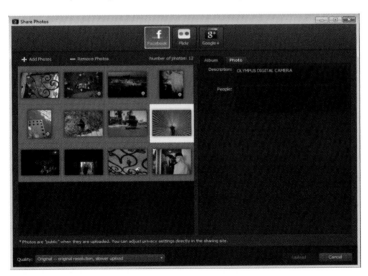

STEP 3 Now click the Facebook button at the top of the Share photos window. A browser window will open and you'll need to login to your Facebook account. If you haven't done so before you'll also need to provide authorization for PaintShop Pro to access your Facebook account. This is also the case for Flickr and Google Plus. Once that's done, you'll see a new field appear below the Description labeled People. If you've tagged your photos with people and linked your People tags with your Facebook friends list, then they'll appear here. That way, you don't have to retag them once they're uploaded. If you're not sure how to do that take a look at page 286.

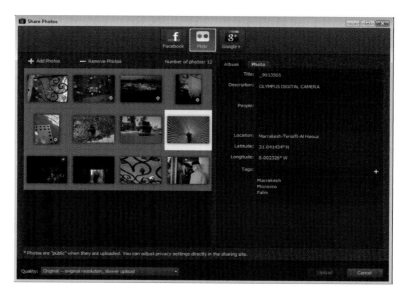

STEP 4 Now click the Facebook button again to turn it off, then click the Flickr button. Once again there's the People field and, as for Facebook this contains any Flickr contacts tagged in your photos provided you've linked them. There's some more information in this panel including the geopositional data (see the step-by-step project on p. 58 for details of how to add that), and tags. If you haven't added tags to your photos, you can do it now, but it's best to do it beforehand (see p. 39 or the step-by-step project on page 51) as tags added here will be appended to your uploaded images, but not in PaintShop Pro.

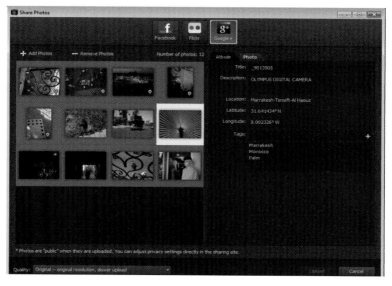

STEP 5 Now uncheck the Flickr button and click the Google+ button. This displays the fields for information that's automatically sent to Google plus along with your photos. Unlike Facebook and Flickr, there are no people tags but, like Flickr, G+ tags your photos with geopositional data. Both Flickr and G+ use the filename as the image tile.

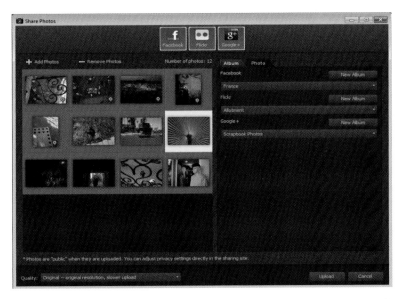

STEP 6 Now click the Album tab and this time check all three buttons – Facebook, Flickr and Google+ at the top. This tab allow you to select a Facebook or G+ album, or Flickr set to add your photos to. Only publicly visible albums are displayed here, so if the visibility of an album or set is restricted you won't see it in the list. Either select a public album or set to add your photos to or create a new one. It's important to be aware that when you upload photos, they're visible to the public. That means you'll have to log in using your Web browser and amend the privacy settings after you've uploaded your photos, but they'll be publicly visible in the meantime.

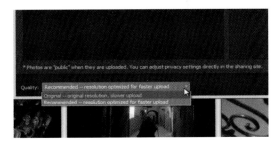

STEP 7 Now you just need to decide whether you want to upload your photos at the full resolution or have PaintShop Pro resize them. There are two options on the Quality pull-down menu – 'Original – original resolution, slower upload' and 'Recommended – resolution optimized for faster upload' (older versions of PaintShop Pro offer specific size options). Select the first option if you want to upload originals, for example if you're uploading photos to Flickr as backups, or if you want others to be able to download the full sized photos for printing. The 'Recommended' option resizes photos to a maximum 1600 × 1200 pixels size, which is big enough for displaying full size on all but the largest screens. The length of time the upload takes will depend on the number of photos and the speed of your Internet connection, but regardless of that, the Recommended reduced resolution upload will be a lot quicker.

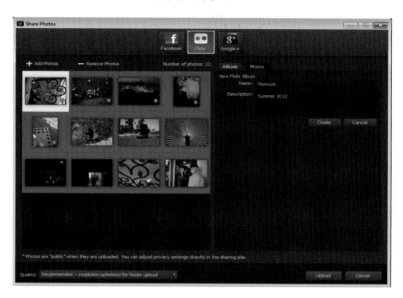

STEP 8 Make one final check to ensure all your photos are captioned and you have selected or created albums for the networks you're uploading to. Check that you've selected the right buttons at the top, selected networks have a white border, plus you'll see them listed in the Album tab. In the screen grab here, I'm uploading 12 photos to a Flickr set called Morocco at reduced resolution. If you have Facebook, Flickr and G+ accounts, it's possible to upload to all three simply by checking all three buttons. When you're ready, click the upload button.

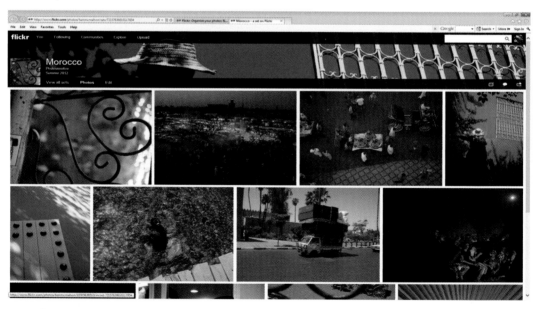

STEP 9 An upload status window appears in which you can monitor the progress of your upload. When it's complete, the window will close. Log in to (in this case) Flickr, to check the photos are there and to make any changes to tags, descriptions, privacy settings and so on.

YEOVIL COLLEGE LIBRARY

Index

YEOVIL COLLEGE
LIBRARY